CASTE SYSTEM IN INDIA
A Historical Perspective

CASTE SYSTEM IN INDIA
A Historical Perspective

Ekta Singh

Publications

KALPAZ PUBLICATIONS
Delhi-110052

Caste System in India : A Historical Perspective

ISBN: 978-81-7835-301-2

Published in 2016 in India by
Kalpaz Publications
C-30, Satyawati Nagar, Delhi – 110052
E-mail: kalpaz@hotmail.com
Ph.: 9212142040

Printed at: G. Print Process, Delhi

Contents

and their Role; Defenders of Caste; Hindu Society; Humanitarian Cause; Shudhi and Hindus; Ethics of Hindus; Role of Reformers; Hindus and Problems; Chances of Success; Vedas and Smritis; Sadachar and Good Acts; Necessity of Religion; Beliefs and Morals.

Preface

The Caste System in India is deep rooted in the long-drawn socio-economic, cultural and political history of our subcontinent. It has brought about a deep and complete division in the Hindu society. Since the days of yore, these divisions had become the symbols of status, from the upper class to the lowest category. Some social reformers and their movements did effect the socio-economic status of the Castes. But the efforts in this direction should not cease and they should remain an ongoing process.

The theme has been well-weaved into eight chapters which have been dealt with in a comprehensive way. They commence from the Introduction, moving ahead with Caste System : the early stages, Caste as status in the family and clan, evolution of Castes, from Rig Veda onward, Castes in India, their mechanism, Genesis and development, views of W.C. Bonnerji, rules for untouchalbes, Social Reform Party, Communal Award, defenders of Caste system, ethics of Hindus, Vedas and Smritis, necessity of religion, beliefs and morals, the social reforms, the theory of Karma, various kinds of rituals, advent of the British rule, Harijan Sevak Sangh, upliftment of the Harijans, role of saints and sadhus, religion and God, Caste System in Modern India, Conversions, Hinduism and culture, Christians in Travancore, temple entry, Vykom Satyagraha, role of Travancore Durbar, the system of Satyagraha and the gospel of spinning and khadi. The Bibliography is fairly comprehensive.

I have collected the research material from several academic institutions, viz, National Archives of India, Nehru

Memorial Museum and Library, Sapru House Library, Central Secretariat Library, Delhi University Library, Indian Council of Historical Research Library, Sahitya Akademi Library and Jawaharlal Nehru University Library. I am grateful to the members of these institutions for affording their academic support to me during my researches. I have used and analysed the material from the writings of well-known authors. I feel much beholden to them.

Ekta Singh

Acknowledgements

I wish to express my deep sense of gratitude to my guide Dr. Manju Singh, Reader, Bundelkhand Degree College, Jhansi for her invaluable support and guidance in fulfillment of the Ph. D. programe.

I also wish to thank Dr.N. N. Awasthi, Director, B. R. Ambedkar Institute of Social Sciences, Bundelkhand University, Jhansi for his constant motivation and generous assistance to complete this programe.

I would like to thank my husband, Surender K. Dass and my parents, Mrs. Uma Singh and Mr. Nihal Singh for their constant encouragement and moral support.

Place : Jhansi
Date : November 2003

Ekta Singh

Introduction

Originating from the Portuguese word, caste, meaning breed, and now defined by the Encyclopedia of Social Sciences as, "an endogamous and hereditary subdivision of ethnic group occupying a position of superior or inferior rank or social esteem in comparison with such other divisions," the caste system of India has now become on of the most rigid and defining social institutions in the world.

Having existed for nearly 3,000 years the caste system has come to dictate the lives and roles of much of India's population by ruling social class and status. This system of defining caste from birth has created a rigid barrier of mobility within the country. Those of lower castes and without caste (the Dalits) are often subject to intense discrimination and are not given the privilege of basic human rights. While efforts have been made, including laws prohibiting discrimination based on caste, in a society as governed by customs as India is, it is difficult to persuade a society to relinquish traditional methods and thought.

A. CASTE PROBLEM IN INDIA

"I have a message for the world, which I will deliver without fear and care for the future. To the reformers I will point out that I am a greater reformer than any one of them. They want to reform only little bits. I want root-and-branch reform."

- Swami Vivekananda

Caste in Society and not in Religion

Though our castes and our institutions are apparently

linked with our religion, they are not so. These institutions have been necessary to protect us as a nation, and when this necessity for self-preservation will no more exist, they will die a natural death. In religion there is no caste. A man from the highest caste and a man from the lowest may become a monk in India and the two castes become equal. The caste system is opposed to the religion of *Vedanta*.

Caste is a social custom, and all our great preachers have tried to break it down. From Buddhism downwards, every sect has preached against caste, and every time it has only riveted the chains. Beginning from Buddha to Raja Rammohun Roy, everyone made the mistake of holding caste to be a religious institution and tried to pull down religion and caste altogether, and failed.

In spite of all the ravings of the priests, caste is simply a crystallized social institution, which after doing its service is now filling the atmosphere of India with its stench, and it can only be removed by giving back to people their lost social individuality. Caste is simply the outgrowth of the political institutions of India; it is a hereditary trade guild. Trade competition with Europe has broken caste more than any teaching.

The Underlying Idea of the Caste System

The older I grow, the better I seem to think of caste and such other time-honoured institutions of India. There was a time when I used to think that many of them were useless and worthless, but the older I grow, the more I seem to feel a difference in cursing any one of them, for each one of them is the embodiment of the experience of centuries.

A child of but yesterday, destined to die the day after tomorrow, comes to me and asks me to change all my plans and if I hear the advice of that baby and change all my surroundings according to his ideas I myself should be a fool, and no one else. Much of the advice that is coming to us from different countries is similar to this. Tell these wiseacres, "I will hear you when you have made a stable society yourselves. You cannot hold on to one idea for two days, you quarrel and fail; you are born like moths in the spring and die like them in five minutes. You come up like bubbles and burst like bubbles too. First form a stable society like ours. First make laws and institutions that remains undiminished in their power through scores of centuries. Then will be the time to talk on the subject with you, but till then, my friend, you are only a giddy child."

Caste is a very good thing. Caste is the plan we want to follow. What caste really is, not one in a million understands. There is no country in the world without caste. Caste is based throughout on that principle. The plan in India is to make everybody Brahmana, the Brahmana being the ideal of humanity. If you read the history of India you will find that attempts have always been made to raise the lower classes. Many are the classes that have been raised. Many more will follow till the whole will become Brahmana. That is the plan.

Our ideal is the Brahmana of spiritual culture and renunciation. By the Brahmana ideal what do I mean? I mean the ideal Brahmana-ness in which worldliness is altogether absent and true wisdom is abundantly present. That is the ideal of the Hindu race. Have you not heard how it is declared he, the Brahmana, is not amenable to law, that he has no law, that he is not governed by kings, and that his body cannot be hurt? That is perfectly true. Do not understand it in the light thrown upon it by interested and ignorant fools, but understand it in the light of the true and original Vedantic conception.. If the Brahmana is he who has killed all selfishness and who lives to acquire and propagate wisdom and the power of love - if a country is altogether inhabited by such Brahmanas, by men and women who are spiritual and moral and good, is it strange to think of that country as being above and beyond all law? What police, what military are necessary to govern them? Why should any one govern them at all? Why should they live under a government? They are good and noble, and they are the men of God; these are our ideal Brahmanas, and we read that in the *SatyaYuga* there was only one caste, and that was the Brahman. We read in the *Mahabharata* that the whole world was in the beginning peopled with Brahmans, and that as they began to degenerate they became divided into different castes, and that when the cycle turns round they will all go back to that Brahmanical origin.

The son of a Brahman is not necessarily always a Brahman; though there is every possibility of his being one, he may not become so. The Brahman caste and the Brahman quality are two distinct things.

As there are sattva, rajas and tamas - one or other of these gunas more or less - in every man, so the qualities which make a Brahman, Kshatriya, Vaishya or a Shudra are inherent in every man, more or less. But at time one or other of these qualities predominates in him in varying degrees and is manifested accordingly. Take a man in his different pursuits, for example : when he is engaged in serving another for pay, he is in Shudra-hood; when he is busy transacting some piece of business for profit, on his account, he is a Vaishya; when he fights to right wrongs then the qualities of a Kshatriya come out in him; and when he meditates on God, or passes his time in conversation about Him, then he is a Brahman. Naturally, it is quite possible for one to be changed from one caste into another. Otherwise, how did Viswamitra become a Brahman and Parashurama a Kshatriya?

The means of European civilization is the sword; of the Aryans, the division into different *varnas*. This system of division into *varnas* is the stepping-stone to civilization, making one rise higher and higher in proportion to one's learning and culture. In Europe, it is everywhere victory to the strong and death to the weak. In the land of Bharata (India), every social rule is for the protection of the weak.

Such is our ideal of caste, as meant for raising all humanity slowly and gently towards the realization of the great ideal of spiritual man, who is non-resisting, calm, steady, worshipful, pure and meditative. In that ideal there is God.

We believe in Indian caste as one of the greatest social institutions that the Lord gave to man. We also believe that through the unavoidable defects, foreign persecutions, and above all, the monumental ignorance and pride of many Brahmans who do not deserve the name, have thwarted in many ways, the legitimate fructification of this glorious

Indian institution, it has already worked wonders for the land of Bharata and it destined to lead Indian humanity to its goal.

Caste should not go; but should be readjusted occasionally. Within the old structure is to be life enough for the building of two hundred thousand new ones. It is sheer nonsense to desire the abolition of caste.

Inequality of Privilege Vitiates the System

It is in the nature of society to form itself into groups; and what will go will be these privileges! Caste is a natural order. I can perform one duty in social life, and you another; you can govern a country, and I can mend a pair of old shoes, but that is no reason why you are greater than I, for can you mend my shoes? Can I govern the country? I am clever in mending shoes, you are clever in reading Vedas, that is no reason why you should trample on my head; why if one commits murder should he be praised and if another steals an apple why should he be hanged? This will have to go.

Caste is good. That is only natural way of solving life. Men must form themselves into groups, and you cannot get rid of that. Wherever you go there will be caste. But that does not mean that there should be these privileges. They should be knocked on the head. If you teach Vedanta to the fisherman, he will say, "I am as good a man as you, I am a fisherman, you are a philosopher, but I have the same God in me, as you have in you." And that is what we want, no privilege for anyone, equal chances for all; let everyone be taught that the Divine is within, and everyone will work out his own salvation. The days of exclusive privileges and exclusive claims are gone, gone for ever from the soil of India.

Untouchability - A Superstitious Accretion

Formerly the characteristic of the noble-minded was - (*tribhuvanamupakara shrenibhih priyamanah*) "to please the whole universe by one's numerous acts of service", but now it is - I am pure and the whole world is impure. "Don't touch me!" "Don't touch me!" The whole world is impure, and I alone am pure! Lucid *Brahmajnana*! Bravo! Great God!

Nowadays, Brahman is neither in the recesses of the heart, nor in the highest heaven, nor in all beings - now He is in the cooking pot!

We are orthodox Hindus, but we refuse entirely to identify ourselves with "Don't- touchism". That is not Hinduism; it is in none of our books; it is an orthodox superstition, which has interfered with national efficiency all along the line. Religion has entered in the cooking pot. The present religion of the Hindus is neither the path of Knowledge or Reason - it is "Don't-touchism". - "Don't touch me", "Don't touch me" - that exhausts its description.

"Don't touchism" is a form of mental disease. Beware! All expansion is life, all contraction is death. All love is expansion, all selfishness is contraction. Love is therefore the only law of life. See that you do not lose your lives in this dire irreligion of "Don't- touchism". Must the teaching (*Atmavat sarvabhuteshu*) - "Looking upon all beings as your own self" - be confined to books alone? How will they grant salvation who cannot feed a hungry mouth with a crumb of bread? How will those, who become impure at the mere breath of others, purify others?

We must cease to tyrannize. To what a ludicrous state are we brought! If a bhangi comes to anybody as a bhangi, he would be shunned as the plague; but no sooner does he get a cupful of water poured upon his head with some muttering of prayers by a *padri*, and get a coat to his back, no matter how threadbare, and come into the room of the most orthodox Hindu, I don't see the man who then dare refuse him a chair and a hearty shake of hands! Irony can go no farther.

Just see, for want of sympathy from the Hindus, thousands of pariahs in Madras are turning Christians. Don't think that this is simply due to the pinch of hunger; it is because they do not get any sympathy from us. We are day and night calling out to them "Don't touch us! Don't touch us!" Is there any compassion or kindliness of heart in the country? Only a class of "Don't-touchists" ; kick such customs out! I sometimes feel the urge to break the barriers of "Don't-touchism", go at once and call out, "Come all who are poor, miserable, wretched and downtrodden", and to bring them all together. Unless they rise, the Mother will not awake.

Each Hindu, I say, is a brother to every other, and it is we, who have degraded them by our outcry, "Don't touch", "Don't touch!" And so the whole country has been plunged to the utmost depths of meanness, cowardice and ignorance. These men have to be lifted; words of hope and faith have to be proclaimed to them. We have to tell them, "You are also men like us and you have all the rights that we have."

Solution of the Caste Problem

Our solution of the caste question is not degrading those who are already high up, is not running amuck through food and drink, is not jumping out of our own limits in order to have more enjoyment, but it comes by every one of us fulfilling the dictates of our Vedantic religion, by our attaining spirituality and by our becoming ideal Brahman. There is a law laid on each one of you in this land by your ancestors, whether you are Aryans, or non-Aryans, rishis or Brahmans or the very lowest outcaste. The command is the same to you all, that you must make progress without stopping, and that from the highest man to the lowest Pariah, every one in this country has to try and become the ideal Brahman. This Vedantic idea is applicable not only here but over the whole world.

The Brahmanhood is the ideal of humanity in India as wonderfully put forward by Shankaracharya at the beginning of his commentary on the *Gita*, where he speaks about the reason for Krishna's coming as a preacher for the preservation of Brahmanhood, of Brahmanness. That was the great end. This Brahman, the man of God, he who has known Brahman, the ideal man, the perfect man, must remain, he must not go. And with all the defects of the caste now, we know that we must all be ready to give to the Brahmans this credit, that from them have come more men with real Brahmanness in them than from all the other castes. We must be bold enough, must be brave enough to speak their defects, but at the same time we must give credit that is due to them.

Therefore, it is no use fighting among the castes. What good will it do? It will divide us all the more, weaken us all the more, degrade us all the more. The solution is not by bringing down the higher, but by raising the lower up to the level of the higher. And that is the line of work that is found in all our books, in spite of what you may hear from some people whose knowledge of their own Scriptures and whose capacity to understand the mighty plans of the ancients are only zero. What is the plan? The ideal at the one end is the Brahman and the ideal at the other end is the Chandala, and the whole work is to raise the Chandala up to the Brahman. Slowly and slowly you will find more and more privileges granted to them.

I regret that in modern times there should be so much discussion between the castes. This must stop. It is useless on both sides, especially on the side of the higher caste, the Brahman, the day for these privileges and exclusive claims is gone. The duty of every aristocracy is to dig its own grave, and the sooner it does so, the better. The more he delays, the more it will fester and the worse death it will die. It is the duty of the Brahman, therefore, to work for the salvation of the rest of mankind, in India. If he does that and so long as he does that, he is a Brahman.

Any one who claims to be a Brahman, then, should prove his pretensions, first by manifesting that spirituality, and next by raising others to the same status. We earnestly entreat the Brahmans not to forget the ideal of India - the production of a universe of Brahmans, pure as purity, good as God Himself : this was at the beginning, says the *Mahabharata* and so will it be in the end.

It seems that most of the Brahmans are only nursing a false pride of birth; and any schemer, native or foreign, who can pander to this vanity and inherent laziness, by fulsome sophistry, appears to satisfy more.

Beware Brahmans, this is the sign of death! Arise and show your manhood, your Brahmanhood, by raising the non-Brahmans around you - not in the spirit of a master - not with the rotten canker of egoism crawling with superstitions and charlatanry of East and West - but in the spirit of a servant.

To the Brahmans I appeal, that they must work hard to raise the Indian people by teaching them what they know, by giving out the culture that they have accumulated for centuries. It is clearly the duty of the Brahmans of India to remember what real Brahmanhood is. As Manu says, all these privileges and honours are given to the Brahman because, "with him is the treasury of virtue". He must open that treasury and distribute to the world.

It is true that he was the earliest preacher to the Indian races, he was the first to renounce everything in order to attain to the higher realization of life, before others could reach to the idea. It was not his fault that he marched ahead of the other castes. Why did not the other castes so understand and do as they did? Why did they sit down and be lazy, and let the Brahmans win the race?

But it is one thing to gain an advantage, and another thing to preserve it for evil use. Whenever power is used for evil it becomes diabolical; it must be used for good only. So this accumulated culture of ages of which the Brahman has been the trustee, he must now give to the people, and it was because he did not open this treasury to the people, that the Muslims invasion was possible. It was because he did not open this treasury to the people from the beginning, that for a thousand years we have been trodden under the heels of everyone who chose to come to India; it was through that we have become degraded, and the first task must be to break open the cells that hide the wonderful treasures which our common ancestors accumulated; bring them out, and give them to everybody, and the Brahman must be the first to do it. There is an old superstition in Bengal that if the cobra that bites, sucks out his own poison from the patient, the man must survive. Well then, the Brahman must suck out his own poison.

To the non-Brahman castes I say, wait, be not in a hurry. Do not seize every opportunity of fighting the Brahman, because as I have shown; you are suffering from your own fault. Who told you to neglect spirituality and Sanskrit learning? What have you been doing all this time? Why have you been indifferent? Why do you now fret and fume because somebody else had more brains, more energy, more pluck and go than you? Instead of wasting your energies in vain discussions and quarrels in the newspapers, instead of fighting and quarreling in your own homes - which is sinful - use all your energies in acquiring the culture which the Brahman has, and the thing is done. Why do you not become Sanskrit scholars? Why do you not spend millions to bring Sanskrit education to all the castes of India? That is the question. The moment you do these things, you are equal to the Brahman! That is the secret power in India.

The only safety, I tell you men who belong to the lower castes, the only way to raise your condition is to study Sanskrit, and this fighting and writing and frothing against the higher castes is in vain, it does no good, and it creates fight and quarrel, and this race, unfortunately already divided, is going to be divided more and more. The only way to bring about the levelling of castes is to appropriate the culture, the education which is the strength of the higher castes.

B. HISTORY OF THE CASTE SYSTEM IN INDIA
What is the Caste System?

The caste system in India can be described as an elaborately stratified social hierarchy distinguishing India's social structure from any other nation. Its history is multifaceted and complex.

Caste is a term, which is used to specify a group of people having a specific social rank and dates back to 1200 BCE. The Indian term for caste is *jati*, and generally designates a group that can vary in size from a handful to many thousands. There are thousands of *jatis* each with its own rules and customs. The various *jatis* are traditionally arranged in hierarchical order and fit into one of the four basic *varnas* the (Sanskrit word for "colours").

- *The varna of Brahmans, commonly identified with priests and the learned class*
- *The varna of Kshatriyas, associated with rulers and warriors including property owners.*
- *The varna of Vaishyas, associated with commercial livelihoods (i.e., traders)*
- *The varna of Shudras, the servile labourers*

The untouchables occupy a place that is not clearly defined by boundaries and is outside of the *varna* scheme. Their jobs (such as toilet cleaning and garbage removal) cause them to be considered impure and thus "untouchable." Historically the untouchables were not allowed in temples and many other public places. In 1950 legislation was passed to prevent any form of discrimination towards the untouchables. Although legislation has affected the status of the people, they are yet very much a visible part of Indian society.

Religious Background

The earliest expressions of caste can be found in one of India's vast bodies of religious scripture known as the *Vedas*, which are though to have been complied between 1500 and 1000 BCE, although the time of their composition is under debate. They were transmitted orally for many generations before being written down. Therefore, centuries may have passed before they were ever committed to writing. These works are considered the source of ancient Indian wisdom. The first of the four basic *Vedic* books is the *Rig Veda*; a collection of over 1,000 hymns containing the basic mythology of the Aryan gods. The *Rig Veda* contains one of the most famous sections in ancient Indian literature in which the first man created, Purusa, is sacrificed in order to give rise to the four *varnas.*

"The Brahmin was his mouth, his two arms were made the Rajanya [Kshatriya, king and warrior], his two thighs [loins] the Vaishya, from his feet the Sudra [servile class] was born."

It can be argued that the composers of the *Vedas*, especially those sections within the *Vedas* called the Brahmans, were concerned with the interconnections that organized reality (Smith, 7). This way of looking at the *varnas* allows us to see how such a system can survive several millennia. It classifies people not only in terms of their different qualities but also with respect to their different privileges. Each class thus has a special role to play in society as well as a unique function: this structure is a means of creating and organizing an effective society. The *varna* system is inter-linked with creation, lending itself a great deal of reverence and validity.

If space, time the congregation of the gods and goddesses, the natural world, scripture and ritual, and the human body itself— if all these realms bear classification according to *varna*, how could an organization of society be regarded as anything other than the way things should be?

An important thing to note is that the Vedas do not mention a concept such as untouchability. It is a part of the system that has been created by society itself.

Society Pre-Colonialism

Although the nation has a long and varied history, the role of the caste system pre-colonialism can be understood by focusing on the major eras in Indian history. Much of India is rural and that which is not, for the most part, is much more urban. With such a drastic difference in the city and the village there is also a difference in the way caste has been interpreted and implemented over the years.

The early system most represented something analogous to the Medieval guild system. It allowed a specialization of society and each member knew their role. Much later in India's history, as India became more and more prevalent in the international scene the concept of the caste sytem began to have different connotations. It was thought of as backward by much of the west. The greatest changes in the perception as well as in reality came with the coming and going of the British.

C. CASTE SYSTEM IN INDIA

Caste marks do not, in fact, exist. The caste system, of course, does but the concept has been grossly degraded by 19th century colonialist historians who saw only its surface rigidities and made sweeping generalizations, (condemnatory for the most part), based on too little knowledge and even less experience. It is however ironic, that they never saw the parallels with the European system of guilds that divided artisans into separate social and economic entities on the basis of their specialization and sub-specializations.

For that is in simplified terms what the caste system is

all about - a stratified and hierarchical socio-economic organization of society that evolved as India's ancient civilizations, (with its own social order, moral and ritual codes), absorbed the nomadic, Sanskrit speaking Aryan populations who crossed the mountain passes from the steppes of Central Asia and settled in Northern India. The ancient Hindus, literally meaning the peoples of the valley of the Indus river, soon took on functions and specializations that had little to do with tilling the soil. The four castes developed out of necessity, for with the evolution of society it was no longer possible for the tiller of the soil to assume the functions of priest, warrior, merchant, and artisan all rolled in one.

A new way of life brought with it a need for governance and order, defence and conquest, learning and trade, labourers and artisans. Roles began to be defined and people were classified according to their function, occupation and economic place in society. Brahmins' were to be the spiritual and temporal guides, teachers and exponents of law; Kshatriya were the warriors, princes and kings - in short, the nobility; Vaishya, took on the tasks of agriculture and merchantry; and Shudra included individuals who performed service communities — manual and agricultural labourers, artisans, masons, etc.The 4th group, Sudra, denotes the service communities - manual and agricultural labourers, artisans, masons, etc. Although they lived on the fringes of society, the "outcastes" or "untouchables", the 5th group in the hierarchy, were still very much a part of the mainstream of society as the tasks of scavenging, cleaning up after funerals, killing or hunting animals for food, working in leather and other unclean materials, all fell to them. Mahatma Gandhi in the 1940s renamed them Harijan, which when literally translated means "the people of God". There was a 6th group too, the *mlechcha*, (outsiders, or foreigners) who, like the Greeks, Kushans, Scythians and other invaders who settled in India, were gradually absorbed in the *varnas* (caste system) according to their profession.

The word caste is not Indian but comes from the Portuguese word *casta* (breed or race). The Sanskrit word applied to the groupings is *varna*, which means several things but is often interpreted to signify colour. In a verse from the first millennium epic, the *Mahabharata*, Brigu, the sage explains: "The Brahmins are fair, the Kshatriyas are reddish, the Vaishyas yellow and the Sudras are black."

According to available evidence, the majority of the people seems to be radically very mixed, and to quote the *Mahabharata* again, "If different colours indicate different castes, then all castes are mixed castes." The Hindus also believe that a man's *varna* is determined by his profession and deeds and not by his birth. Besides, the ancients were not racists. The truth of the matter probably lies in the fact that *varna*, like a lot of Sanskrit words, changes its meaning according to the context it is used in and can denote form, quality, class, category, race, merit or virtue.

Eventually, however, *varna* came to signify an endogamic group, its members linked by heredity, marriage, custom and profession. Professions became diversified with the evolution of society and whole groups of people took on a new identity which was associated with the economic activity of their *gotra* (clan) and became subdivisions of the *varna*s. The laws that govern the *varna*s, and particularly the taboo on inter-caste marriages, have maintained the "purity" of the "breed" thus denoting "caste."

The most peculiar of the social institutions of India is the caste system. It is peculiar in the sense that it is confined to India and is found nowhere else in the world. It is peculiar because of the extreme social segmentation which it produces; it is also peculiar because it is not a purely social system but is so closely interwoven with Hinduism as to have certain religious elements. Each member of the Hindu community belongs to one or other of over 2,000 castes, which divide into groups arranged in a complex system of social differentiation. As between its members, a caste is a bond of union, but the system splits up society into sections which, owing to the prohibitions not only against inter-marriage, but also against eating, drinking, and even smoking together, prevent social fusion more perhaps than any other institution in the world. The caste system thus at once unites and divides thousands of groups, but its salient feature is mutual exclusiveness, for each caste regards other castes as separate communities with which it has no concern. The system does not however preclude association for common purposes or social intercourse, for subject to the restrictions which it imposes on mutual hospitality and matrimonial connections, members of different castes may be on terms of intimacy or even friendship. The caste system is the antithesis of the principle that all men are equal, for there is a hierarchy of castes, based on the principle that men neither are nor can be equal. The different castes rank as high or low according to the degree of honour in which they are held by the Hindu community as a whole, subject to the pre-eminence of the Brahman, who forms, as it were, the apex of a pyramid in which other castes are superimposed in layers, one upon another.

A man belongs to, and, except in rare cases, remains till death in, the caste in which he is born. The social position of each individual is fixed by heredity and not by personal qualifications and material considerations. Differences of status are justified by the religious doctrines of *Karma* and the transmigration of souls. *Karma*, which many Hindus regard as the central doctrine of their religion, is briefly the belief that a man reaps as he sows, that he benefits by goods deeds and is doomed to suffer as a consequence of evil deeds... A man's caste, is, therefore, determined by his past. It is his birthright by the working of an eternal and inexorable law. ...Though his caste is fixed unalterably in this life, he may be reborn in a higher caste as a reward for righteous conduct and faithful performance of duty... The number of castes is not immutable...The Lingayat sect, for example, which arose in the twelfth century, had as one of its objects the abolition of caste distinctions; besides this, it was so imbued with the spirit of reform that it repudiated the practice of infant marriage and allowed the marriage of widows. By the seventeenth century the sect had introduced caste divisions, and had split up into sections which allowed no intermarriage...They still deny the religious supremacy of Brahmans, but they are not singular in this respect, for certain artisan castes in Madras also contend that there is no need for the religious services of Brahmans and themselves claim the status of Brahmans. ...So far from waging a war of extermination the Aryans formed alliances with non-Aryans whose power made them formidable, converted them to Hinduism, and admitted them to their ranks.

This is a process which has continued down to modern times, for it is a well-known fact that among the Rajputs, who represent the Kshatriyas (the fighting men of the Aryans), there are many descendents of aboriginals whose fighting qualities entitled them to respect... There were thus divisions based primarily on race and partly on occupation. To these were added a more subtle and lasting differentiation based on religious status. The last appears in the classification of society found in the Laws of Manu. This is a Brahman work of comparatively late date—in its present form it is ascribed to between the second century B.C. and the second century A.D.—which is regarded by the Hindus as the highest authority on their social institutions and family law. According to this work there were four classes arranged in order of precedence, viz. Brahmans, an order of priests and law-givers, who represented the world of religion and learning; Kshatriyas, the fighting and ruling class; Vaishyas, who were engaged in commercial, agricultural, and pastoral pursuits; and Sudras, whose life was one of service to the other three classes and who also obtained a living by handicrafts. These four classes were called *varnas*, a word meaning colour, which undoubtedly had racial implications. The distinction between the four was, however, not based on race but partly on occupation and partly on religion. The first three classes had a spiritual birth right which was denied to the Sudras. They were recognized as 'twice-born', i.e., they went through a ceremony of initiation at an early age which made them eligible for religious rites.

The Sudras had no such religious privilege and were from birth to death under a religious disability marking their inferior status. Below these four classes again was a fifth class consisting of degraded races, such as that known as *Chandal*, which were regarded as completely outside the pale. The existing system is the growth of centuries, as major divisions have split into minor divisions and castes have been divided and subdivided over and over again, and eventually become stereotyped. The continual process of segmentation is the result of many causes, such as racial, religious and occupational distinction, territorial distribution, and, to some extent also, the regulations made by Hindu kings on the advice of their Brahman councilors in different parts of India. The caste system...It governs such matters as diet; it lays down marriage laws; it regulates to some extent the actual means of livelihood. There is an almost bewildering variety of usages as the combined result of many factors. One is that some castes have traces of a tribal organization, which affects their marriage laws. Another is that physical geography affects customs, especially of diet, in different areas: fish, for example, is a popular dish in the land of great rivers like Bengal, where it is abundant and cheap, but is eschewed in places where it is scarce and dear. A third is the fact that a caste is largely an autonomous unit. Certain principles, especially those relating to religion, may be laid down by the Brahmans, but their application and the enunciation of others are left to the castes themselves, and the castes often act in entire independence both of the Brahmans and of one another.

Much also depends on the extent to which the different castes follow Brahmanical teaching and observe the orthodox tenets of Hinduism; and it must be remembered that many of the lower castes, though recognizing the great Hindu deities, have animistic beliefs and worship gods and godlings unknown to Brahmanism. In the great majority of cases their religious rites are conducted by non-Brahmans; Brahmans neither officiate at their domestic ceremonies nor act as their religious preceptors; and they live in ignorance of Brahmanical doctrines, whereas higher castes base their social code on the Hindu scriptures... The caste system splits up society into a multitude of little communities, for every caste, and almost every local unit of a caste, has its own peculiar customs and internal regulations. The members of each caste believe that they are all descended from a common ancestor, who may have been either a real or a mythical personage. The idea of kinship is, as pointed out by Sir Herbert Risley, 'certainly the oldest and perhaps the most enduring factor in the caste system and seems to have supplied the framework and the motive principles of the more modern restrictions based upon ceremonial usage and community of occupation'. It is probably on this account that the most important and the most rigid of the rules laid down by caste are those which are concerned with marriage. The principal rule is that of endogamy, under which the members of each caste must marry within, and may not marry outside, the caste. The internal organization of the caste is also determined by regulations as to marriage. It is subdivided into sub-castes, which again are further subdivided into groups, and both the sub-castes and these groups are delimited on matrimonial lines. The three bodies may be compared to concentric circles, the caste being an outer circle, the sub-caste an inner circle, and the nuclear matrimonial group, the innermost circle. The sub-castes generally resemble the caste in being endogamous, for marriage to any one other than a member of the same sub-caste is unlawful. On the other hand the innermost group, which is known by various names (such as *gotra, got, kul*), is exogamous. The members of each are, or believe themselves to be, descended in the male line from a common ancestor, and intermarriage between them is looked on as little sort of incest, so that they are obliged to marry outside the group but within the sub-caste. The fission of castes into sub-castes is due to many causes. One of the most frequent is the adoption of different occupation: it is common, for example, for the members of a caste who sell an article to separate from, and claim superiority to, those who produce it. Differences of social customs are another cause of division, e.g., those who prohibit the remarriage of widows and those who permit it form separate sub-castes. Membership of different religious sects is a third line of demarcation. For instance, one sub-caste may be Vaishnava, i.e., Vishnu is the object of adoration, and will not intermarry with a Saiva sub-caste, which specially venerates Siva. Territorial distribution also operates in the same way, members of a caste who have different places of origin or present residence being grouped in distinct sub-castes.

Difference of language is yet another barrier to union in some parts of Madras, where members of a caste who speak

Tamil, Telugu and Kanarese belong to as many different sub-castes... The conception of purity and impurity is the key to many of the apparent enigmas of the caste system, and Dr. Ketkar regards it as the chief principle on which the system depends. "The Brahman is at the top of society because he is more pure and sacred than other castes, while Mahar and Paraiyan are at the bottom because they are impure. Thus purity is the pivot on which the entire system turns. Rank, social position, economic condition have no direct effect on the gradation from the standpoint of caste...Caste in India is strong and rigid because the ideas of the people regarding purity and pollution are rigid. "The idea of relative purity and consequent social inequality underlies the rules as to eating and drinking together... ...the Laws of Manu forbade the higher castes to reside outside the land of their birth, and this injunction is still observed by orthodox circles... ...The ideas as to what are honourable and what are dishonourable occupations are so extraordinarily varied that they can be reduced to no common factor. One idea which is generally prevalent, and which has its roots in the remote past, is that industrial occupations and labourer's manual work are base pursuits. There is no conception of the dignity of labour in India. The higher castes despise manual work and consider it beneath their dignity. Those castes whose hereditary means of livelihood is some handicraft, such as carpentry, pottery-making, oil manufacture, blacksmith's work, etc., all come within the lower grades of castes. Neither Brahmans nor Rajputs, many of whom are land-holders, may undertake the physical labour of cultivation, above all, they must not, however poor, drive the plough. To do so is derogatory to their high estate, and they must maintain themselves as gentleman farmers...

One main object (of the Laws of Manu) was undoubtedly to maintain the Brahman in a privileged position as a sacrosanct order with a monopoly of learning. This position they long maintained, and under early Hindu rule they were like the clergy of the Catholic Church in medieval times, who, as Froude points out in Times of Erasmus and Luther, reigned supreme over prince and peasant by the magic of sanctity, and the monopoly of learning, and enjoyed the secular power which learning, combined with sanctity and assisted by superstition, can bestow... ...whatever may have been the case in ancient times, caste can no longer be said to determine occupation... ...the Rajputs and Jats, who number many millions, are organized on tribal lines, and though they have caste rules, do not observe the rule of endogamy which is generally characteristic of the caste system. They occasionally intermarry, the Rajputs, who have the higher status, taking Jat wives but refusing to marry their daughters to Jat husbands... ...the Marathas and the Maratha Kunbis, and the Marathas, who claim to be the higher of the two, will marry Marathi Kunbi women but will not give their own women in marriage to them... Kathis (of Kathiawar)...divided into two sections called Sakhayat (land-owners) and Awartya (landless), and a member of one must marry a member of the other... The caste system is seen in its greatest rigour and precision in the south of India...an almost complete absence of what may be called the middle castes, the representatives of the Kshatriyas and Vaishyas...A number of the castes belong to one or other of two great factions called Right-hand and Left-hand, a division unknown in any other part of India. The Right-hand faction consists mainly of cultivating and trading castes, the Left-hand of industrial castes. The schism dates back many centuries...one theory is that it originated in a revolt by artisan castes against Brahman domination and was connected with the struggle between Jainism and Brahmanism, the former religion, which was stronger in urban areas, finding adherents in the artisan class, which was largely urban, while the latter was upheld by the conservative cultivators. Certain it is that the artisan class, who lead the Left-hand faction, deny the supremacy of Brahmans, call themselves Viswa Brahmans, and wear the sacred thread. The two factions are bitterly hostile.

The caste system has infected to some extent the social system of the lower classes of Moslems, tough it is utterly at variance with the precepts and traditions of Islam... 'As the twice-born Aryan is to the mass of Hindus, so is the Mohammedan of alleged Persian, Afghan or Moghal origin to the rank and file of his co-religionists, although now, since many descendants of converts from Hinduism have by education and position sprung to the fore, they too are receiving more honour than formerly and are even sought after for marriage with daughters of foreign extraction. Saiyids again have objections to women of their families marrying Sheikhs, though they will take wives from the latter, whom they raise to their own level. There are further two main social groups called Ashraf and Ajlaf, and as a rule a member of the former will not willingly give his daughter in marriage to a man of the latter.

The Depressed Classes covers not only low status in the hierarchy of caste combined with religious and social disabilities, but also a low economic condition. ...Most of the depressed classes obtain their livelihood by labour, chiefly agricultural. A minority are artisans, village servants and small cultivators... ...Educationally, the depressed classes are on as low a level as they are economically: the census of 1931 has shown that only 3 per cent are literate...some have risen in secular professions, and the present leader of the depressed classes, Dr. Ambedkar, a Mahar by caste, who has been a Delegate to the Round Table Conference, has distinguished himself in the sphere of politics... ..(Arya Samaj) has admitted the depressed classes in large numbers to its membership...Mr. Gandhi himself has advocated their social claims for many years. He has adopted a girl of an untouchable caste as his daughter, and in his seminary (ashram) no sweepers are kept... Dr. Ambedkar observed: "Hindu society does not think rationally about its conduct towards the depressed classes. It leads its customary life and is not prepared to relinquish it even at the bidding of Mr. Gandhi. It refuses to reassess its old values. As regards temple entry, the depressed classes all over India have made it clear to Mr. Gandhi that they will have nothing to do with it regarded as a final solution of the problem of removal of untouchability. They would accept it only if Mr. Gandhi would make it clear that it was the first step in a general reform of Hindu society involving the break-up of the caste system."

As Surendranath Banerjea quoted: "You cannot think

of a social question affecting the Hindu community that is not bound up with religious considerations...The social reformer in India has to fight against forces believed to be semi-divine in their character and more or less invulnerable against the commonplace and mundane weapons of expediency and common sense."

(The view of Brahmans) of Hinduism is like that of Judaism expressed by Isaac Disraeli, viz. that everything in it is ancient and nothing is obsolete... ...Now that others have the key to the Vedas, the position of the Brahmans as the only arbiters in social, as well as religious, matters has been undermined. An appeal can be and is, made by Hindu reformers to the picture of pristine society as given in the Vedas, which knew nothing of the present elaborate caste system, and did not recognize child marriages or purdah, but allowed women to lead a free and natural life. Practices of the present day are shown to have no sanction in the most ancient of the Hindu scriptures, and to be not an essential component of Hinduism, but later accretions... 'Back to the Vedas' was the slogan of Swami Dayanand Saraswati, the founder of the Arya Samaj, which seeks to restore an earlier and simpler form of Hinduism and, by ridding it of excrescencies, to effect both religious and social reform. It advocates monotheism, it denounces idolatry, the evil of child marriages, and the ban on the remarriage of widows, and it favours the abolition of untouchability and reform of the caste system, which, it announces, should rest on the basis of worth, not birth... Castes which, though ranking above the depressed classes are still of low status, are also pressing for admission to a higher place in the gradation of castes. There is, however, no general demand for the abolition of caste and for the levelling down of the higher castes. What is aimed at by the lower castes is levelling up. So far from advocating any destruction of the social pyramid which the system has built up, they desire merely a higher place in it. Nothing is more noticeable than their anxiety to be recognized as twice-born castes, their assumption in some cases of the sacred thread, which is the outward and visible sign of the twice-born castes, and the increasing solidarity resulting from the formation of caste associations, which seek to better their position by means of organization and agitation as well as by education. ...In Madras, again, the political domination of the Brahmans has been shaken by the Justice Party, which represents non-Brahman and stands for justice and equality between all men irrespective of caste, while a branch of the party called 'the self-respect movement' preaches the same doctrine in social matters, and advocates the independence and self-assertion of the non-Brahman... ...An immense majority of the population is characterized by an ingrained conservatism, an intense reluctance to disturb the existing order of things.. the main structure of caste remains intact with its mutually exclusive communities, its carefully regulated gradations of rank, and the ban on intermarriage which prevents any fusion of classes: it is as if some superficial cracks had appeared on the stucco front of a building, while the brickwork behind it remains solid...In spite of its obvious defects, the artificial barriers which it maintains between classes, the irrational customs which it sanctions, and the rational practices which it forbids, it is not only the basis of social order, but also in a large measure the source and inspiration of social morality, and its destruction would be a dangerous revolution unless its place can be taken by another and a better system.

The Theories of the Caste System

There are different theories about the establishment of the caste system. There are religious-mystical theories. There are biological theories. And there are socio-historical theories.

The religious theories explain how the four *varnas* were founded, but they do not explain how the Jats in each *varna* or the untouchables were founded. According to the *Rig Veda*, the ancient Hindu book, the primal man - *Purush* - destroyed himself to create a human society. The different *varnas* were created from different parts of his body. The Brahmans were created from his head; the Kshatrias from his hands; the Vaishyas from his thighs and the Sudras from his feet. The *varna* hierarchy is determined by the descending order of the different organs from which the *varnas* were created.

Other religious theory claims that the *varnas* were created from the body organs of Brahma, who is the creator of the world.

The biological theory claims that all existing things, animated and inanimated, inherent three qualities in different apportionment. *Sattva* qualities include wisdom, intelligence, honesty, goodness and other positive qualities. Rajas include qualities like passion, pride, valour and other passionate qualities. *Tamas* qualities include dullness, stupidity, lack of creativity and other negative qualities. People with different doses of these inherent qualities adopted different types of occupation. According to this theory the Brahmans inherent *Sattva* qualities. Kshatrias and Vaishyas inherent Raja's qualities. And the Sudras inherent *Tamas* qualities.

Like human beings, food also inherent different dosage of these qualities and it affects its eater's intelligence. The Brahmans and the Vaishyas have *Sattvic* diet which includes fruits, milk, honey, roots and vegetables. Most of the meats are considered to have *Tamasic* qualities. Many Sudra communities eat different kinds of meat (but not beef) and other *Tamasic* food. But the Kshatrias who had *Rajasic* diet eat some kinds of meat like deer meat which is considered to have *Rajasic* qualities. Many Marathas who claim to be Kshatrias eat mutton. The drawback of this theory is that in different parts of India the same food was sometimes qualified to have different dosage of inherent qualities. For example, there were Brahmans who eat meat which is considered *Tamasic* food.

The social historical theory explains the creation of the *varnas*, *Jats* and of the untouchables. According to this theory, the caste system began with the arrival of the Aryans in India. The Aryans arrived in India around 1500 BC. The fair skinned Aryans arrived in India from south Europe and north Asia. Before the Aryans there were other communities in India of other origins. Among them Negrito, Mongoloid, Austroloid and Dravidian. The Negrito have physical features similar to people of Africa. The Mongoloid have Chinese features. The Austroloids have features similar the aboriginals of Australia. The Dravidians originate from the

Mediterranean and they were the largest community in India. When the Aryans arrived in India their main contact was with the Dravidians and the Austroloids. The Aryans disregarded the local cultures. They began conquering and taking control over regions in north India and at the same time pushed the local people southwards or towards the jungles and mountains in north India.

The Aryans organized among themselves in three groups. The first group was of the warriors and they were called Rajayana, later they changed their name Rajayana to Kshatria. The second group was of the priests and they were called Brahmans. These two groups struggled politically for leadership among the Aryans. In this struggle the Brahmans got to be the leaders of the Aryan society. The third group was of the farmers and craftsmen and they were called Vaisia. The Aryans who conquered and took control over parts of north India subdued the locals and made them their servants. In this process the Vaishyas who were the farmers and the craftsmen became the landlords and the businessmen of the society and the locals became the peasants and the craftsmen of the society.

In order to secure their status the Aryans resolved some social and religious rules which, allowed only them to be the priests, warriors and the businessmen of the society. For example, take Maharashtra. Maharashtra is in west India. This region is known by this name for hundreds of years. Many think that the meaning of the name Maharashtra is in its name, Great Land. But there are some who claim that the name, Maharashtra, is derived from the Jat called Mahar who are considered to be the original people of this region. In the caste hierarchy the dark skinned Mahars were outcasts. The skin colour was an important factor in the caste system. The meaning of the word "*varna*" is not class or status but skin colour.

As in most of the societies of the world, so in India, the son inherited his father's profession. And so in India there developed families, who professed the same family profession for generation in which, the son continued his father's profession. Later on as these families became larger, they were seen as communities or as they are called in Indian languages, *Jat*. Different families who professed the same profession developed social relations between them and organized as a common community, meaning *Jat*.

Later on the Aryans who created the caste system, added to their system non-Aryans. Different *Jats* who professed different professions were integrated in different *varnas* according to their profession. Other foreign invaders of ancient India - Greeks, Huns, Scythians and others - who conquered parts of India and created kingdoms were integrated in the Kshatria *varna* (warrior castes). But probably the Aryan policy was not to integrate original Indian communities within them and therefore many aristocratic and warrior communities that were in India before the Aryans did not get the Kshatria status.

Most of the communities that were in India before the arrival of the Aryans were integrated in the Sudra *varna* or were made outcast depending on the professions of these communities. Communities who professed non-polluting jobs were integrated in Sudra *Varna*. And communities who professed polluting professions were made outcastes. The Brahmans are very strict about cleanliness. In the past people believed that diseases can also spread also through air and not only through physical touch. Perhaps because of this reason the untouchables were not only disallowed to touch the high caste communities but they also had to stand at a certain distance from the high castes.

The Religious Aspect of Caste System

In Hinduism there exists four castes arranged in a hierarchy. Anyone who does not belong to one of these castes is an outcast. The religious word for caste is 'varna'. Each *varna* has certain duties and rights. Each *varna* members have to work in certain occupation which only that *varna* members are allowed. Each *varna* has certain type of diet. The highest *varna* is of the Brahman. Members of this class are priests and the educated people of the society. The *varna* after them in hierarchy is Kshatriya. The members of this class are the rulers and aristocrats of the society. After them are the Vaishya. Members of this class are the landlords and businessmen of the society. After them in hierarchy are the Sudra. Members of this class are the peasants and working class of the society who work in non-polluting jobs. The caste hierarchy ends here. Below these castes are the outcastes who are untouchable to the four castes. These untouchables worked in degrading jobs like cleaning, sewage, etc.

The first three castes had social and economical rights which the Sudra and the untouchables did not have. The first three castes are also seen as 'twice born'. The intention in these two births is to the natural birth and to the ceremonial entrance to the society at a much later age.

Each *varna* and also the untouchables are divided into many communities. These communities are called *Jat* or *Jati* (The caste is also used instead of *Jat*). For example, the Brahmans have Jats called Gaur, Konkanash, Saraswat, Iyer and others. The outcastes have Jats like Mahar, Dhed, Mala, Madiga and others. The Sudra is the largest *varna* and it has the largest number of communities. Each *Jat* is limited to professions worthy of their *varna*. Each *Jat* is limited to the *varna* diet. Each *Jat* members are allowed to marry only with their *Jat* members. People are born into their *Jat* and it cannot be changed.

This is the how the caste system is supposed to be in its religious form. But in reality it is much more complicated and different from its religious form.

References

Rapsom, E.J., *The Cambridge History of India*, Volume I.
Macdonell and Keith, *Vedic Index of Names and Subjects*, London, 1912.
The Aryan Household, ed, 1891.
Ketkar, S.V., *History of Caste in India*, New Delhi, 1995.
Monie Williams, Sanskrit Dictionary.
The Indian Empire, Vol.II, Oxford, 1909.
Dutt, N.K., *Origin and Growth of Caste in India.*
Senart, Emile, *Caste in India.*
Vedic Index I.
Vedic Index II.
Ibbetson, Denzil, *The Races, Castes and Tribes of the People*, 1881.
Miller, S.M., *Comparative Social Mobility.*
Ghurye, G.S., *Caste and Race*, Bombay, 1932.
Hartog Committee's Report.

1

Caste System : Early Stages

In May 1901 the Government of India issued orders for the
commencement of the Ethnographical Survey of the
Provinces (Bombay, Madras, Bengal, Punjab, Burma, Assam,
United Provinces and Central Provinces), and proposed that
the inquiries into the origin, social configuration, customs
and occupations of the numerous castes and tribes should
be spread over a period of four or five years. These inquiries
were to follow closely the lines of certain questions approved
by Messrs. Nesfield, Ibbetson and Risley at a conference
held in 1885. They were to be carried out by the
Superintendents in addition to their ordinary official duties.

It was not found possible to allow more than a few
thousand rupees annually to each province for the work of
the Survey; and before the work was half done, i.e., in 1909,
even this small financial provision was withdrawn. The
Survey has since been practically dependent on the
voluntary labours of the Superintendent in charge, with such
assistance as he was able to secure without the expenditure
of funds. This voluntary assistance has been forthcoming
from three sources. Certain scholars such as D. R.
Bhandarkar and B. A. Gupte have placed their knowledge
at the disposal of the Superintendent and assisted the work
of the survey in the capacity of Honorary Assistants. A
number of gentlemen have furnished valuable materials in

the capacity of Honorary Correspondents. Finally, certain local committees organized by the Superintendent during the course of census operations in 1901 for the purposes of investigating and reporting on caste questions have supplied materials of considerable value and interest. With this assistance it has been possible to complete the survey of the tribes and castes in the Presidency, excluding Sind, by the beginning of the present year. The work has involved the preparation of nearly 500 articles. These have been published in draft form and circulated for criticism before being finally embodied in the Survey record.

It may at once be admitted that the work could not possibly have been completed, even in this greatly extended period, had it not been for the very full materials available in the pages of the Bombay Gazetteers compiled by the late James Campbell. Much of the work of the Survey has indeed consisted of the re-arrangement of these materials, which were drawn up originally on a district basis instead of dealing with tribes and castes as a whole. When compared with more recent information, the original district accounts have been found to be remarkably accurate in detail. With the assistance described, and in such leisure as was available to the Superintendent, in spite of the pre-occupation of more important official duties, a considerable amount of new information has been collected regarding the tribes and castes of the Bombay Presidency. The ensuing pages thus contain much new matter, though the main source of, information has been found in the pages of the Bombay District Gazetteers, which contain accounts remarkable both for their fullness and accuracy.

At the time of issuing the first of the draft Monographs, of which the complete series is now published in these volumes, I indicated that the tribes and castes recorded in the Census Tables of 1901, and numbering over 500, would be dealt with in three classes :

Class 1, being those containing one hundred thousand members, were to be described as fully as possible;

Class 2, being those between one hundred thousand and five thousand, were to be dealt with in less detail;

Class 3, being those under five thousand, was for the most part to be described merely by rearranging the materials on the line of the Ethnographical questions.

This scheme has been adhered to. The only important departure from the general scheme outlined in 1903 at the time of publishing the first monograph, dealing with the Ahir, is the omission of the tribes and castes of Sind.

In the course of revising existing materials for the caste accounts a number of new caste divisions have been discovered, both in connection with the groups inside which marriage is essential, and the smaller divisions inside which marriage is forbidden. These are referred to in this work respectively as endogamous and exogamous groups. They are of special interest as the interior structure of a caste is frequently valuable evidence of its origin. It has also been found that certain caste names are synonyms. Castes have in such cases been re-grouped. In connection with castes of converts from Hinduism to Islam, useful information has been obtained from the marriage registers of the *Kazis,* showing the cases in which intermarriage between such castes is allowed. Many Musalman castes adhere to the Hindu practice of endogamy. Among those Musalman caste which intermarry are found armourers, butchers, farriers, elephant-drivers, and similar occupational groups which are probably descendants of the camp followers of the Mughal armies. It is interesting to note that contact with the Muhammdan armies has left its influence in the greater freedom with which intermarriage is allowed. The social prejudice which prevents members of many Mohammadan castes from marrying outside the caste is a relic of the previously existing Hindu custom, such castes being clearly traceable to a Hindu origin before conversion.

Muslim Rule

They are found chiefly in areas where Musalman rule has stimulated conversion, either by example, as in Bijapur, or by force as in north Kanara, once under the dominion of Hyder and Tipu. A great deal of new information has been obtained regarding the interesting Lingayat community, which is found to be based partly on religious and partly on caste distinctions. The special interest of the community lies in the fact that it exhibits the process by which a religious movement, starting with the abolition of caste distinctions, develops slowly into a community of which the most recent converts adhere strictly to the non-intermarrying caste distinctions of their Hindu ancestors.

The survey has brought to light a great deal of new information regarding totemistic divisions in the Deccan and Southern Maratha Country. The identification of Maratha guardians or devakas with Kanarese *balis* is an indication of a similarity of origin between certain castes and tribes of the Presidency, which has not hitherto been suspected.

Tribe Defined

Broadly speaking, the term tribe is used for a unit based on common descent as opposed to the term caste which is applied to a social unit founded on common occupation, common residence, common language or common political control. A social unit based on religion is described as a sect.

From the dawn of history India has been subject to invasion by land and sea, and the invaders who were themselves very probably of mixed origin, have seldom refrained from intermarriage with the heterogeneous population already established in the country. In the Institutes of Manu we find an attempt to classify the resulting units of mixed descent under different names. The process of admixture of blood has continued to the present day. Probably its influence was especially marked during the series of post-Aryan invasions between the third century B.C. and the sixth century A.D. By this time Aryan, Dravidian, and mixed Aryo-Dravidian castes were numerous. *Intermarriage with the invading tribes such as the Ahirs, Gujars and other Scythian units must have led to a great* complexity of racial types, each naturally tending to preserve, itself from further admixture of blood, by forming a marriage group excluded by the purer groups from intermarriage, and itself refusing to countenance unions with those who were members of groups regarded as inferior owing to greater impurity of blood.

To the influence of race, in itself of great importance, would shortly be added the effect of varying occupations as the tribal units passed from the pastoral to the agricultural state and from that to the practice of arts and handicrafts. Thus true castes were formed; but occupation would not ordinarily obliterate the racial distinctions already referred to. The occupational group would contain various ethnic groups remaining endogamous. In this way, if we start with the idea of descent, we can show the population in tribes divided into groups (castes) following different occupations; or, starting from the occupations, we may show the caste including a number of different tribal groups. The Ahirs and Gujars, immigrant tribe of great importance, are now broken into many caste sections such as those found in the Shimpis, Sonars, Sutars, Chamars, etc. We may, therefore, show Ahirs and Gujars with their occupational divisions as forming part of the tribe, or the castes as a whole, with Ahir and Gujar as sub-castes. In both cases, the sub-divisions are the endogamous units.

Tribe and Caste

Tribe and caste, therefore, are different ways of looking at the same social groups, the tribe being the forerunner of the caste. Unfortunately, the question of the correct classification of such groups is further complicated by other influences besides those of descent and occupation. Of these the principal are religion and domicile.

The effect of religious movements, such as Jainism, Lingayatism, Islam and Christianity on social grouping is especially interesting. Jains, found almost entirely in Gujrat and Bombay City, usually form an endogamous division of the occupational caste, though dining with the Hindu element may be permissible. Lingayatism is more complex. Starting with a repudiation of caste distinctions, Lingayats have passed through several phases, the earlier converts coming in time to separate themselves from those who joined later; and ultimately, as in the case of Jains, Lingayats merely form an endogamous division of the Hindu group from which they were converted. Islam should not recognize caste; but the practice varies. There are Muhammdan castes that marry with other castes of the same faith. There are many that will not marry within their own caste, though of course not with the Hindu members. Even Christianity has been a source of caste division in places; for there are three caste divisions of Christians in Goanese territory, known as Brahman, Chardo and Sudra; and certain castes such as Bhandaris, Kolis and Kunbis contain Christian sections that only marry within such sections.

Most important in its effect on caste formation is the influence of domicile and language. A portion of a caste separated by migration from its parent body tends to develop certain differences in customs, occupation or interest. Owing to the common tendency to exaggerate the importance of such differences which is a specially Indian characteristic, marriage with the original body of the caste is frequently abandoned on account of these small differences. In the past, no doubt, the difficulty *of* communication accelerated this process. Marriages with caste fellows separated by a lengthy and tedious journey from a remote section of the caste would tend to be of rare occurrence, and eventually be looked on as in someway contrary to caste practice, that is to say, as unlawful. The result can be traced in numerous cases where the sub-castes have a territorial name.

A.M.T. Jackson has drawn attention to the fact that a change of domicile on the part of a portion of a caste was peculiarly liable to create new sub-caste owing to the powers exercised by Hindu rulers over the caste organizations. As supreme authority, the king must decide questions of caste practice; and he might well do so in such a way as to create local practices at variance with the custom of sections of the caste under another jurisdiction. Here again the proneness of the people to attach undue importance to small points of difference would lead to intermarriage being abandoned between the sections of the caste under different political control. This is no doubt a good instance of the effect of domicile on caste fission. Jackson's theory will be found to derive much support from the close resemblance between the sub-divisions of the two leading castes in Gujarat, the Brahmins and Vanis, which have many of the same territorial names.

In the Deccan, where in Hindu times political control was more uniform than in Gujarat, Castes have retained a greater measure of cohesion. This has been preserved under Muhammdan rule, even though the Deccan was then divided between five, and subsequently three, kingdoms. Mohammdan kings, who did not interfere in caste disputes, ruled these territories, unlike the early Gujarat States. That Bijapur, Ahmednagar and Golconda have not given their names to caste divisions is not therefore evidence against the validity of Jackson's political theory.

It will be gathered from the foregoing remarks that caste is in reality a system of self-determination based on the habit of attaching more importance to the differences between social groups than to that which they have in common. Social union is fostered and maintained by attaching importance to all that human beings, whatever their race, occupation or domicile, may have in common with each other. Social cleavage is inevitable when an exaggerated importance is attached to differences of race, occupation or domicile between one group of individuals and another. The barrier of religion may be expected to give rise to groups that will not intermarry, for it is based on fundamentals. But when to this is added an endless series of social fences erected on account of differences in origin, occupation or custom, it is inevitable that society should break into a number of self-contained elements to which there can scarcely be a limit. Too frequently the bar on inter-marriage and inter-dining, which is the essence of caste organization, is based on an assumed superiority of one group of individuals over another, so that, broadly speaking, the Indian caste system might be described as the most complete system of social exclusiveness that the world has ever witnessed. A common sentiment of Indian nationality might provide in time a sufficient motive for pulling down caste barriers. But in India habits and customs readily formed, are adhered to with great tenacity. An inter-caste marriage law does not promise to achieve any great measure of success. Recently inter-marriages have been recorded between endogamous castes such as Deshasth and Chitpavan Brahmans. These however, are exceptional; and there is no present indication that caste barriers on inter-dining and inter-marriage are likely to be rapidly removed.

The survey, therefore, has had to deal with a number of groups, which cannot accurately be described as being racial, occupational, sectarian or geographical though one or more of these influences has produced the group in each case.   It is almost impossible in such circumstances to avoid divisions when drawing up a list of caste units particularly in the case of Lingayats. The aim of the survey has been to show in each case the groups that form endogamous units; combined for convenience of description under the heading of a major group which must in some cases be religious, e.g., Lingayats, some times occupational, e.g., Vanis and in rarer instances tribal, as for instance Bhils, Kolis, Kathis, etc.

Caste Evolution

It is of interest to note that when, owing to the influence of the four main causes of caste evolution already described, a group, divides into sub-castes the process occasionally has two distinct stages. To commence with a group that formerly allowed inter-marriage, freely between all its members develops a section, that for racial, functional or similar reasons hold itself superior in status to the rest of the group. This is shown by the former declining to allow their daughters to marry the sons of the other caste members, but accepting brides for their own sons from the main body of the caste. In Punjab, many castes are thus related to each other to the present day, and completely endogamous Castes are of rare occurrence. In the Bombay Presidency the practice is less common; but it is found among Rajputs, Marathas Lingayats and even among the lowest castes. Marathas, who were once one with Kunbis will still, marry Kunbi girls in some parts of the Presidency. Lingayat Panchamsalis are divided into Jangams and Banjigs, of which the former will marry the daughters of the latter after a process of initiation, though in no circumstances, would they allow their own daughters to marry Banjigs. Two such groups, of which the lower is known technically hypergamous, will usually tend to develop into completely separate castes in course of time. The marriage of girls from the lower section is abandoned as soon as the breach between the social status of the two sections is sufficiently wide. One of the lowest castes of the Presidency, the Mahars, developed an embryo new caste recently in this way, owing to a number of Mahars having learnt to drive motor vehicles. The added wealth and prestige that this occupation brought with it showed itself in a "Driver" section, which was disinclined to continue free inter-marriage with the caste as a whole. It only requires time in such circumstances for the caste to develop a completely endogamous driver division.

In the course of the work of the survey, it has been able to accumulate some interesting facts bearing on the extent which primitive, i.e., pre-Aryan as well as foreign or immigrant elements can be traced in the castes of the Presidency excluding Sind. The result of investigations in the southern portion of the Presidency, where castes are clearly organized on primitive lines, has brought to light a regular system of totemistic divisions of special interest and significance. These divisions are known locally as *balis* and are named after animals such as the elk, the hog deer, the elephant, the monkey, and the tortoise, certain fish and trees or plants such as the banyan, pipal, screwpines plantain, etc.

There is a division named after the white ants nest. These *balis* are exogamous, and display the usual totemistic feature, i.e., members worship the tree, plant, animal or other objects giving its name to the *bali,* on special occasions such as marriage or the occupation of a new house. They will not cut or injure it in any way, and in no circumstances those who have a common *bali* be allowed to inter-marry. Children appear originally to have inherited the mother's totem. Later this system has been modified into one of tracing the totem through the male parent.

Further north in the Presidency we find that many castes show traces of having originally possessed a similar organization. There is remarkable resemblance traceable between the guardians or *devaks* of the Maratha castes in the Deccan and the *balis* of North Kanara. The same trees

as for instances the Nagchampa *(Mesua ferrea)* and screw
pine *(Pandanus odoratissimus)* are found as *devaks* and as
balis. In the article on Marathas information will be found
regarding these *devaks*. Being regularly worshipped
carefully preserved and governing inter-marriages, they
appear to possess the leading characteristics of totems. It
is reasonable to assume that the *devak* with its suggestive
resemblance to the *bali* is strong evidence of the primitive
origin of at least an important element in the castes in
which it is found. From this assumption very interesting
results may follow. It is not possible within the limits of
this brief survey to develop the argument to its logical
conclusion; but clearly Marathas contain a much stronger
pre-Aryan element than has hitherto been supposed.

We are on more difficult ground when we endeavour to
trace the remains of foreign elements in the caste
formations of the Presidency. The late Sir James Campbell
attached much importance to the survival of the names of
post-Aryan invading tribes such as Yavans, Parthians,
Ahirs, Gajars and Yadavs or of the early ruling Indian
dynasties, e.g., Maurya, Kadamba, Chalukhya among the
castes of the Presidency. It has been seen that Ahir and
Gujar divisions are still found in many castes. Maurya,
Kadamba and Chalukhya survive in the form of surnames,
i.e., More, Kadam and Cholke, among Marathas, Kunbis,
Mahars and Kolis. But it is unsafe to attach much
significance to names in India. They probably bear little
more significance than the term Shivajis which was
formerly applied by the English to numerous castes enlisted
under the banner of the Maratha hero that is to say, they
indicate subservience to a common leader or dynasty, but
do not connote common descent. The Ahir, anti-Gujar
elements stand on a somewhat different footing to the
surnames; but it is impossible at the present day to strive
at the exact relation, which such sub-castes bear to the
original Ahir and Gujar tribes. The subject has been, very
ably treated by D. R. Bhandarkar in his study of the foreign
elements in Hindu society, where both Nagar Brahman and
Sisodia Rajput have been shown to be Gujars originally. It
is certain that inter-marriage with local elements has

largely obscured the extent to which Ahir and Gujar have contributed to modern caste formations, even in cases where the name survives.

The general impression conveyed by the survey is that the original foreign element in many of the castes has been greatly obscured by inter-marriage with the indigenous population. Even the Parsis, the most exclusive of immigrant castes, have admittedly mixed with the jungle tribes of Gujarat and the issue, until recently, has been admitted to the Parsi community. Ultimately we may perhaps be prepared to the conclusion that the tribes and castes of the Presidency have far more in common as regard of their origin than has hitherto been admitted. The pages of the survey contain much evidence in support of this contention. There is scarcely a caste that is not found to posses a section known as Akaramashes, Bande, Shinde, Dasa, Kale, etc., signifying that there has been irregular union either with women of a lower caste or with men of a higher one. The institutes of Manu allow seven generations of marriage within the caste to restore the full status to the issue of such a union. The evidence available tends to show that a much less drastic test was imposed in recent times. The Abyssinian Angria married a Maratha girl and history equally records instances of Koli chieftains who have been allowed a similar privilege, the children being doubtless classed as Marathas in both instances. For many years Maratha Kunbi women have served in Brahman houses in the Konkans the issue being classed as Shinde under Marathas.

Birth, Marriage and Death

A good deal of space is devoted under each of the caste heads to a description of birth, marriage, death and other important social ceremonies. The conclusions to be drawn from a comparison of these ceremonies must await the results of a detailed study. There are certain special ceremonies derived from Dravidian castes in Southern India which tend to occur in the Deccan and thus suggest some connection with non-Aryan elements. Until recently the social status of a caste has been greatly affected by the prevalence of infant or adult marriages, and the existence or prohibition of widow re-marriage. It is of interest to note that, while low-castes have been endeavouring raise their social status by introducing child marriages and abandoning the marriage of widows, a reform movement among the highest castes is aiming at a return to adult marriage and the re-marriage of widows. The development is one that may have far-reaching effects in the near future.

A number of reports have been witness to the prevalence, among certain wild tribes and low-castes, of the practice of marriage with trees. The occasion selected is when a bachelor desires to marry a widow. In this case the unmarried partner first goes through the ceremony with one of the totem trees, e.g., the Shami *Prosopis spicigera* or *Rui Calotropis gigantea*. The tree is then cut down and destroyed. It seems probable that the tree bride is intended to form a spirit companion to the widow's first partner who might, if not so satisfied, devote an unwelcome amount of attention to the re-married couple. This curious custom is in vogue in all parts of the Presidency. It is not to be confused with the ceremony known as *Ark-vivaha,* i.e., marriage with a *rui* bush, prescribed in the sacred books for Hindus who lose *two* wives, before they marry a third, time. Most probably the primitive custom gave rise to the Hindu rite, which is restricted to special cases of marriages with third wives; but the original ceremony is clearly a spirit-scaring rite designed to protect a bachelor who marries a widow.

In the early days of the Survey a trained operator was employed for a short time, under the direction of the late Herbert Risley, in taking anthropometrical records of some of the leading caste types in Bombay. The number selected for measurement in the case of each caste was very small, and this in iself would render it desirable to view the results with caution. As they stand in their published form they exhibit such an unexpected jumble of castes and tribes, whether placed by cephalic measurement or index, that it is impossible to deduce from them conclusions of value. Risley was at one time inclined to the view that measurements recorded among the Marathas afforded evidence of their Scythic origin. He based this conclusion on the discovery of broad-headed people in the Deccan. But measuremens, which bring together the Brahman and the Mahar, require a great deal of collateral evidence from reliable sources before they can safely be used as the basis of a theory of racial origin. A reference to Risley tables will show the Bombay castes of which measurements were taken grouped in the following order: -

A. By Cephalic Index	**B. By Nasal Index**
1. Deshasth Brahman.	1. Deshasth Brahman.
2. Mahar.	2. Nagar Brahman
3. Chitpavan Brahman	3. Shenvi Brahman.
4. Kunabi.	4. Vania.
5. Koli.	5. Prabhu.
6. Maratha	6. Koli.
7. Shenvi Brahman.	7. Chitpavan Brahman.
8. Vania.	8. Kunabi.
9. Nagar Brahman.	9. Desasth Brahman.
10. Prabhu.	10. Maratha
	11. Mahar.

It will be seen that in the first of these groups a low cephalic index is shared by the Mahar, one of the lowest castes of the Presidency, with the Deshasth and Chitpavan Brahmans. This is at least disconcerting. The Mahar would not be expected in such strange company. Again in the case of the nasal index, to which Risley at one time attached so much importance as to hazard the theory that a man's social status would be found to vary in inverse ratio to the mean relative width of his nose, we find the lead rightly taken by three Brahman castes, which are followed by Vani and Prabhu. After that, the classification is very, suspicious. The Koli is found above the Chitpavan Brahman; the Maratha Kunbi above the Deshasth Brahman; and both of these are higher in the scale than the Maratha. It is impossible from the known facts to find any satisfactory explanation of these two lists of precedence. Mahars and Kolis must be as typical representatives of the early types in the Presidency as can well be found. Yet these measurements give them a place close to the Brahmans, and even above the Deshasth. The Maratha is found below the Koli and the Mahar in cephalic measurement, and placed below the Koli by nasal index. His history and social position would lead to the expectation that the position should be reversed. Unfortunately, it has not been found possible, owing to the withdrawal of financial support from the Survey, to pursue these inquiries and test the recorded data by making additional measurements for each selected caste or by measuring other typical castes not included in the scope of Risleys' observations. This might have thrown some further light on the very curious results already recorded. If any theory at all is to be based on the Risley tables it would seem to be that the tribes and castes of the Bombay Presidency are much more closely connected, racially, from the highest to the lowest, than history, tradition, customs and appearance have hitherto led us to suppose.

It is my intention on some future occasion to deal in a separate work with the full results of the Ethnographical Survey. Within the limits of an introductory note space can be found only for a few points of special interest; and these have necessarily been very summarily treated. To illustrate the difficulties in which the classification of the people of the Presidency by tribe and caste is involved it will describe briefly a few typical groups representing important units of the population: Vanis, Marathas, Lingayats, Bhils and Kolis.

Ideology of Manu

The Vani, Banya or Banjig is a trader corresponding to the Vaishya of the fourfold classification of Manu. As Vaishyas they claim a twice-born status; but here their common interest ceases, for they are divided into a large number of groups that will not intermarry. Of these in Gujarat, the following divisions are common to Brahman and Vani: -

1.	Agarval	10.	Nagar
2.	Jharola	11.	Nanddora
3.	Desaval	12.	Osval
4.	Gujar	13.	Palival
5.	Harsola	14.	Porvad
6.	Khadyata	15.	Shrimali

7. Kapol	16. Sorathia
8. Mevada	17. Vayada
9. Modh	

These being mainly geographical in origin, tend to bear out Mr. Jacksons theory of caste fission to which reference has already been made. These numerous groups contain Jain and Hindu divisions, known as *Shravak* and *Meshri that* will not intermarry. They have also divisions known as Visa (20), Dasa (10), Panch (5), Adhich (2 ½), representing an increasing admixture of some lower element.

In the Deccan the Vani caste is more homogeneous, only a few divisions being found, owing no doubt to the fact that political control has been more uniform in that area than in Gujarat. Further South, the Vani is known as a Banjig, and is generally a Lingayat. As such, he will not marry with Hindu or Jain Vanis.

Marathas are the chief unit in the Deccan and Konkan, probably deriving their name from Maharashtra, i.e., the Deccan, and representing a tribe with some Northern element but largely aboriginal. There is probably no substantial difference in origin between the landholding and warrior section, i.e., Marathas Proper, the cultivators, i.e., Maratha Kunbis, and the numerous local occupational castes such as Maratha Vanis, Sonars, Sutars, Parits, etc. Intermarriage is not ordinarily allowed between these groups, although in remote parts: Marathas Proper will take girls marriage from the Kunbi of Kulvadi caste. They will not marry their girls to boys of the Kuladi caste. The Kunbis again, is at times recruited from the Koli who settled down to agriculture and acquires a "Kunbi" or cultivator status. The rise of the Maratha power in the seventeenth century induced the fighting classes (land-holders) to claim for themselves Kshatriya rank, and to discourage widow remarriage. It is chiefly on this ground that they claim to be superior to the Kunbis. But by descent the Maratha appears to be one with the Maratha, Kunbi and certain other occupational castes in the Deccan.

The Lingayats are a religious body dating from the eleventh century, when they separated from the Hindu fold by denying the authority of the Brahman, rejecting the scriptures, and abandoning Hindu ceremonies and pilgrimages. Largely recruited from Jain traders or Banjigs, these with their priests, known as Jangams, formed originally one's body ignoring caste distinctions. Later converts, however were in course of time relegated to an inferior social status thus giving rise to endogamous groups, resembling the ordinary Hindu caste in exclusiveness, though adopting the special, religious rites of Lingayatism. Hindus and Lingayats do not intermarry, even if they have a common caste name and occupation. The original rejection of castes distinctions has thus, it will be seen, given place to the formation of castes containing Lingayats bearing the same, relation to Hindus in such castes as the Jains in the Vani divisions of Gujarat bear to the Hindu members.

Bhils and Kolis are aboriginal tribes, which probably do not differ at all in origin. They are doubtless the former inhabitants of the greater part of the Presidency, now largely confined to hilly or jungle tracts of the country. The common bond between Bhils is one of descent, as is the case, with Kolis. Changes of occupation and a certain admixture of foreign blood have led to the formation of a number of divisions in each case. Among Kolis we find divisions with the names of Ahir, Bhil, Dhangar and Maratha as Ahirs and divisions with Maratha names are found among the Bhils. Other primitive tribes besides *Kolis,* Berads, have Bhil divisions. It has been seen that the Koli, by taking to cultivation, may rise to the position of a Maratha Kunbi. For the most part Bhils and Kolis remain good examples of purely tribal stocks. Inter-marriage with inferior Rajputs has in places produced mixed castes from both sources.

During the progress of the survey, the Superintendent has automatically become a tribunal for settling disputes regarding caste precedence. The circulation of the draft monographs led to the formulation of claims such, for instance, as those of Panchals to be classed as Vishva Brahmans, Sonars to be described as Daivadnya Brahmans, and of Vadavals to be admitted to rank as Panchkalshis, or Somvanshi Kshatriyas. Interesting documents have been produced bearing on these disputed points. Manbhavs have been proved to be entirely distinct from the degraded caste of Mangs with which they were formerly supposed to be connected. The Savashe Brahmans have established their appeal against their former classification as degraded Deshasth Brahmans and have been reclassed as Sahavasi Brahmans. If in the decisions arrived at on these and similar points the Superintendent's views fail to meet with general acceptance, it may at least be agreed in support of them that the evidence on both sides has been very carefully re-examined in arriving at these results.

References

Ketkar, S.V., *History of Caste in India*, New Delhi, 1995.

Brown, A.R., *Structure and Function in the Primitive Society*, London, 1959.

Biswas, D.K., *Political Sociology*, Calcutta, 1978.

Lal, S.K., *The Urban Elite*, Delhi, 1974.

Levy, M., *The Structure of Society*, New Jersey, 1952.

History of the Marathas, Vol. I.

Selected Works of Jawaharlal Nehru, (ed) by S. Gopal.

Khandait, *Tribes and Castes of Bengal.*

Blunt, E.A.H., *The Caste System of Northern India.*

Memoir of Central India, Vol. II.

Monier Williams, Sanskrit Dictionary.

Rapson, E.J., *The Combridge History of India*, Vol. I.

Central Provinces Gazetteer, Calcutta, 1908.

Indian Annual Register, relevant volumes.

2

Caste Determines Social Positions

The word 'caste,' Dr. Wilson states, is not of Indian origin, but is derived from the Portuguese *casta,* signifying race, mould or quality. The Indian word for caste is *Jat* or *Jati,* which has the original meaning of birth or production of a child, and hence denotes good birth or lineage, respectability and rank. *Jatha* means wellborn. Thus *Jat* now signifies a caste, as every Hindu is born into a caste, and his caste determines his social position through life.

The two main ideas denoted by a caste are a community of or persons following a common occupation and a community whose members marry only among them. A third distinctive feature is that the members of a caste do not as a rule eat with outsiders with the exception of other Hindu castes of a much higher social position than their own. None of these will, however, serve as a definition of a caste. In a number of castes the majority of members have abandoned their traditional occupation and taken to others. Less than a fifth of the Brahmans of the Central Provinces are performing any priestly or religious functions, and the remaining four-fifths are landholders or engaged in Government service as magistrates, clerks of public offices, constables and orderlies, or in railway service in different grades, or in the professions as barristers and pleaders, doctors, engineers and so on. The Rajputs and Marathas were originally soldiers, but only an infinitely small proportion belong to, the Indian Army, and the remainder are ruling chiefs, landholders, cultivators, labourers or in the various grades or Government service and the police. Of the Telis or oil-pressers only 9 per cent are engaged in their traditional occupation, and the remainder are landholders, cultivators and shopkeepers. Of the Ahirs or graziers only 20 per cent tend and breed cattle. Only 12 per cent of the Chamars are supported by the tanning industry, and so on. The Bahnas or cotton-cleaners have entirely lost their occupation, as cotton is now cleaned in factories; they are cartmen or cultivators, but retain their caste name and organization. Since the introduction of machine-made cloth has reduced the profits of handloom weaving, large numbers of the weaving castes have been reduced to manual labour as a means of subsistence. The abandonment of the traditional occupation has become a most marked feature of Hindu society as a result of the equal opportunity and freedom in the choice of occupations afforded by the British Government, coupled with the rapid progress of industry and the spread of education. So far it has had no very markedly disintegrating effect on the caste system, and the status of a caste is still mainly tied by its traditional occupation; but signs are not wanting of a coming change. Again, several castes have the same traditional occupation; about forty of the castes of the Central Provinces are classified as agriculturists, eleven as weavers, seven as fishermen, and so on. Distinctions of occupation therefore are not a sufficient basis for a classification of castes. Nor can a caste be simply defined as a body "of persons who marry only among themselves, or, as it is termed, an endogamous group; for almost every important caste is divided into a number of subcastes which do not marry and frequently do not eat with each other. But it is a distinctive and peculiar feature of caste as a social institution that it splits up the people into a multitude of these divisions and bars their intermarriage; and the real unit of the system and the basis of the fabric of Indian society is this endogamous group or subcaste.

Status and Occupation

The subcastes, however, connote no real difference of status or occupation. They are little known exception within the caste itself, and they consist of groups within the caste which marry among themselves, and attend the communal feasts held on the occasions of marriages, funerals and meetings of the caste *panchayat* or committee for the' judgment of offences against the caste rules and their expiation by a penalty feast; to these feasts all male adults of the community, within a certain area, are invited. In the Central Provinces the 250 groups, which have been classified as castes, contain perhaps 2000 subcastes. Except in some cases other Hindus do not know a man's subcaste, though they always know his caste; among the ignorant lower castes men may often be found who do not know whether their caste contains any subcastes or whether they themselves belong to one. That is, they will eat and marry with all the members of their caste within a circle of villages, but know nothing about the caste outside those villages, or even whether' it exists elsewhere. One subdivision of a caste may look down upon another on the ground of some difference of occupation, of origin, or of abstaining from or partaking of some article of food, but these distinctions are usually confined to their internal relations and seldom recognized by outsiders. For social purposes the caste consisting of a number of these endogamous groups generally occupies the same position, determined roughly according to the respectability of its traditional occupation or extraction.

No adequate definition of caste can thus be obtained from community of occupation or intermarriage; nor would it be accurate to say that every one must know his own caste and that all the different names returned at the census may be taken as distinct. In the Central Provinces about 900 caste names were returned at the census of 190 1, and these were reduced in classification to about 250 proper castes.

In some cases synonyms are commonly used. The caste of *pan* or betel-vine growers and sellers is known indifferently as Barai, Pansari or Tamboli. The great caste of Ahirs or herdsmen has several synonyms—as Gaoli in the Northern

Districts, Rawat or Gahra in Chhattisgarh, Gaur among the Uriyas, and Golkar among Telugus. Lohars are also called Khati and Kammari; Masons are called Larhia, Raj and Beldar. The more distinctly occupational castes usually have different names in different parts of the country, as Dhobi, Warthi, Baretha, Chakla and Parit for washermen; Basor, Burud, Kandra and Dhulia for bamboo-workers, and so on. Such names may show that the subdivisions to which they are applied have immigrated from different parts of India, but the distinction is generally not now maintained, and many persons will return one or other of them indifferently. No object is gained, therefore, by distinguishing them in classification, as they correspond to no differences of status or occupation, and at most denote groups which do not intermarry, and which may therefore more properly be considered as subcastes.

Titles

Titles or names of offices are also not infrequently given as caste names. Members of the lowest or impure castes employed in the office of Kotwar or village watchmen prefer to call themselves by this name, as they thus obtain a certain rise in status, or at least they think so. In some localities the Kotwars or village watchmen have begun to marry among themselves and try to form a separate caste. Chamars (tanners) or Mahars (weavers) employed as grooms will call themselves Sais and consider themselves superior to the rest of their caste. The Thethwar Rawats or Ahirs will not clean household cooking-vessels, and therefore look down on the rest of the caste and prefer to call themselves by this designation, as 'Theth' means 'exact' or 'pure,' and Thethwar is one who has not degenerated from the ancestral calling. Salewars are a subcaste of Koshtis (weavers), who work only in silk and hence consider themselves as superior to the other Koshtis and a separate caste. The Rathor subcaste of Telis in Mandla have abandoned the hereditary occupation of oil-pressing and become landed proprietors. They now wish to drop their own caste and to be known only as Rathor, the name of one of the leading Rajput clans, in the hope that in time it will be forgotten that they ever were Telis, and they will be admitted into the community of Rajputs.

It occurred to them that the census would be a good opportunity of advancing a step towards the desired end, and accordingly they telegraphed to the Commissioner of Jubbulpore before the enumeration, and petitioned the Chief Commissioner after it had been taken, to the effect that they might be recorded and classified only as Rathor and not as Teli; this method of obtaining recognition of their claims being, as remarked by Sir Bampfylde Fuller, a great deal cheaper than being weighed against gold. On the other hand, a common occupation may sometimes amalgamate castes originally distinct into one. The sweeper's calling is well-defined and under the generic term of Mehtar are included members of two or three distinct castes, as Dom, Bhangi and Chuhra; the word Mehtar means a prince or headman, and it is believed that its application to the sweeper by the other servants is ironical. It has now however, been generally adopted as a caste name. Similarly, Darzi, a tailor, was held by D. Ibbetson to be simply the name of a profession and not that of a caste; but it is certainly a true caste in the Central Provinces, though probably of comparatively late origin. A change of occupation may transfer a whole body of persons from one caste to another. A large section of the Banjara caste of carriers, who have taken to cultivation, have become included in the Kunbi caste in Berar and are known as Wanjari Kunbi. Another subcaste of the Kunbis called Manwa is derived from the Mana tribe. Teli or oilmen, who have taken to vending liquor, now form a subcaste of the Kalar caste called Teli-Kalar; those who have become shopkeepers are called Teli-Bania and may in time become an inferior section of the Bania caste. Other similar subcastes are the Ahir-Sunars or herdsmen-goldsmiths, the Kayasth-Darzis or tailors, the Kori-Chamars or weaver-tanners, the Gondi Lohars and Barhais, being Gonds who have become carpenters and blacksmiths and been admitted to these castes; the Mahar Mhalis or barbers, and so on.

It would appear, then, that no precise definition of a caste can well be formulated to meet all difficulties. In classification, each doubtful case must be taken by itself, and it must be determined, on the information available, whether any body of persons, consisting of one or more endogamous groups, and distinguished by one or more separate names, can be recognized as holding, either on account of its traditional occupation or descent, such a distinctive position in the social system, that it should be classified as a caste. But not even the condition of endogamy can be accepted as of universal application; for Vidurs, who are considered to be descended from Brahman fathers and women of other castes will, though marrying among themselves, still receive the offspring of such mixed alliances into the community; in the case of Gosains and Bairagis, who, from being religious orders, have become castes, admission is obtained by initiation as well as by birth, and the same is the case with several other orders; some of the lower castes will freely admit outsiders; and in parts of Chhattisgarh social ties are of the latest description, and the intermarriage of Gonds, Chamars and other low castes are by no means infrequent. But not withstanding these instances, the principle of the restriction of marriage to members of the caste is so nearly universal as to be capable of being adopted as a definition.

Division of Aryans

The well-known traditional theory of caste is that the Aryans were divided from the beginning of time into four castes: Brahmans or priests, Kshatriyas or warriors, Vaishyas or merchants and cultivators, and Sudras or menials and labourers, all of whom had a divine origin, being born from the body of Brahma—the Brahmans from his mouth, the Kshatriyas from his arms, the Vaishyas from his thighs, and the Sudras from his feet. Intermarriage between the four castes was not at first entirely prohibited, and a man of any of the three higher ones, provided that for his first wife he took a woman of his own caste, could subsequently marry others of the divisions beneath his own. In this manner the other castes originated. Thus, the Kaivarttas or Kewats were the offspring of a Kshatriya father and Vaishya mother, and so on. Mixed marriages in the opposite direction, of a woman of a higher caste with a man of a lower one, were reprobated as strongly as possible, and the offspring of these were relegated to the lowest position in society; thus the Chandals, or descendants of a Sudra father and Brahman mother, were of all men the most base. It has been recognized that this genealogy, though in substance the formation of a number of new castes through mixed descent may have been correct, is, as regards the details, an attempt made by it priestly law-giver to account, on the lines of orthodox tradition, for a state of society which had ceased to correspond to them.

In the ethnographic description of the people of Punjab, which forms the caste chapter of Denzil Ibbetson's *Census. Report of 1881,* it was pointed out that occupation was the chief basis of the division of castes, and there is no doubt that this is true. Every separate occupation has produced a distinct caste, and the status of the caste *depends now mainly or almost entirely on its occupation. The fact that there may be several castes practising such important callings as agriculture or weaving does not invalidate* this in any way, and instances of the manner in which such castes have been developed will be given subsequently. If a caste changes its occupation it may, in the course of time, alter its status in a corresponding degree. The important Kayasth and Gurao castes furnish instances of this. Castes, in fact, tend to rise or fall in social position with the acquisition of land or other forms of wealth or dignity much in the same manner as individuals do nowadays in European countries. Hitherto in India it has not been the individual who has undergone the process; he inherits the social position of the caste in which he is born, and, as a rule, retains it through life without the power of altering it. It is the caste, as a whole, or at least one of its important sections or subcastes, which gradually rises or falls in social position, and the process may extend over generations or even centuries.

In the *Brief Sketch of the Caste System of the North-Western Provinces and Oudh,* J.C. Nesfield puts forward the view that the whole basis of the caste system is the division of occupations, and that the social gradation of castes corresponds precisely to the different periods of civilization during which their traditional occupations originated. Thus, the lowest castes are those allied to the primitive occupation of hunting, Pasi, Bhar, Bahelia, because the pursuit of wild animals was the earliest stage in the development of human industry. Next above these come the fishing castes, fishing being considered somewhat superior to hunting, because water is a more sacred element among Hindus than land, and there is less apparent cruelty in the capturing of fish than the slaughtering of animals; these are the Kahars, Kewats, Dhimars and others. Above these come the pastoral castes—Ghosi, Gadaria, Gujar and Ahir; and above them the agricultural castes, following the order in which these occupations were adopted during the progress of civilisation. At the top of the system stands the Rajput or Chhatri, the warrior, whose duty is to protect all the lower castes, and the Brahman, who is their priest and spiritual guide. Similarly, the artisan castes are divided into two main groups —the lower one consists of those whose occupations preceded the age of metallurgy, as the Chamars and Mochis or tanners, Koris or weavers, the Telis or oil-pressers, Kalars or liquor-distillers, Kumhars or potters, and Lunias or salt-makers. The higher group includes those castes whose occupations were coeval with the age of metallurgy, that is, those who work in stone, wood and metals, and who make clothing and ornaments, as the Barhai or worker in wood, the Lohar or worker in iron, the Kasera and Thathera, brass- workers, and the Sunar or worker in the precious metals, ranking precisely in this order of precedence, the Sunar being the highest. The theory is still further developed among the trading castes, who are arranged in a similar manner, beginning from the Banjara or forest trader, the Kunjra or greengrocer, and the Bharbhunja or grain-parcher, up to the classes of Banias and Khatris or shopkeepers and bankers.

It can hardly be supposed that the Hindus either consciously or unconsciously arranged their gradation of society in a scientific order of precedence in the manner described. The main divisions of social precedence are correctly stated by Nesfield, but it will be suggested in this essay that they arose naturally from the divisions of the principal social organism of India, the village community.

Nevertheless Nesfield's book will always rank as a most interesting and original contribution to the literature of the subject and his work did much to stimulate inquiry into the origin of the caste system.

In his Introduction to the *Tribes and Castes of Bengal* Herbert Risley laid stress on the racial basis of caste showing that difference of race and difference of colour were the foundation of the Indian caste system or division of the people into endogamous units. There seems reason to suppose that the contact of the Aryans with the indigenous people of India was, to a large extent, responsible for the growth of the caste system, and the main racial divisions may perhaps even now be recognized, though their racial basis has to a great extent, vanished. But when we come to individual castes and subcastes, the scrutiny of their origin, which has been made in the individual articles, appears to indicate that caste distinctions cannot, as a rule, be based on supposed difference of race. Nevertheless Risley's *Castes and Tribes of Bengal* and *Peoples of India* will, no doubt, always be considered as standard authorities, while as Census J Commissioner for India and Director of Ethnography he probably did more to foster this branch of research in India generally than any other man has ever done.

M. Emile Senart, in his work *Les Castes dans I' Inde*, gives an admirable sketch of the features marking the entry of the Aryans into India and their acquisition of the country from which the following account is largely taken. The institution of caste as it is understood at present did not exist among the Aryans of the Vedic period, on their first entry into India. The word *varna*, literally colour which is afterwards used in speaking of the four castes, distinguishes in the Vedas two classes only: there are the Arya Varna and the Dasa Varna —the Aryan race and the race of enemies. In other passages the Dasyus are spoken of as black, and Indra is praised for protecting the Aryan colour. In later literature the black race, Krishna Varna, are opposed to the Brahmans, and the same word is used of the distinction between Aryas and Sudras. The word *varna* was thus used, in the first place, not of four castes, but of two hostile races, one white and the other black. It is said that Indra divided the fields among his white coloured people after destroying the Dasyus by whom may be understood the indigenous barbarian races. The word Dasyu, which frequently recurs in the Vedas probably refers to the people of foreign countries or provinces like the Goim or Gentiles of the Hebrews. The Dasyus were not altogether barbarians, for they had cities and other institutions showing a partial civilization, though the Aryas lately from more bracing climes than those which they inhabited, proved too strong for them. To the Aryans the word Dasyu had the meaning of one who not only did not perform religious rites, but attempted to harass their performers. Another verse says, "Distinguish, O Indra, between the Aryas and those who are Dasyus punishing those who perform no religious rites; compel them to submit to the sacrifices; be thou the powerful, the encourager of the sacrificer.

Rakshas was another designation given to the tribes with whom the Aryans were in hostility. Its meaning is strong, gigantic or powerful, and among the modern Hindus it is a word for a devil or demon. In the Satapatha Brahmana of the white Yajur-Veda the Rakshasas are represented as prohibiters that is prohibiters of the sacrifice. Similarly, at a later period, Manu describes Aryavarrta, or the abode of the Aryas, as the country between the eastern and western oceans, and between the Himalayas and the Vindhyas, that is Hindustan, the Deccan being not then recognised as an abode of the Aryans. And he thus speaks of the country "From a Brahman born in Aryavarrta let all men on earth learn their several usages." "That land on which the black antelope naturally grazes, is held fit for the performance of sacrifices; but the land of Mlechchhas (foreigners) is beyond it." "Let the three first classes (Brahmans, Kshatriyas and Vaishyas) invariably dwell in the above-mentioned countries; but a Sudra distressed for subsistence may sojourn wherever he chooses.'

Another passage states: "If some pious king belonging to the Kshatriya or some other caste should defeat the Mlechchhas and establish a settlement of the four castes in their territories, and accept the Mlechchhas thus defeated as Chandalas (the most impure caste in ancient Hindu society) as is the case in Aryavarrta, then that country also becomes fit for sacrifice. For no land is impure of itself. A land becomes so only by contact." This passage is quoted by a Hindu writer with the same reference to the Code of Manu as the preceding one, but it is not found there and appears to be a gloss by a later writer, explaining how the country south of the Vindhyas, which is excluded by Manu, should be rendered fit for Aryan settlement.   Similarly in a reference in the Brahmanas to the migration of the Aryans eastward from the Punjab it is stated that Agni the fire-god flashed forth from the mouth of a priest invoking him at a sacrifice and burnt across all the five rivers, and as far as he burnt Brahmans could live. Agni, as the god of fire by which the offerings were consumed, was addressed as follows: "We kindle thee at the sacrifice, O wise Agni, the sacrificer, the luminous, the mighty." The sacrifices referred to were, in the early period, of domestic animals, the horse, ox or goat, the flesh of which was partaken of by the worshippers, and the sacred Soma liquor, which was drunk by them; the prohibition or discouragement of animal sacrifices for the higher castes gradually came about at a later time, and was probably to a large extent due to the influence of Buddhism.

The early sacrifice was in the nature of a communal sacred meal at which the worshippers partook of the animal or liquor offered to the god. The *Dasyus* or indigenous. Indian races could not worship the Aryan Gods nor join in the sacrifices offered to them, which constituted the act of worship. They were a hostile race, but the hostility was felt and expressed on religious rather than racial grounds, as the latter term is understood at present.

Views of Senart

M. Senart points out that the division of the four castes appearing in post-Vedic literature, does not proceed on equal lines. There were two groups, one composed of the three higher castes and the other of the Sudras or lowest. The higher castes constituted a fraternity into which admission was obtained only by a religious ceremony of initiation and investment with the sacred thread. The Sudras were excluded and could take no part in sacrifices. The punishment for the commission of the gravest offences by a Brahman was that he became a Sudra, that is to say an outcaste. The killing of a Sudra was an offence no more severe than that of killing certain animals. A Sudra was prohibited by the severest penalties from approaching within a certain distance of a member of any of the higher castes. In the Sutras it is declared that the Sudra has not the right (Adhikara) of sacrifice enjoyed by the Brahman, Kshatriya and Vaishya. He was not to be invested with the sacred thread, nor permitted, like them, to hear, commit to memory, or recite Vedic texts. For listening to these texts he ought to have his ears shut up with melted lead or lac by way of punishment; for pronouncing them, his tongue cut out; and for committing them to memory, his body cut in two. The Veda was never to be read in the presence of a Sudra; and no sacrifice was to be performed for him. The Sudras, it *is* stated in the Harivansha, are sprung from vacuity and are destitute of ceremonies, and so are not entitled to the rites of initiation. Just as upon the friction of wood, the cloud of smoke which issues from the fire and spreads around is of no service in the sacrificial rite, so too the Sudras spread over the earth are unserviceable, owing to their birth, to their want of initiatory rites, and the ceremonies ordained by the Vedas. Again it is ordained that silence is to be observed by parties of the three sacrificial classes when a Sudra enters to remove their natural defilements, and thus the servile position of the Sudra is recognised. Here it appears that the Sudra is identified with the sweeper or scavenger, the most debased and impure of modem Hindu castes.

In the Dharmashastras or law-books it is laid down that a person taking a Sudra's food for a month becomes a Sudra and after death becomes a dog. Issue begotten after eating a Sudra's food is of the Sudra caste. A person who dies with Sudra's food in his stomach becomes a village pig, or is reborn in a Sudra's family. An Arya who had sexual intimacy with a Sudra woman was to be banished; but a Sudra having intimacy with an Arya was to be killed. If a Sudra reproached a dutiful Arya or put himself on equality with him on a road, on a couch or on a seat, he was to be beaten with a stick. A Brahman might without hesitation take the property of a Sudra; he, the Sudra, had indeed nothing of his own; his master might, doubtless, take his property. According to the *Mahabharata* the Sudras are appointed servants to the Brahmans, Kshatriyas and Vaishyas. A Brahman woman having connection with a Sudra was to be devoured by dogs, but one having connection with a Kshatriya or Vaishya was merely to have her head shaved and be carried round on an ass. When a Brahman received a gift from another Brahman he had to acknowledge it in a loud voice from a Rajanya or Kshatriya, in a gentle voice; from a Vaishya, in a whisper; and from a Sudra, in his own mind. To a Brahman he commenced his thanks with the sacred syllable Om ; to a king he gave thanks out the sacred Om; to a Vaishya he whispered his thanks; to a Sudra he said nothing, but thought in his own mind, *svasti* or 'This is good.' It would thus seem clear that the Sudras were distinct from the Aryas and were a separate and inferior race, consisting of the indigenous people of India. In the Atharva-Veda the Sudra is recognised as distinct from the Arya, and also the Dasa from the Arya, as in the Rig-Veda. Dr. Wilson remarks, "The aboriginal inhabitants again who conformed to the Brahmanic law, received certain privileges, and were constituted as a fourth caste under the name of Sudras, whereas all the rest who kept aloof were called Dasyus, whatever their language might be. The Sudras, though treated by Manu and Hindu legislation in general as a component, if enslaved, part of the Indian community, not entitled to the second or sacramental birth, are not even once mentioned in the older parts of the Vedas. They are first locally brought to notice in the *Mahabharata*, along with the Abhiras, dwelling on the banks of the Indus. There are distinct classical notices of the Sudras in this very locality and its neighbourhood. In historical times, says Lassen, "their name reappears in that of the town Sudros on the lower Indus, and, what is especially worthy of notice, in that of the people Sudroi, among the Northern Arachosians."

Thus their existence as a distinct nation is established in the neighbourhood of the Indus, that is to say in the region in which, in the oldest time, the Aryan Indians dwelt. The Aryans probably conquered these indigenous inhabitants first; and when the others in the interior of the country were subsequently subdued and enslaved, the name Sudra was extended to the whole servile caste. There seems to have been some hesitation in the Aryan community about the actual religious position to be given to the Sudras. In the time of the liturgical Brahmanas of the Vedas, they were sometimes admitted to take part in the Aryan sacrifices. Not long afterwards, when the conquests of the Aryans were greatly extended, and they formed a settled state of society among the affluents of the Jamuna and Ganges, the Sudras were degraded to the humiliating and painful position which they occupy in Manu. There is no mention of any of the Sankara or mixed castes in the Vedas.

From the above evidence it seems clear that the Sudras were really the indigenous inhabitants of India, who were subdued by the Aryans as they gradually penetrated into India. When the conquering race began to settle in the land, the indigenous tribes, or such of them as did not retire before the invaders into the still unconquered interior, became a class of menials and labourers, as the Amalekites were to the children of Israel. The Sudras were the same people as the Dasyus of the hymns, after they had begun to live in villages with the Aryans, and had to be admitted, though in the most humiliating fashion, into the Aryan polity. But the hostility between the Aryas and the Dasyus or Sudras, though in reality racial, was felt and expressed on religious grounds, and probably the idea of what is now understood by difference of race or deterioration of type from mixture of races. The Sudras' were despised and hated as worshippers of a hostile god. They could not join in the sacrifices by which the Aryans renewed and cemented their kinship with their god and with each other; hence they were outlaws towards whom no social obligations existed. It would have been quite right and proper that they should be utterly destroyed, precisely as the Israelites thought that Jehovah had commanded them to destroy the Canaanites. But they were too numerous, and hence they were regarded as impure and made to live apathy so that they should not pollute the places of sacrifice, which among the Aryans included their dwelling-houses. It does not seem to have been the case that the Aryans had any regard "for the preservation of the purity of their blood or colour." From an early period men of the three higher castes might take a Sudra woman in marriage, and the ultimate result has been an almost complete fusion between the two races in the bulk of the population over the greater part of the country.

Nevertheless the status of the Sudra still remains attached to the large community of the impure castes formed from the indigenous tribes, who have settled in Hindu villages and entered the caste system. These are relegated to the most degrading and menial occupations, and their touch is regarded as conveying defilement like that of the Sudras. The status of the Sudras was not always considered so low, and they were sometimes held to rank above the mixed castes. And in modern times in Bengal Sudra is quite a respectable term applied to certain artisan castes which there have a fairly good position. But neither were the indigenous tribes always reduced to the impure status. Their fortunes varied, and those who resisted subjection were probably sometimes accepted as allies. For instance, some of the most prominent of the Rajput clans are held to have been derived from the aboriginal 2 tribes. On the Aryan expedition to southern India, which is preserved in the legend of Raffia, as related in the *Ramayana,* it is stated that Rama was assisted by Hanuman with his army of apes. The reference is generally held to be to the fact that the Aryans had as auxiliaries some of the forest tribes, and these were consequently allies, and highly thought of, as shown by the legend and by their identification with the mighty god Hanuman. And at the present time the forest tribes who live separately from the Hindus in the jungle tracts are, as a rule, not regarded as impute. But this does not impair the identification of the Sudras with those tribes who were reduced to subjection and serfdom in the Hindu villages, as shown by the evidence here given. The view has also been held that the Sudras might have been a servile class already subject to the Aryans, who entered India with them. And in the old Parsi or Persian community four classes existed, the

Athornan or priest, the Rathestan or warrior, the Vasteriox or husbandman, and the Hutox or craftsman. The second and third of these names closely resemble those of the corresponding Hindu classical castes, the Rajanya or Kshatriya and the Vaishya, while Athornan, the name for a priest, is the same as Atharvan, the Hindu name for a Brahman versed in the Atharva-Veda. Possibly then Hutox may be connected with Sudra, as frequently changes into. But on the other hand the facts that the Sudras are not mentioned in the Vedas, and that they succeeded to the position of the Dasyus, the black hostile Indians, as well as the important place they fill in the later literature, seem to indicate clearly that they mainly consisted of the indigenous subject tribes. Whether the Aryans applied a name already existing in a servile class among themselves to the indigenous population whom they subdued, may be an uncertain point.

In the Vedas, moreover, M. Senart shows that the three higher castes are not definitely distinguished; but there are three classes—the priests, the chiefs and the people, among whom the Aryans were comprised. The people are spoken of in the plural as the clans who followed the chiefs to battle. The word used is Visha. One verse speaks of the Vishas (clans) bowing before the chief (Rajan), who was preceded by a priest (Brahman). Another verse says: "Favour the prayer (Brahma), favour the service; kill the Rakshasas, drive away the evil; favour the power *(khatra)* and favour the manly strength; favour the cow *(dharm)*, the representative *of* property; and favour the people (or house, *visha)."*

Similarly, Wilson states that in the time of the Vedas, *visha* (related to *vesha,* a house or district) signified the people in general; and Vaishya, its adjective, was afterwards applied to a householder, or that appertaining to an individual of the common people. The Latin *vicus* and the Greek *dicos* are the correspondents of *visha.* The conclusion to be drawn is that the Aryans in the Vedas, like other early communities, were divided by rank or occupation into three classes—priests, nobles and the body of the people. The Vishas or clans afterwards became the Vaishyas or third classical caste. Before they entered India the Aryans were a migratory pastoral people, their domestic animals being the horse, cow, and perhaps the sheep and goat. The horse and cow were especially venerated, and hence were probably their chief means of support. The Vaishyas must therefore have been herdsmen and shepherds, and when they entered India and took to agriculture, the Vaishyas must have become cultivators. The word Vaishya signifies a man who occupies the soil, an agriculturist, or merchant.

The word Vasteriox used by the ancestors of the Parsis, which appears to correspond to Vaishya, also signifies a husbandman, as already seen. Dr. Max Mueller states: "The three occupations of the Aryas in India were fighting, cultivating the soil and worshipping the gods. Those who fought the battles of the people would naturally acquire influence and rank, and their leaders appear in the Veda as Rajas or kings. Those, who did not share in the fighting would occupy, a more humble position; they were called Vish, Vaishyas or householders, and would no doubt have to contribute towards the maintenance of the armies. According to Manu, God ordained the tending of cattle, giving alms, sacrifice, study, trade, usury, and also agriculture for a Vaishya." The Sutras state that agriculture, the keeping of cattle, and engaging in merchandise, as well as learning the Vedas, sacrificing for himself and giving alms, are the duties of a Vaishya. In the *Mahabharata* it is laid down that the Vaishyas should devote themselves to agriculture, the keeping of cattle and liberality. In the same work the god Vayu says to Bhishma: "And it was Brahma's ordinance that the Vaishya should sustain the three castes (Brahman, Kshatriya and Vaishya) with money and corn; and that the Sudra should serve them."

Yajur-Veda

In a list of classes or occupations given in the White Yajur-Veda, and apparently referring to a comparatively advanced state of Hindu society, tillage is laid down as the falling of the Vaishya, and he is distinguished from the Vani or merchant, whose occupation is trade or weighing. Manu states that a Brahman should swear by truth; a Kshatriya by his steed and his weapons; a Vaishya by his cows, his seed and his gold; and a Sudra by all wicked deeds.

Yellow is the colour of the Vaishya, and it must apparently be taken from the yellow corn, and the yellow colour of *ghi* or butter the principal product of the sacred cow; yellow is also the colour of the sacred metal gold, but there can scarcely have been sufficient gold in the hands of the body of the people in those early times to enable it to be especially associated with them. The Vaishyas were thus, as is shown by the above evidence, the main body of the people referred to in the Vedic hymns. When these settled down into villages the Vaishyas became the house-holders and cultivators, among whom the village lands: were divided; the Sudras or indigenous tribe, who also lived in the villages or in hamlets adjoining them, were labourers and given all the most disagreeable tasks in the village community as is the case with the impure castes at present.

The demonstration of the real position of the Vaishyas is important, because the Hindus themselves no longer recognize this. The name Vaishya is now frequently restricted to the Bania caste of bankers, shopkeepers and moneylenders, and hence the Banias are often supposed: to be the descendants and only modern representatives of the original Vaishyas. Evidence has been given in the article on Bania to show that the existing Bania caste is mainly derived from the Rajputs. The name 'Bania', a merchant or trader, is found at an early period, but whether, it denoted a regular Bania caste may be considered as uncertain. In any case it seems clear that this comparatively small caste, chiefly coming from Rajputana, cannot represent the Vaishyas, who were the main body or people of the invading Aryans. At that time the Vaishyas cannot possibly have been traders, because they alone provided the means of subsistence of the community, and if they produced nothing, there could be no material for trade. The Vaishyas must, therefore, as already seen, have been shepherds and cultivators, since in early times wealth consisted almost solely of cow and cattle. At a later period, with the increased religious veneration for all kinds of life, agriculture apparently fell into some kind of disrepute as involving the sacrifice of insect life, and there was a tendency to emphasise trade as the Vaishya's occupation in view of its greater respectability.

It is considered very derogatory for a Brahman or Rajput to touch the plough with his own hands, all the act has hitherto involved a loss of status: these castes however, did not, object to hold land but, on the contrary, ardently desired to do so like all other Hindus. Ploughing was probably despised as a form of manual labour, and hence an undignified action for a member of the aristocracy, just as a squire or gentleman farmer in England might consider it beneath his dignity to drive the plough himself. No doubt also, as the fusion of races proceeded, and bodies of the indigenous tribes who were cultivators adopted Hinduism, the status of a cultivator, sank, to some extent and his Vaishyan ancestry was forgotten. But though the Vaishya himself has practically disappeared, his status as a cultivator and member of the village community appears to remain in that of the modern cultivating castes, as will be shown subsequently.

Aryan in Villages

The settlement of the Aryans in India was in villages and not in towns, and the Hindus have ever since remained a rural people. In 1911 less than a tenth of the population of India was urban, and nearly three-quarters of the total were directly supported by agriculture. Apparently, therefore, the basis or embryo of the gradation of Hindu society or the caste system should be sought in the village. Two main divisions of the village community may be recognised in the Vaishyas or cultivators and the Sudras or impure serfs and labourers. The exact position held by the Kshatriyas and the constitution of their class are not quite clear, but there is no doubt that the Brahmans and Kshatriyas formed the early aristocracy, ranking above the cultivators, and a few' other castes have since attained to this position. From early times, as is shown by an ordinance of Manu, men of the higher castes or classes were permitted, after taking a woman of their own class for the first wife, to have second and subsequent wives from any of the classes beneath them. This custom appears to have been largely prevalent. No definite rule prescribed that the children of such unions should necessarily be illegitimate, and in many cases no doubt seems to exist that if not they themselves, their descendants at any rate ultimately became full members of the caste of the first ancestor. According to Manu, if the child of a Brahman by a Sudra woman intermarried with Brahmans and his descendants after him, their progeny in the seventh generation would become full Brahmans and the same was the case with the child of a Kshatriya or a Vaishya with a Sudra woman. A commentator remarks that the descendants of a Brahman by a Kshatriya woman could attain Brahmanhood in the third generation, and those by a Vaishya woman in the fifth. Such children also could inherit. According to the *Mahabharata*, if a Brahman had four wives of different castes, the son by a Brahman wife took four shares, that by a Kshatriya wife three, by a Vaishya wife two, and by a Sudra wife one share. Manu gives a slightly different distribution, but also permits to the son by a Sudra wife a share of the inheritance. Thus, the fact is clear that the son of a Brahman even by a Sudra woman had a certain status of legitimacy in his father's caste as he could marry in it, and must therefore have been permitted to partake of the sacrificial food at marriage and he could also inherit a small share of the property.

The detailed rules prescribed for the status of legitimacy and inheritance show that recognised unions of this kind between men of a higher class and women of a lower one were at one time fairly frequent, though they were afterwards prohibited. And they must necessarily have led to much mixture of blood in the different castes. A trace of them seems to survive in the practice of hypergamy, still widely prevalent in northern India, by which men of the higher subcastes of a caste will take daughters in marriage from lower ones, but will not give their daughters in return. This custom prevails largely among the higher castes of the Punjab, as the Rajputs and Khatris and among the Brahmans of Bengal. Only a few cases are found in the Central Provinces, among Brahmans, Sunars and other castes. Occasionally intermarriage between two castes takes place on a hypergamous basis; thus Rajputs are said to take daughters from the highest clans of the cultivating caste of Dangis. More commonly families of the lower sub-castes or clans in the same caste consider the marriage of their daughters into a higher group a great honour and will give large sums of money for a bridegroom. Until quite recently a Rajput was bound to marry his daughters into a clan of equal or higher rank than his own, in order to maintain the position of his family. It is not easy to see why so much importance should be attached to the marriage of a daughter, since she passed into another clan and family, to whom her offspring would belong. On the other hand, a son might take a wife from a lower group without loss of status, though his children would be the future representatives of the family. Another point, possibly connected with hypergamy, is that a peculiar relation exists between a man and the family into which his daughter has married. Sometimes he will accept no food or even water in his son-in-law's Village. The word *sala,* signifying wife's brother, when addressed to a man, is also a common and extremely offensive term of abuse. The meaning is now perhaps supposed to be that one has violated the sister of the person spoken to, but this can hardly have been the original significance as *sasur* or father-in-law is also considered in a minor degree an opprobrious term of address But though among the our classical castes it was possible I: for the descendants of mixed unions between fathers of higher and mothers of lower caste to be admitted into their father's caste, this would not have been the general rule. Such connections were very frequent and the Hindu classics account through them for the multiplication of castes.

Long lists are given of new castes formed by the children of mixed marriages. The details of these genealogies seem to be destitute of any probability, and perhaps, therefore, instances of them are unnecessary. Matches between a man of higher and a woman of lower caste were called *anuloma,* or with the hair' or grain, and were regarded as suitable and becoming. Those between a man of lower and a woman of higher caste were, on the other hand, known as *pratiloma* or against the hair, and were considered as disgraceful and almost incestuous. The offspring of such unions are held to have constituted the lowest and most impure castes of scavengers, dog-eaters and so on. This doctrine is to be accounted for by the necessity of safeguarding the morality of women in a state of society where kinship is reckoned solely by male descent. The blood of the tribe and clan, and hence the right to membership and participation in the communal sacrifices, is then communicated to the child through the father; hence if the women are unchaste, children may be born into the family who have no such rights, and the whole basis of society is destroyed. For the same reason, since the tribal blood and life is communicated through mates, the birth and standing of the mother are of little importance, and children are, as has been seen, easily admitted to their father's rank. But already in Manu's time the later and present view that both the father and mother must be of full status in the clan, tribe or caste in order to produce a legitimate child, has begun to prevail, and the children of all mixed marriages are relegated to a lower group. The offspring of these mixed unions did probably give rise to a class of different status in the village community. The lower-caste mother would usually have been taken into the father's house and her children would be brought up in it. Thus, they would eat the food of the household, even if they did not participate in the sacrificial feasts; and a class of this kind would be very useful or the performance of menial duties in and about the household, such as personal service, bringing water, and so on, for which the Sudras, owing to their impurity, would be unsuitable. In the above manner a new grade of village menial might have arisen and have gradually been extended to the other village in industries, so that a third group would be formed in the village community ranking between the cultivators and labourers. This gradation of the village community may perhaps still be discerned in the main social distinctions of the different Hindu castes at present. And an attempt will now be made to demonstrate this hypothesis in connection with a brief survey of the castes of the province.

An examination of the social status of the castes of the Central Provinces, which, as already seen, are representative of a great part of India, shows that they fall into five principal groups. The highest consists of those castes who now claim to be directly descended from the Brahmans, Kshatriyas or

Vaishyas, the three higher of the four classical castes. The second comprises what are generally known as pure or good castes. The principal mark of their caste status is that a Brahman will take water to drink from them, and perform ceremonies in their houses. They may be classified in three divisions: the higher agricultural castes, higher artisan castes, and serving castes from whom a Brahman will take water. The third group contains those castes from whose hands a Brahman will not take water but their touch does not convey impurity and they are permitted to enter Hindu temples. They consist mainly of certain cultivating castes of low status, some of them recently derived from the indigenous tribes, other functional castes formed from the forest tribes, and a number of professional and menial castes, whose occupations are mainly pursued in villages, so that they formerly obtained their subsistence from grain-payments or annual allowances of grain from the cultivators at seedtime and harvest. The group includes also some castes of village priests and mendicant religious orders, who be from the cultivators. In the fourth group are placed the non-Aryan or indigenous tribes. Most of these cannot properly be said to form part of the Hindu social system at all, but for practical purposes they are admitted and are considered to rank below all castes except those who can- not be touched. The lowest group consists of the impure castes whose touch is considered to defile the higher castes. Within each group there are minor differences of status some of which will be noticed, but the broad divisions may be considered as representing approximately the facts the rule about Brahmans taking water from the good agricultural and artisan castes obtains, for instance, only in northern India. Maratha Brahmans will not take water from any but other Brahmans, and in Chhattisgarh Brahmans and other high castes will take water only from the hands of a Rawat (grazier), and from no other caste. But nevertheless the Kunbis, the great cultivating caste of the Maratha country, though Brahmans do not take water from them, are on the same level as the Kurmis, the cultivating caste of Hindustan, and in tracts where they meet Kunbis and Kurmis are often considered to be the same caste. The evidence of the statements made as to the origin of different castes in the following account will be found in the articles on them in the body of the work.

The castes of the first group are noted below:

Brahman Khitri   Bania   Bhil

Rajput   Kayasth and Prabhu Karan Gurao

Status of Brahmans

The Brahmans are, as they have always been, the highest caste. The Rajputs are the representatives of the ancient Kshatriyas or second caste, though the existing Rajput clans are probably derived from the Hun, Gujar and other invaders of the period before and shortly after the commencement of the Christian era, and in some cases from the indigenous or non-Aryan tribes. It does not seem possible to assert in the case of a single one of the present Rajput clans that any substantial evidence is forthcoming in favour of their descent from the Aryan Kshatriyas, and as regards most of the clans there are strong arguments against such a hypothesis. Nevertheless the Rajputs have succeeded to the status of the Kshatriyas, and an alternative name for them, Chhatri is a corruption of the latter word. They are commonly identified with the second of the four classical castes, but a Hindu law-book gives Rajaputra as the offspring of a Kshatriya father and a mother of the Karan or writer caste. This genealogy is absurd, but may imply the opinion that the Rajputs were not the same as the Aryan Kshatriyas. The Khatris are an important mercantile caste of the Punjab, who in opinion of most authorities are derived from the Rajputs. The name is probably a corruption of Kshatri or Kshatriya. The banias are the great mercantile, banking and shopkeeping caste among the Hindus and a large proportion of the trade in grain and *ghi* (presented butter) is in their hands while they are also the chief moneylenders. Most of the important Bania subcastes belonged originally to Rajputana and Central India, which are also the homes of the Rajputs, and reasons have been given in the article on Bania for holding that they are derived from the Rajputs. They, however, are now commonly called Vaishyas by the Hindus, as, I think, under the mistaken impression that they are descended from the original Vaishyas. The Bhats are the bards, heralds and genealogists of India and include groups of very varying status. The Bhats who act as genealogists of the cultivating and other castes and eat cooked food from their clients may perhaps be held to rank with or even below them. But the high-class Bhats are undoubtedly derived from Brahmans and Rajputs, and rank below those castes. The bard or herald had a sacred character, and his person was inviolable like that of the herald elsewhere, and this has given a special status to the whole caste. The Kayasths are the writer caste of Hindustan, and the Karans and Prabhus are the corresponding castes of Orissa and Bombay.

The position of the Kayasths has greatly risen during the last century on account of their own ability and industry and the advantages they have obtained through their high level of education. The original Kayasths may have been village accountants and hence have occupied a lower position, perhaps below the cultivators. They are an instance of a caste whose social position has greatly improved on account of the wealth and importance of its members. At present the Kayasths may be said to rank next to Brahmans and Rajputs. The origin of the Prabhus and Karans is uncertain, but their recent social history appears to resemble that of the Kayasths. The Guraos are another caste whose position has greatly improved. They were priests of the village temples of Siva, and accepted the offerings of food which Brahmans could not take. But they also supplied leaf plates for festivals, and were village musicians and trumpeters in the Maratha armies, and hence probably ranked below the cultivators and were supported by contributions of grain from them. Their social position has been raised by their sacred character as priests of the god Siva and they are now sometimes called Shaiva Brahmans. But a distinct recollection of their former status exists.

Thus, all the castes of the first group are derived from the representatives of the Brahmans and Kshatriyas, the two highest of the four classical castes, except the Guraos, who have risen in status owing to special circumstances. The origin of the Kayasths is discussed in the article on that caste. Members of the above castes usually wear the sacred thread which is the mark of the Dwija or twice-born, the old Brahmans, Kshatriyas and Vaishyas. The thread is not worn generally by the castes of the second group, but the more wealthy and prominent sections of them frequently assume it. The second group of good castes from whom a Brahman can take water falls into three sections as already explained the higher agricultural castes, the higher artisans, and the serving or menial castes from whom a Brahman takes water from motives of convenience. These last do not properly belong to the second group but to the next lower one of village menials. The higher agricultural castes or those of the first section are noted below:

Agharia	Daharia	Jat	Kurmi	Mina or Deswali
Ahir	Dangi	Khandait	Lodhi	Panwar Rajput
Bhilala	Dumal	Kirar	Mali	Raghuvansi
Bishnoi	Gujar	Kolta	Maratha	Velama
Chasa	Jadum	Kunbi		

In this division the Kurmis and Kunbis are the typical agricultural castes of Hindustan or the plains of northern India, and the Bombay or Maratha Deccan. Both are very numerous and appear to be purely occupational bodies. The name Kurmi perhaps signifies a cultivator or worker. Kunbi may mean a householder. In both castes, groups of diverse origin seem to have been amalgamated owing to their common calling. Thus the Kunbis include a subcaste derived from the Banjara (carriers), another from the Dhangars or shepherds, and a third from the Manas, a primitive tribe. In Bombay it is considered that the majority of the Kunbi caste are sprung from the 'non-Aryan' or indigenous tribes, and this may be the reason why Maratha Brahmans do not take water from them. But they have now become one caste with a status equal to that of the other good cultivating castes. In many tracts of Berar and elsewhere practically all the cultivators of the village belong to the Kunbi caste, and there is every reason to suppose that this was once the general rule and that the Kunbis or 'householders' are simply the cultivators of the Maratha country who lived in village communities. Similarly H. Risley considered that some Kurmis of Bihar were of the Aryan type, while others of Chota

Nagpur are derived from the indigenous tribes. The *Chasas* are the cultivating caste of Orissa and are a similar occupational group. The word *Chasa* has the generic meaning of a cultivator, and the caste are said by H. Risley to be for the most part of non-Aryan origin, the loose organisation of the caste system among the Uriyas making it possible on the one hand for outsiders to be admitted into the caste, and on the other for wealthy *Chasas*, who gave up ploughing with their own hands and assured the respectable title of Mahanti, to raise themselves to membership among the lower classes of Kayasths. The Koltas are another Uriya caste, probably an off shoot of the *Chasas*, whose name may be derived from the *kulthi* pulse, a favourite crop in that locality.

In Tamil Region

Similarly the Vellalas are the great cultivating caste of the Tamil country, to whom by general consent the first place in social esteem among the Tamil Sudra castes is awarded. In the *Madras Census Report of 1901* Francis gives an interesting description of the structure of the caste and its numerous territorial, occupational and other subdivisions. He shows also how groups from lower castes continually succeed in obtaining admission into the Vellala community in the following passage:

"Instances of members of other castes who have assumed the name and position of Vellalas are the Vettuva Vellalas, who are only Puluvans; the Illam Vellalas, who are Panikkans; the Karaiturai (lord of the shore) Vellalas, who are Karaiyans; the Karukamattai (palmyra leaf-stem) Vellalas, who are Balijas; the Guha (Rama's boatmen) Vellalas, who are Sembadavans; and the Irkuli Vellalas, who are Vannans. The children *of* dancing-girls also often call themselves Mudali, and claim in time to be Vellalas, and even Paraiyans assume the title of Pillai and trust to its eventually enabling them to pass themselves off as members of the caste."

This is an excellent instance of the good status attaching to the chief cultivating caste of the locality and of the manner in which other groups, when they obtain possession of the land, strive to get themselves enrolled in it.

The Jats are the representative cultivating caste of the Punjab. They are probably the descendants of one of the Scythian invading hordes who entered India shortly before and after the commencement of the Christian era. The Scythians, as they were called by Herodotus, appear to have belonged to the Mongolian racial family, as also did the white Huns who came subsequently. The Gujar and Ahir castes, as well as the Jats, and also the bulk of the existing Rajput clans, are believed to be descended from these invaders; and since their residence in India has been comparatively short in comparison with their Aryan predecessors, they have undergone much less fusion with the general population, and retain a lighter complexion and better features, as is quite perceptible to the ordinary observer in the case of the Jats and Rajputs. The Jats have a somewhat higher status than other agricultural castes because in the Punjab they were once dominant, and one of the ruling chiefs belonged to the caste. The bulk of the Sikhs were also Jats. But in the Central Provinces, where they are not large landholders, and have no traditions of former dominance, there is little distinction between them and the Kurmis. The Gujars for long remained a pastoral freebooting tribe, and their community was naturally recruited from all classes of vagabonds and outlaws, and hence the caste is now of a mixed character, and their physical type is not noticeably distinct from that of other Hindus. G. Campbell derived the Gujars from the Khazars, a tribe of the same race as the white Huns and Bulgars who from an early period had been settled in the neighbourhood of the Caspian. They are believed to have entered India during the fifth or sixth century. Several clans of Rajputs, as well as considerable sections of the Ahir and Kunbi castes were, in his opinion, derived from the Gujars. In the Central Provinces the Gujars have now settled down into respectable cultivators. The Ahirs or cowherds and graziers probably take their name from the Abhiras, another of the Scythian tribes. But they have now become a purely occupational caste, largely recruited from the indigenous Gonds and Kawars, to whom the business of tending cattle in the jungles is habitually entrusted. 1n the Central Provinces Ahirs live in small forest villages with Gonds, and are sometimes scarcely considered as Hindus. On this account they have a character for bucolic stupidity, as the proverb has it: 'When he is asleep he is an Ahir and when he is awake he is a fool.' But the Ahir caste generally has a good status on account of its connection with the sacred cow and also with the god Krishna, the divine cowherd.

The Marathas are the military caste of the Maratha country, formed into a caste from the cultivators, shepherds and herdsmen, Who took service under Shivaji and subsequent Maratha leaders. The higher clans may have been constituted from the aristocracy of the Deccan states, which was probably of Rajput descent. They have now became a single caste, ranking somewhat higher than the Kunbis, from whom the bulk of them originated, on account of their former military and dominant position. Their status was much the same as that of the Jats in the Punjab. But the ordinary Marathas are mainly engaged in the subordinate Government and private service, and there is very little distinction between them and the Kunbis. The Khandaits or swordsmen (from *khanda,* a sword) are an Uriya caste, which originated in military service, and the members of which belonged for the most part to the non-Aryan Bhuiya tribe. They were a sort of rabble, half military and half police, H. Risley states, who formed the levies of the Uriya zamindars. They have obtained grants of land, and their status has improved. In the social system of Orissa the Sreshta (good) Khandaits rank next to the Rajputs, who are comparatively few in number, and have not that intimate connection with the land which has helped to raise the Khandaits to their present position. The small Rautia landholding caste of Chota Nagpur, mainly derived from the Kol tribe, was formed from military service, and obtained a higher status with the possession of the land exactly like the Khandaits.

Rajput Clans

Several Rajput clans, as the Panwars of the Wain ganga Valley, the Raghuvansis, the Jadums derived from the

Yadava clan, and the Daharias of Chhattisgarh, have formed distinct castes, marrying among themselves. A proper Rajput should not marry in his own clan. These groups have probably in the past taken wives from the surrounding population, and they can no longer be held to belong to the Rajput caste proper, but rank as ordinary agricultural castes. Other agricultural castes have probably been formed through mixed descent from Rajputs and the indigenous races. The Agharias of Sambalpur say they are sprung from a clan of Rajputs near Agra, who refused to bend their heads before the king of Delhi. He summoned all the Agharias to appear before him, and fixed a sword across the door at the height of a man's neck. As the Agharias would not bend their heads they were as a natural consequence all decapitated as they passed through the door. Only one escaped, who had bribed a Chamar *to* go instead of him. He and his village fled from Agra and came to Chhattisgarh, where they founded the Agharia caste. And, in memory of this, when an Agharia makes a libation to his ancestors, he first pours a little water on the ground in honour of the dead Chamar. Such stories may be purely imaginary, or may contain some substratum of truth, as that the ancestors of the caste were Rajputs, who took wives from Chamars and other low castes. The Kirars are another caste with more or less mixed descent from Rajputs. They are also called Dhakar, and this means one of illegitimate birth. The Bhilalas are a caste formed of the offspring of mixed alliances between Rajputs and Bhils. In many cases in Nimar Rajput immigrants appear to have married the daughters of Bhil chieftains and landholders, and succeeded to their estates. Thus, the Bhilalas include a number of landed proprietors, and the caste ranks as a good agricultural caste, from whom Brahmans will take water.

Among the other indigenous tribals, several of which have in the Central Provinces retained the possession of large areas of land and great estates in the wilder forest tracts a sub-caste has been formed of the landholding members of the tribe. Such are the Raj-Gonds among the Gonds, the Binjhals among Baigas, and the Tawar sub-tribe of the Kawar tribe of Bilaspur, to which all the zamindars belong. These last now claim to be Tomara Rajputs, on the basis of the similarity of the name. These groups rank with the good agricultural castes, and Brahmans sometimes consent to take water from them. The Dangis of Saugor appear to be the descendants of a set of freebooters in the Vindhyan hills, much like the Gujars in northern India. The legend of their origin is given in B. Robertson's *Census Report* of 1891. The chief of Garhpahra or old Saugor detained the palanquins of twenty-two married women and kept them as his wives. The issue of the illicit intercourse were named Dangis, and there are thus twenty-two subdivisions of these people. There are also three other subdivisions who claim descent from pure Rajputs, and who will take daughters in marriage from the remaining twenty-two, but will not give their daughters to them. Thus, the Dangis appear to have been a mixed group, recruiting their band from all classes of the population, with some Rajputs as leaders. The name probably means hillman, from *dang,* a hill. *Khet men bami gaon mein dangi"* A Dangi in the village is like the hole of a snake in one's field, is a proverb showing the estimation in which they were formerly held. They obtained estates in Saugor and a Daogi dynasty formerly, governed part of the District, and they are now highly respectable cultivators. The Minas or Deswalis belonged to the predatory Mina tribe of Rajputana, but a section of them have obtained possession of the land in Hoshangabad and rank as a good agricultural caste. The Lodhas of the United Provinces are placed lowest among the agricultural castes by Nesfield, who describes them as little better than a forest tribe. The name is perhaps derived from the bark of the *lodh* tree, which was collected by the Lodhas of northern India and sold for use as a dyeing agent.

In the Central Provinces the name has been changed to Lodi, and they are said to have been brought into the District by a Raja of the Gond-Rajput dynasty of Mandla in the seventeenth century, and given large grants of waste land in the interior in order that they might clear it of forest. They have thus become landholders, and rank with the higher agricultural castes. They are addressed as Thakur, a title applied to Rajputs, and Lodhi landowners usually wear the sacred thread.

The above details have been given to show how the 21 different agricultural castes originated. Though their origin is so diverse they have, to a great extent, the same status, and it seems clear that this status is dependent on their possession of the land. In the tracts where they reside they are commonly village proprietors and superior tenants. Those who rank a little higher than the others, as the Jats, Marathas, Dangis and Lodhis, include in their body some ruling chiefs or large landed proprietors, and as a rule were formerly dominant in the territory in which they are found. In primitive agricultural communities the land is the principal, if not almost the sole, source of wealth. Trade in the modern sense scarcely exists, and what interchange of commodities there is affects, as a *rule,* only a trifling fraction of the population. India's foreign trade is mainly the growth of the last century, and the great bulk of the exports are of agricultural produce, yet in proportion to the population the trading community is still extremely small. It thus seems quite impossible that the Aryans could have been a community of priests, rulers and traders, because such a community would not have had means of subsistence. And if the whole production and control of the wealth and food of the community had been in the hands of the Sudras, they could not have been kept permanently in their subject, degraded position. The flocks and herds and the land, which constituted the wealth of early India, must thus have been in the possession of the Vaishyas; and grounds of general probability, as well as the direct evidence already produced, make it clear that they were the herdsmen and cultivators, and the Sudras the labourers. The status of the modern cultivators seems to correspond to that of the Vaishyas, that is, of the main body of the Aryan people, who were pure and permitted to join in sacrifices. The status, however, no longer attaches to origin, but to the possession of the land; it is that of a constituent member of the village community, corresponding to a citizen of the city states of Greece and Italy. The original Vaishyas have long disappeared; the Brahmans themselves say that there are no Kshatriyas and no Vaishyas left, and this seems to be quite correct. But the modern good cultivating castes retain the status of the

Vaishyas' as the Rajputs retain that of the Kshatriyas. The case of the Jats and Gujars supports this view. These two castes are almost certainly derived from Scythian nomad tribes, who entered India long after the Vedic Aryans. And there is good reason to suppose that a substantial proportion, if not the majority, of the existing Rajput clans were the leaders or: aristocracy of the Jats and Gujars. Thus, it is found that in the case of these later tribes the main body were shepherds and cultivators, and their descendants have the status of good cultivating castes at present, while the leaders became the Rajputs, who have the status of the Kshatriyas; and it therefore seems a reasonable inference that the same had previously been the case with the Aryans themselves. It has been seen that the word Visha or Vaishya signified one of the people or a householder. The name Kunbi appears to have the same sense, its older form being *kutumbika,* which is a householder or one who has a family; a *pater familias.*

It has been seen also that *Visha* in the plural signified clans. The clan was the small body which lived together, and in the patriarchal stage was connected by a tie of kinship held to be derived from a common ancestor. Thus, it is likely that the clans settled down in villages, the cultivators of one village being of the same exogamous clan. The existing system of exogamy affords evidence in favour of this view, as will be seen. All the families of the clan had cultivating rights in the land, and were members of the village community; and there were no other members, unless possibly a Kshatriya headman or leader. The Sudras were their labourers and serfs, with no right to hold land, and a third intermediate class of village menials gradually grew up. The law of Mirasi tenures in Madras is perhaps a survival of the social system of the early village community. Under it only a few of the higher castes were allowed to hold land, and the monopoly was preserved by the rule that the right of taking up waste lands belonged primarily to the cultivators of the adjacent holdings; no one else could acquire land unless the first bought them out. The pariahs or impure castes were not allowed to hold land at all. This rule was pointed out by Slocock, and it is also noticed by Henry' O

Maine: "There are in Central and Southern India certain villages to which a class of persons is hereditarily attached, in such a manner that they form no part of the natural and organic aggregate to which the bulk of the villagers belong. These persons are looked upon as essentially impure; they never enter the village, or only enter reserved portions of it; and their touch is avoided as contaminating. Yet they bear extremely plain mark of their origin. Though they are not included in the village, they are an appendage solidly connected with it; they have, definite village duties, one of which is the settlement of boundaries, on which their authority is allowed to be conclusive. They evidently represent a population of alien blood whose lands have been occupied by the colonists or invaders forming the community. Elsewhere, Henry Maine points out that in many cases the outsiders were probably admitted to the possession of land, but on an inferior tenure to the primary holders or freemen who formed the cultivating body of the village; and suggests that this may have been the ground for the original distinction between occupancy and non-occupancy tenants. The following extract from a description of the Maratha villages by Grant Duff may be subjoined to this passage: "The inhabitants are principally cultivators, and are now either Mirasidars or ooprees. These names serve to distinguish the tenure by which they hold their lands. The *oopree* is a mere tenant-at-will, but the Mirasidar is a hereditary occupant whom the Government cannot displace so long as he pays the assessment on his field. With various privileges and distinctions in his village of minor consequence, the Mirasidar has the important power of selling or transferring his right of occupancy at pleasure. It is a current opinion in the Maratha country that all the lands were originally of this description."

Maine's Ideas

As regards the internal relations of clans and village groups, H. Maine states: 'The men who composed the primitive communities believed themselves to be kinsmen in the most literal sense of the word; and, surprising as it may seem, there are a multitude of indications that in one stage of thought they must have regarded themselves as equals. When these primitive bodies first make their appearance as landowners as claiming an exclusive enjoyment in a definite area of land, not only do their shares of the soil appear to have been originally equal, but a number of contrivances survive for preserving the equality, of which the most frequent, is the periodical redistribution of the tribal domain." A Similarly Professor Hearn states: The settlement of Europe was made by-clans. Each clan occupied a certain territory. The land thus occupied was distributed by *metes* and bounds to each branch of the clan; the remainder, if any, continuing the property or the clan. And again: "In those cases where the land had been acquired by conquest there were generally some remains of the conquered population who retained more or less interest in the lands that had once been their own. But as between the conquerors them-selves it was the clansmen, and the clansmen only, who were entitled to derive any advantage from the land that the clan had acquired. The outsiders, the men who lived with the clan but were not of the clan, they were no part of the folk, and had no share in the folkland. No services rendered, no participation in the common danger, no endurance of the burden and heat of the day, could create in an outsider any colour of right. Nothing short of admission to the clan, and of initiation in its worship, could enable him to demand as of right the grass of a single *cow* or the wood for a single fire.

Thus, it appears that the cultivating community of each village constituted an exogamous clan, the members of which believed themselves to be kinsmen. When some caste or tribe occupied a fresh area of land they were distributed by clans in villages, over the area, all the cultivators of a village being of one caste or tribe, as is still the case with the Kunbis in Berar. Sometimes several alien castes or groups became amalgamated into a single caste, such as the Kurmis and Kunbis; in others they were remained as a separate caste or became one. When the non-Aryan tribes retained possession of the land, there is every reason to suppose that they also were admitted into Hinduism, and either constituted a fresh caste with the cultivating status, or were absorbed into an existing one with a change of name. Individual ownership of land was probably unknown. The *Patel* or village headman, on whom proprietary right was conferred by the British Government, certainly did not posses it previously. He was simply the spokesman and representative of the village community in its dealings with the central or ruling authority. But it seems scarcely likely either that the village community considered itself' to *own* the land. Cases in which the community as a corporate body has exercised any function of ownership other than that of occupying and cultivating the soil, if recorded at all, must be extremely rare, and I do not know that any instance is given by Henry Maine. A tutelary village god is to be found as a rule in every Hindu village. In the Central Provinces the most common is Khermata, that is the goddess of the village itself or the village lands. She is a form of Devi, the general earth goddess. When a village-is -founded the first thing to be done is to install the village god. Thus, the soil of the village is venerated as a goddess, and it seems doubtful whether the village community considered itself the owner.

In the Maratha Districts, Hanuman or Mahabir, the monkey god, is the tutelary deity of the village. His position seems to rest on the belief of the villagers that the monkeys were the lords and owners of the soil before their own arrival. For the worship of these and the other village gods there is usually a village priest, known as Bhumka, Bhumia, Baiga or Jhankar, who is taken from the non-Aryan tribes. The reason for his appointment seems to be that the Hindus still look on themselves to some extent as strangers and interlopers in relation to the gods of the earth and the village, and consider it necessary to approach these through the medium of one of their predecessors. The words Bhumka and Bhumia both mean lord of the soil, or belonging to the soil. As already seen, the authority of some menial official belonging to the indigenous tribes is accepted as final in cases of disputed boundaries, the idea being apparently that as his ancestors first occupied the village, he has inherited from them the knowledge of its true extent and limits. All these points appear to tell strongly against the view that the Hindu village community considered itself to own the village land as we understand the phrase. They seem to have looked on the land as a god, and often their own tutelary deity and protector. What they held themselves to possess was a right of occupancy, in virtue of prescriptive settlement, not subject to removal or disturbance, and transmitted by inheritance to persons born to the membership of the village community. Under the Muhammadans the idea that the state ultimately owned the land may have been held, but prior to them the existence of such a belief is doubtful. The Hindu king did not take rent land, but a share of the produce for the support of his establishments.

The Rajput princes did not call themselves after the name of their country, but of its capital town, as if their own property consisted only in the town, as Jodhpur, Jaipur and, Udaipur, instead of Marwar, Dhundhar and Mewar. Just as the village has a priest of the non-Aryan tribes for propitiating the local gods, so the Rajput chief at his accession was often inducted to the royal cushion by a Brut or Mina, and received the badge of investiture as if he had to obtain his title from these tribes. Indeed the right of the village community to the land was held sometimes superior to that of the state. J. Malcolm relates that he was very anxious to get the village of Bassi in Indore State repopulated when it had lain waste for thirty-six years. He had arranged with the Bhil headman of a neighbouring village to bring it under cultivation on a favourable lease. The plan had other advantages, and Holkar's minister was most anxious to put it into execution, but said that this could not be done until every possible effort had been made to discover whether any descendant of the former *Patel* or of any *watandar* hereditary cultivator of Bassi was still in existence; for if such were found, he said, "even we Marathas, bad as we are, cannot do anything which interferes with their rights." None such being found at the time, the village was settled as proposed by Malcolm; but some time afterwards, a boy was discovered who was descended from the old *patel's* family, and he was invited to resume the office of headman of the village of his forefathers, which even the Bhil, who had been nominated to it, was forward to resign to the rightful inheritor! Similarly the Maratha princes, Sindhia,

Holkar and others, are recorded to have set more store the headship of the insignificant Deccan villages, which were the hereditary offices of their families, than the great principalities which they had carried out for themselves with the sword. The former defined and justified their position in the world as the living link and representative of the continuous family comprising all their ancestors and all their descendants; the latter was at first regarded merely as a transient, secular possession, and a source of wealth and profit. This powerful hereditary right probably rested on a religious basis. The village community was considered to be bound up with its village god in one joint life, and hence no one but they could in theory have the right to cultivate the lands of that village. The very origin and nature of this right precluded any question of transfer or alienation. The only lands in which any ownership, corresponding to our conception or the term, was held to exist, were perhaps those granted free of revenue or the maintenance — temples, which were held to be the property of the god. In Rome and other Greek and Latin cities the idea of private or family ownership of land also developed from a religious sentiment. It was customary to bury the dead in the fields, which they had held, and here the belief was that their spirits remained and protected the interests of the family. Periodical sacrifices were made to them and they participated in all the family ceremonies. Hence the land in which the tombs of ancestors were situated was held to belong to the family, and could not be separated from it. Gradually, as the veneration for the spirits of ancestors decayed, the land came to be regarded as the private property of the family, "and when this idea had been realised it was made alienable, though not with the same freedom as personal property. But the word *pecunia* for money, from *pecus* a flock, like the Hindi *dhan,* which means wealth and also flocks of goats and sheep, and feudal *from* the Gaelic *fin,* cattle, point to conditions of society in ,which land was not considered a form of private property or wealth. M. Fustel de Coulanges notices other primitive races who did not recognise property in land: "The Tartars understand the term property as applying to cattle, but not as applying to land. According to some authors, among the ancient Germans there was no ownership of land; every year each member of the tribe received a holding to cultivate, and the holding was changed in the following year. The German owned the crop; he did not own the soil. The same was the case among a part of the Semitic race and certain of the Slav peoples."

In large areas of the Nigeria Protectorate at present, land has no exchangeable value at all; but by the native system of taxation a portion of the produce is taken in consideration of the right of use. In ancient Arabia, Baal meant the lord of some place or district, that is, a local deity, and hence came to mean a god. Land naturally moist was considered as irrigated by a god and the special place or habitation of the god. To the numerous Canaanite Baalims, or local deities, the Israelites ascribed all the natural gifts of the land, the corn, the wine, and the oil, the wool and the flax, the vines and fig trees. Pasture land was common property, but a man acquired rights in the soil by building a house, or, by quickening a waste place, that is, bringing it under cultivation. The Israelites thought that they derived their title to the land of Canaan from Jehovah, having received it as a gift from Him. The association of rights over the land with cultivation and building, pointed out by Professor Robertson Smith, may perhaps explain the right over the village lands which was held to appertain to the village community. They had quickened the land and built houses on it, establishing the local village deity on their village sites, and it was probably thought that their life was bound up with that of the village god, and only they had a right to cultivate his land. This would explain the great respect shown by the Marathas for hereditary title land, as seen above; a feeling which must certainly have been based on some religious belief, and not on any moral idea of equity or justice; no such deep moral principle was possible in the Hindu community at the period in question. The Hindu religious conception of rights to land was thus poles apart from the secular English law of proprietary and transferable right, and if the native feeling could have been understood by the early British administrators the latter would perhaps have been introduced only in a much modified form.

Aryan Immigrants

The suggested conclusion from the above argument is that the main body of the Aryan immigrants, that is the Vaishyas, settled down in villages by exogamous clans or septs. The cultivators of each village believed themselves to be kinsmen descended from a common ancestor, and also to be akin to the god of the village lands from which they drew their sustenance. Hence their order had an equal right to cultivate the village land and their children to inherit it, though they did not conceive of the idea of ownership of land in the sense in which we understand this phrase.

The original status of the Vaishya, or a full member of the Aryan community who could join in sacrifices and employ Brahmans to perform them, was gradually transferred to the cultivating member of the village communities. In process of time as land was the chief source of wealth, and was also regarded as sacred, the old status became attached to castes or groups of persons who obtained or held land irrespective of their origin, and these are what are now called the good cultivating castes. They have now practically the same status, though, as has been seen, they were originally of most diverse origin, including bands of robbers and freebooters, cattle-lifters, non-Aryan tribes, and sections of any castes which managed to get possession of an appreciable quantity of land.

The second division of the group of pure or good castes, or those from whom a Brahman can take water, comprises higher artisan castes:

Barhai	Halwai	Komti	Sunar Vidur
Bharbbunja	Kasar	Sansia	Tamera

The most important of these are the Sunar or goldsmith the Kasar or worker in brass and bell-metal; the Tamera or coppersmith; the Barhai or carpenter; and the Halwai and Bharbhunja or confectioner and grain-parcher. The Sansia or stone-mason of the Uriya country may perhaps also be included. These industries represent a higher degree of civilization than the village trades, and the workers may probably have been formed into castes at a later period, when the practice of the handicrafts was no longer despised.

The metal-working castes are now usually urban, and on the average their members are as well-to-do as the cultivators. The Sunars especially include a number of wealthy men, and their importance is increased by their association with the sacred metal, gold; in some localities they now claim to be Brahmans and refuse to take food from Brahmans. The more ambitious members abjure all flesh-food and liquor and wear the sacred thread. But in Bombay the Sunar, was in former times one of the village menial castes, and here, before and during the time of the Peshwas, Sunars were not allowed to wear the sacred thread, and they were forbidden to hold their marriages in public, as it was considered unlucky to see a Sunar bridegroom. Sunar bridegrooms were not allowed to see the state umbrella *or to ride in a palanquin, and had to be married at night and in secluded places, being subject to restrictions and annoyances from* which even Mahars were free.

Thus, the goldsmith's status appears to vary greatly according as his trade is a village or urban industry. Copper is also a sacred metal, and the Tameras rank next to the Sunars among the artisan castes, with the Kasars or brass-workers a little below them; both these castes sometimes wearing the sacred thread. These classes of artisans generally live in towns. The Barhai or carpenter is sometimes a village menial, but most carpenters live in towns, the wooden implements of agriculture being made either by the blacksmith or by the cultivators themselves. Where the Barhai is a village menial he is practically on equality with the Lohar or blacksmith; but the better-class-carpenters, who generally live in towns, rank higher. The Sansia or stone-mason of the Uriya country works, as a rule, only in stone, and in past times therefore his principal employment must have been to build temples. He could not thus be a village menial, and his status would be somewhat improved by the sanctity of his calling. The Halwai and Bharbhunja or confectioner and grain-parcher are castes of comparatively low origin, especially the latter; but they have to be given the status of ceremonial purity in order that all Hindus may be able to take sweets and parched grain from their hands. Their position resembles that of the barber.

References

Banerjea, Surendranath, A *Nation in Making.*

Vedic Index, Volume I.

Vedic Index, Volume II.

Ketkar, S.V., *History of Caste*, New York, 1909.

Census of India, Volume XXV.

Senart, Emile, *Caste in India.*

Russell, R.V., *The Tribes and Castes of the Central Provinces.*

Imperial Gazetteer of India, Vol. I, 1907.

The Collected works of Mahatama Gandhi, relevant volumes.

Rig Veda, Muller II.

Talbe, J., *Islam in Bengal, The Modern World*, 1914.

Richards, F.J., *Side Lights on the Dravidian Problem,* Part II.

Iyer, L.K.A., *Lectures on Ethnography*, Chapter IV.

Srinivas, M.N., *Caste in India*, 1962.

Roy, Burman, B.K., Social Mobility Movements among Scheduled Castes and Tribes, New Delhi AICC papers.

3

Evolution of Castes

Few topics within the sphere of Indian sociology present more difficulties than those connected with the origin and evolution of caste. Scholars have devoted considerable time to research and study of the subject, and have come to no conclusion. Various theories have been propounded by scholars. They can be roughly divided into two schools. The older school based its arguments on the sacred literature of the Hindus, and arrived at different conclusions; but all agree in ascribing to caste extreme antiquity, and regard the system as the artificial product of the Brahmanic hierarchy. Of late fresh light has been thrown on the subject by the study of inscriptions, and by the patient investigations of Buddhist and Jain literature, the authors of which were directly opposed to the Brahmans, and gave quite a different account of early society. And there is the new school of theorists "who post-date the origin of caste to comparatively modern late times by looking for its origin in the nature of the elements composing the early Indian society, and for its development in the working of social forces on these lines." Thus, none of the theories so far advanced commands universal approval. Further, information on the early Hindu society is still meager, and the discovery of any new fact will lead to the revision of the best of the theories. "The majority," says Blunt, "are infected with disease common to many theories—the lack of a sense of proportion, in that far too much importance is attached to some one point which is certainly cardinal to the particular theory, but is also regarded as the cardinal point in the "hole inquiry."

Rig Veda

The earliest reference to caste is found in the *Rig Veda,* in which mention is made of *four* castes which originated from Brahma, the Supreme Being. The Brahman came from his mouth, the Kshatriya from his arm, the Vaisya from his thighs, and the Sudras from his feet. This statement is somewhat allegorical. It means that the Brahmans are the instructors of mankind, the Kshatriya as are the warriors, and the Vaisyas and Sudras are the agriculturists and servants respectively. Similar references to the origin of caste are found in *Satapatha Brahmanas* (II-4-11), the *Taittiriya Brahmana* (III-12- 9, 3), *Vajaseniya Samhita,* and the *Atharva Veda.* But from an examination of the legends contained in the *Brahmanas,* it is seen that the accounts vary.

From the beginning of the Vedic period to the middle of the *Sutra* or Buddhist period, the fourfold division represented only classes, and this can be proved by the statements in the *Srauta-Sutra* of Blunt, E.A.H.: *The Caste System of Orthodox India,* Chap. II, pp. 11.12. *Rig Veda,* X.90, 11-12. *Drahyana* and in the *Puranas* regarding the functions of priests and warriors.

In the ninth book of the Rig *Veda,* there is a famous passage referring to various crafts. It is said that the organization of castes is *fully* developed at the period of *Brahmanas,* and is codified in the laws of Manu. The four castes are fully established. The rites and duties of *Brahmans* are in complete accord With modern descriptions, and the necessary purity of the race is fully inculcated. The caste is ignored by the persistent neglect of initiation.

The orthodox Hindu, on the other hand, considers the caste system to be a divine institution, and that there have existed since the beginning four distinct orders of men, Brahman or priest, Rajanya, Kshatriya or noble, Vaisya or tiller of the soil, and Sudra or the servile class. There is a great difference between the first three and the last. The

former are said to be the conquering Aryan and the latter
the conquered Sudra or Dasyu. The Aryans are said to
possess light colour, and the Dasyus dark colour. It is also
said that before the end of the Rigvedic period, a belief in
the divine origin of the four orders of men was firmly
established, but there are no references to the sub-division
of these orders. "In the next period, the period of the *Yajur
Veda* and the *Brahmanas,* are found the division of the Aryan
Society into four classes with distinct functions. The term
denotes a social order, independently of any actual difference
of colour, and we hear of the mixed *varnas,* the offspring of
parents belonging to distant orders." Descent is the chief
factor, though not the sole one. Tribal connection, religion,
and occupation combine with descent to consolidate the
social groups and keep them apart. "Throughout the Vedas"
says Blunt, "there is not a single reference to connubial or
communal restrictions to any of the characteristics of the
modern Hindu social system."

Jatakas and Hindu Society

"In the *Jatakas,* a collection of folk-tales, there is an
account of the Hindu society in early Buddhist times. The
colour distinction so prominent in the *vedas* has faded into
the background, though its memory survives in the word
varna, used for the social classes, namely, Kshatriya,
Brahman, Vaisya and Sudra. Here the Kshatriya heads the
list. The lords spiritual has not assumed the pride of place
the expense of the lords temporal. The Brahman is held in
status inferior to the Kshatriya nobility. The v*arnas* have
not yet become castes. The birth qualification has not yet
developed to make them close corporations. *Vaisyas* and
Sudras rise to the rank of Kshatriyas. Anybody can become
a Brahman by becoming a priest. There is no endogamous
restriction; a Brahman marries a Kshatriya widow, and
according to one *Jataka,* Buddha himself, a Kshatriya,
marries a poor cultivator's daughter. Marriage within the
clan is considered preferable to marriage outside it. But
social prejudice and social convention stand in the way of
the latter. Below the v*arnas* there are *hina jatyo,* low tribes,
of barbers, potters or weavers, for example, a remnant of

the *Dasya* tribes on the outskirts of civilization. The lowest
of all are the *Chandalas* and other outcaste tribes."

Megasthenes, who was an ambassador in the court of
Chandragupta (Sandrokotus of the Greeks) in 300 B.C.,
wrote an account of the social system of his day in a work
compiled by him, and this was preserved by Strabo, Arrian
and other writers. His classification of the people of his day
into seven groups is somewhat confusing. He speaks of the
philosophers, the husbandmen, the herdsmen and hunters,
the traders and labourers, the fighting men, the overseers,
the councilors, and the judges and administrators. From
the above list, *Brahmans* and *Kshatriyas* are easily identified.
The third and fourth groups include Vaisyas and Sudras.
The fourth would include all the guilds of armourers and
ship-builders of which Megasthenes speaks as possessing
special privileges. The sixth and the seventh of
Megasthenes' groups refer to professional classes. According
to Strabo's version, "no one is allowed to marry out of his
own caste or to exchange one profession for another or to
follow more than one business. An exception is made in
the case of the philosopher, who for his virtue is allowed
this privileges." Arrian endorses this view. From the facts
mentioned above may be inferred three important things,
namely, prohibition of intercaste marriages, the importance
of heredity, and the exemption of Brahmans from the above
rules. Nevertheless there were violations. Chandragupta
was of mixed descent. There were mixed marriages at a
much later date, and perhaps there were exceptional
instances as early as the fourth century B.C.

Regarding the six centuries between 300 B.C. and 300
A.D., information bearing on the development of caste is
rather scanty. Some attempts were made to prevent the
intermixture of caste. During this period, there occurred
the invasions of the Sakas, the Yavanas, the Pahlavas and
the Kushans. These must have left their mark on the Hindu
society, though very little is known, except in the case of
the Huns, about their intermixture with the population of
the country.

The Institutes of Manu and the chief *Puranas* in their
present form are ascribed to the Golden Age of Sanskrit

Literature under the early Gupta Kings (330-450 A.D.). The Brahmanas and Kshatriyas, the 'sacerdotal' and ruling and military castes respectively are shown as occupational. The Vaisyas and Sudras are not clearly defined. They are identical probably with trading, industrial and menial classes. The *Vratya* and *Vrishala* castes are the degenerate descendants of the twice-born classes who have neglected to perform the prescribed rites. Among them are included Khasa, Dravira, Yavana, Saka, Pahlava and China, and these names clearly show what Manu's *Vratyas* and *Vrishalas* were. These must have been the names of the aboriginal tribes and races, that have partly or wholly merged in the then Hindu tribes and castes. Manu's *Institutes* contain a fairly good account of the social system as it existed in his time. Many tribal castes must have sprung from foreign invaders, after their adoption of Hinduism. In this connection, it must be remembered that many of the invaders were barbarous, and their manners and customs would have become repugnant to the Hindus. It is very likely that these groups would have gradually become endogamous communities. Further, the real position of the Kshatriyas cannot be ascertained. It is said that Chandragupta Maurya was of mixed birth; the Andhra dynasty is usually regarded as of Sudra extraction. Harsha of Thanesvar, the last great Hindu king, was a Vaishya, but ranked as a Kshatriya. It seems, therefore, that the ancient Kshatriyas, like the modern Rajputs were a social class to which all rulers by virtue of their sovereignty were recognized as belonging. The Kshatriyas, like the modern Rajputs, may be regarded as an occupational caste following the Hindu ritual, and becoming rulers.

Buddhist Period

In the early Buddhist period the Kshatriya was socially supreme. In Manu's account, the supremacy passed to the Brahman. That the Kshatriya power decayed and reverted to the Brahman, it cannot be denied. In fact, as Blunt says, the causes may be found in the history of the time. During the three centuries from 200 B.C. to 500 A.D. India was subject to foreign invasions by powerful barbarian hordes, which led to the extirpation of the ancient Kshatriyas, who were also liable to be attacked from within Buddhism, which was a Kshatriya religion, founded by a Kshatriya prince, was opposed to Brahmanism. The two religions went on side by side for ten centuries till at last Brahmanism gained the ascendancy after the death of Harsha of Thanesvar in the middle of the seventh century A.D. It is also said that Parasurama extirpated the Kshatriyas. Thus the Kshatriya became extinct, and his power as ruler passed by right of sword to the foreign Sakas, Pahlavas and Kushans, each of whom in turn usurped the throne with the title of Kshatriya. Thus the kings and king- "lots of India were often Hinduised foreigners who never attained to the rank and pre-eminence of the ancient Kshatriyas. This low position of the Jater Kshatriyas afforded an opportunity to the Brahman, who, in the meantime, increased his authority and consolidated his position. In the Vedic period he was an acolyte at sacrifices, and assistant to the head of the family who officiated as priest. During the period which ended with the advent of Buddha in the midst of a people that was intensely religious, and still more intensely ritualistic, he had become the hereditary priest, the sole master of religious ceremonial and doctrine, and as such had won for himself an almost unassailable supremacy. Further, as philosopher and statesman, by sheer force of learning he had acquired considerable temporal power.

The king's minister was a Brahman and was no more a figure head. Vasishta, the family priest of Trayyaruna, king of Kosala, acted as regent in his master's absence. Chanakya overthrew Nanda kings, put Chandragupta Mauryas on the throne, and acted as his minister. The first Brahman dynasty after the Kanvas was the Shahya dynasty of Sindh in the tenth century. During the Buddhist period Brahman power suffered a little; Buddhism and the Kshatriya religion were revolts against Brahminism and its metaphysics. But Brahminism was never entirely destroyed. Under the Gupta dynasty the Brahmanic culture was widely diffused. The Brahman ascendancy both temporal and spiritual revived. It increased during the troubled period, which came with destruction of the old Arya nobility. The Brahman, the chief remaining link with the past, obtained the social hegemony', never again to lose it.

During the 'Vedic period, V*isha* (a house or district) signified people in general, and its adjective V*aisya* was afterwards applied to a householder. The *Vishas* or clans afterwards became the 'Vaisyas,' the third classical caste. Before they entered India, the Aryans were pastoral people, their domestic animals being the horse, the cow and, perhaps, the sheep and the goat. The horse and the cow were specially venerated, and they were the chief means of transport. The Vaisyas must, therefore, have been herdsmen and shepherds who entered India, took to agriculture and settled down to the practice of cultivation. The word V*aisya* signifies a man who occupies the soil, a cultivator or a merchant. According to Manu, God ordained them to tend cattle, give alms, offer sacrifice, to study, to cultivate, to trade, and learn the Vedas.

In the Buddhist period, Dr. Dutt opines, that Vaisyas and Sudras were not to be found as pure castes, nor did they represent groups anywhere. There is no mention anywhere of a member of any particular professional caste belonging to either Dasya v*arna* or Sudra v*arna*. The real distinction existed only during the Vedic period. Even during the early period of the Brahmanas, the distinction had almost vanished, and in later periods still more so. It was so in practice as well. In the early Buddhist period, mention is made of Gahapat or Grahapati, as a landowning and mercantile class which ranked below Kshatriyas and Brahmans. The word is synonymous with Kudumbika (house-holder) living in towns and villages. Gradually the Vaisyas underwent a kind of social degradation, and the reasons are given below:

1. The rapid increase in number of the Kshatriyas, coupled with the expansion of the Aryan domination, and the advance from tribalism towards feudalism and oligarchy;

2. The advancement and separation of the sacerdotal class from the common people, and their domination over them. The Vaisya, according to *Taittiriya Samhita*, lived only to be exploited by the Brahmans and Kshatriyas.

Numerous passages attest to their inferiority to the first two twice-born classes;

3. The abundant supply of slave labour in farming, pasturing and industrial arts, and the close association with certain branches of industry, together with a growing contempt for manual labour which brought the industries themselves low in the estimation of the higher classes. The separation of *Rathakaras* (chariot-makers), *Takshan* (carpenters) and *Kamaras* (workers in brass) from the Vaisya community is an instance in point. Thus, the artisan classes became separated from the Vaisyas, among whom there were merchants and farmers. At the outset there was no distinction, and gradually a Vaisya farmer was looked upon as inferior in status to a Vaisya merchant. In the *Jataka* literature, it is said that merchants alone formed what might be called the Vaisya community, while others sank to the status of Sudras;

4. During the Vedic period all professions and industries were in the hands of the Aryans. But after the intermingling of the Aryan with non-Aryan races the industrial and economic life of the people became very much changed. A large number of occupations fell to the lot of lower classes;

5. When the colour bar and purity of blood came to be considered, the cultured and the ruling classes adopted a policy of segregation and refrained from intermarriage and interlining with the non-Aryan peoples. The rank and file of the Vaisyas, owing to their number and association with the Sudras in various fields of activity, received a large admixture of non-Aryan blood. This also resulted in a lowering of the status of the Vaisyas.

M. Senart points out that the division of the four castes appearing in the post-Vedic literature does not continue on the same lines. There were two groups, one composed of the three higher castes, the other of the Sudras, or the lowest. The higher caste constituted the fraternity to which admission was obtained only by the religious ceremony of initiation and investment of the sacred thread. The Sudras were excluded, and could take no part in sacrifice. The punishment for the commission of grave offence by a

Brahman was degradation to a Sudra or outcaste. Dr. Wilson remarks: "They were the original inhabitants of the land, who conformed to the Brahmanic rules, and received certain privileges. They constituted the fourth caste, with the designation of Sudras. Manu has ordained that if Sudras are unable to maintain their families, they might subsist by handicrafts. The Sudras were ordained not to wear the sacred thread. They were regarded as a servile class, whose duty it was to minister to the twice-born."

Chandalas' Status

The *Chandalas* were the most despised of the Hindu society. They were not allowed to live within the walls of the town. The Pukkasa and *Chandalas* were also despised classes. They were excluded from the category of castes. In the *Dharmasastras* the occupation of a Chandala is to carry the dead bodies of men who have no relations or friends, and to execute criminals. In the fivefold division of society in the *Madhyadesa* (Middle country), Brahman, Kshatriya, Vaisya, Sudra, and Nishada are given. In the Buddhist Jataka literature also, the social divisions are on similar lines. The authors of *Dharmasastras,* relying on the Vedic texts as authority, excluded them from the fourfold division. The fifth caste was rejected, and the *Nishadas, Chandalas* and *Pukkasas* were under casteless classes privileges. So strong is the proprietary sense that the recognized rights of certain families are sometimes sold like a good-will, mortgaged and even given in dowry. An encroachment on another man's rights is severely dealt with, even to outcasting in some places. In fact, encroachment of any kind was vehemently resisted.

It is in these guilds that Dahlman and other modern writers find the germs of modern functional castes. Corporations so powerful and well-organized must have exercised a considerable influence on the development of the Hindu social system. A survival of it is found at present in Bombay and Baroda.

The word *caste* is derived from Portuguese *Casta, (Lat. castus)* pure or chaste. It is used to denote the division of the Hindu society into various sections, or *Jati,* based on *varna* or colour. The main ideas involved in the conception of caste are a homogeneous community, hereditary membership, inter-marriage and inter-dining. The above data are not sufficient, for a definition of caste, because in many of the castes there is a tendency for the members to give up their traditional occupation in favour of a more lucrative one.

The word *caste* has been variously defined, and none of the definitions is satisfactory. These are given below:

1. Caste is defined "as an endogamous group or a collection of such groups bearing a common name, and having the same traditional occupation, claiming a common descent from the same source, and commonly regarded as forming a single homogeneous community."

2. Herbert Risley defines caste, "as a collection of families bearing a common name, claiming a common descent from a mythical ancestor, human or divine, professing to follow the game hereditary calling and (are) regarded by those who are competent to give an opinion as forming a single homogeneous community. The name is always associated with a specific occupation."

3. Emile Senart has a more comprehensive definition. "Caste, according to him, is a close corporation, exclusive and in theory at any rate, rigorously hereditary; equipped with certain traditional and independent organizations including a chief and council; meeting on occasion in assemblies of more or less plenary authority, and joining in the celebration of certain festival, bound together by a common occupation; observing certain usage which relate more particularly to marriage, to food and to questions of occasional pollution; and ruling its members by the exercise of jurisdiction, the extent of which varies, but which succeeds, by the sanction of certain penalties and, above all, by the power of final or revocable exclusion from the group in making the authority of the community effectively felt."

Defilement

The test of caste is not intermarriage and inter-dining, but defilement by eating and touching what is unclean. On this consideration, *Sutras* show only the beginning of that formal theory of defilement which results in a pure man of the upper class being defiled by the shadow of an impure man and in the taboo of all contact with the impure. "According to Gautama *(Dharma Sutra XVII,* I), a Brahman may not eat food given by any of the reborn who are the worthy members of his caste, and in need of food to support his life, he may take food and other things even from a Sudra. Food forbidden is that defiled by hair or insects falling into it, and that touched by a woman in her mensus, by a black bird (crow) or by its foot or given by an outcaste, a woman of bad character, a person accused, an hermaphrodite, a police officer *(dandika),* a carpenter, a miser, a jailer, a physician, a man who hunts without using a bow, i.e., a non-snarer of animals, a man who eats refuse or the food of a multitude, of an enemy." The list contains the taboo of food offered disrespectfully and of certain animals. "Apastamba *(Dharma Sultra,* 1, 6. 18. 11) allows the acceptance of gifts, including a house and land from the low caste *(Ugra),* though like the later law books his code states that a priest may not eat in the house of anyone of the three orders *(varnas)* below him, but he may eat the food of any caste except that of the Sudras, and eat even their food in times of distress. Forbidden by him is the food of an artisan, of people who let houses or lands, a spy, an unauthorized priest (a Buddhist), besides that of a surgeon, usurer and others. Caste is *varna* or *jati,* colour and kin, the former embracing the latter, as a social order including clans and families."

Different Theories

Various theories on caste have been formulated by scholars, the most important of which are given below :-

1. According to Denzil Ibbetson, occupation is the chief basis of the division of caste. Every separate occupation has produced a distinct caste, the status of which depends now either partially or entirely on its occupation. The fact that there may be several castes pursuing the same occupation, as agriculture or weaving, does not invalidate this any way. If a caste changes its occupation,

it may gradually change its status in a corresponding degree. Caste sometimes tends to rise or fall in social position with the acquisition of land or other forms of wealth or dignity. Strictly speaking, a man inherits the social position of the caste in which he is born, and retains it, through life without the power of altering it. It is now the caste as a whole, or at least one of its important sections or sub-castes, which rises or falls in social position, and the process may extend over generations or centuries. This theory, though applicable to a large number of castes, does not cover the whole ground.

2. Caste, according to Nesfield, is used to designate common occupation. It is the centre round which caste has grown up, and its social gradation corresponds precisely to the different periods of civilization during which their traditional occupation originated. The primitive tribes inhabiting the hills pursue the occupation of hunting, and the pursuit of wild animals was the earliest stage in the development of human industry. Next in order comes the fishing caste, fishing being considered superior to hunting, because the water is a more sacred element than land among the Hindus. There is less apparent cruelty in capturing fish than in the slaughtering of animals. Above these come the pastoral castes. Above the pastoral castes are the agricultural castes and the various tribes included in them. Following the order in which these occupations are adopted during the progress of civilization, the others are mentioned. Above them are the various occupational castes. The higher group includes those castes, whose occupations were coeval with the age of metallurgy, those who work in stone, wood, metal, and make ornaments. At the top of the system stands the Kshatriyas, or the warrior class, whose duty it is to protect all the lower castes, and the Brahman who is their priest and spiritual guide.

The gradation of society given above is in the scientific order of precedence, and it is likely that these divisions arose from the divisions of the principal social organization of India in the village community.

According to this theory, the caste system springs from the regular evolution of social life, starting from the lowest level and following in its slow progression. This theory cannot be reconciled with the relatively late date to which Nesfield refers to the constitution of society. He also affirms that the Brahman was the first born of castes, the model upon, which all the other castes were subsequently formed, extending gradually from king or warrior to the tribes practicing hunting and fishing, whose rank is no higher than that of a savage. The Brahmans who formed themselves into the Levite guild set an example that was followed by others. It was he who invented for himself, the rule prohibiting marriage with a woman of another caste. There is a curious contradiction of later passages where he derives the regulation of marriage from the traditional usage of the tribe, The Vaisyas, according to him, and the Sudras in particular, have never been anything except a kind of rubric intended to embrace a multitude of heterogeneous elements.

Ibbetson's thesis is less complete and less forced than that of Nesfield, but is based on the same data. He summarizes the various stages that are to be discerned in the history of caste: -

(i)   The organization of the tribe common to all primitive societies

(ii)   the guilds founded on heredity of occupation

(iii)   the exaltation peculiar to India of sacerdotal function

(iv)   the exaltation of Levitical blood by the importance attributed to heredity

(v)   the consolidation of the principle, by the elaboration of a series of entirely artificial laws derived from Hindu beliefs, regulating marriage and fixing the limits within which it may be concentrated, declaring certain occupations and foods to be impure, and determining the conditions and extent of the relations permitted between the castes. It is seen that great importance is attached to the community of occupation and the constitution of the tribe. The status of the Brahman is reversed. They are represented as contributing to the spontaneous organization of the country. The real weakness of the system consists in the inordinate importance attributed to community of occupation, if this really constituted the primitive bond of castes, the latter would have shown less tendency to split up and disintegrate. The medium, which originally united it, would have maintained its cohesion.

The Occupation Theory

Many castes take their name from their dominant occupation. The thirty-four castes of Mysore based mostly on occupation afford striking examples. *Neygi* (weaver) is like *Brahman,* a designation under which it would be incorrect to include a number of groups, and to do so would be to unite a number of groups having neither the right to intermarry, nor to inter-dine with distinct castes. The agricultural and weaving castes are numbered by dozens in Mysore. So are the Vellalans of the Madras Presidency, and the Reddies of Mysore. It is the same everywhere.

3.　It is in race, that Risley unlike Nesfield, seeks the soul of caste. He lays stress on the difference of colours between the dark Dravidian or Non-Aryan races and their conquerors the fair skinned Aryans. The conquerors take the daughters of the land as concubines, but give their own daughters in marriage only among themselves. Race is substituted as the generating principle. The nasal index is the formula for the proportions of the nose, and is the most unerring criterion of race. There seems reason to suppose that the contact of the Aryans with the indigenous people of India is mainly responsible for the growth of the caste system, and the main racial divisions may perhaps even be recognized, though their basis has to a great extent vanished. But when we come to individual castes and sub-castes, the scrutiny of their origin is based more on certain Puranic stories, than on the supposed racial traits. Risley bases his argument upon the use of the word *Varna* and the meaning attributed to it. In this, he sees the natural enmity between the conquering and conquered races, the white and the black, as the germ of distinction. The endogamous laws are the foundation of the system. He arrives indirectly at the general acceptance of the orthodox Brahmanic system, and believes in the dominance gradually acquired by the priesthood. The theory of mixed castes is, according to him, an invaluable proof of cross-breeding. For Nesfield, caste is a matter of profession; for Risley, it is a matter of marriage.

From early times, by an ordinance of Manu, men of the higher castes or classes were permitted, after marrying a woman of their own caste, to have subsidiary wives from any of the classes below them. This custom seems to have been prevalent, and no definite rule was prescribed that the children of such unions should necessarily be illegitimate, and in many cases there is no doubt that their descendants ultimately became full members of the caste of the first ancestor. According to Manu, the children of a Brahman by a Kshatriya woman could attain Brahmanhood in the third generation, and those by a Vaisya woman in the fifth.

Such children could also inherit. According to the *Mahabharata,* (Chap. xlvii) if a Brahman had four wives of different castes, the son by a Brahman wife took four shares, that by a Kshatriya wife three, that by a Vaisya wife two, and that by a Sudra wife one share. Manu gives a slightly different distribution, but also permits the son by a Sudra wife to have a share of the inheritance. Thus, the fact is clear that the son of a Brahman even by a Sudra woman had a certain status of legitimacy in his father's caste, as he could marry in it, and must therefore have been permitted to partake of the sacrificial food at marriage, and could also inherit a small share of the property. The detailed rules prescribed for the state of legitimacy and inheritance shows that recognized unions of this kind between a man of higher class and a woman of lower class were once fairly frequent in spite of subsequent prohibitions. This must have led to mixture of blood in the different castes. There is still a survival of it in the practice of hypergamy.

Both *tribe* and *caste* are loosely applied to a social group. The tribe is defined as "the largest body of people, speaking about what they themselves regard as one language, and having a common language for themselves as well as a sense of solidarity which expresses itself in regarding other people as strangers." A tribe is not a close corporation. In its original form, it is an aggregate of persons who have or believe themselves to have a common origin. This, together with common political interests, and mutual defense, holds them together. Sometimes, it admits of aliens who wish to throw in their lot with it especially women obtained by purchase or capture. It is not endogamous though circumstances tend to favour endogamy. It differs from caste inasmuch as the common name does not usually imply occupation. Its members occupy or profess to occupy a definite tract, but they do not necessarily marry among themselves. The modern tendency for such tribes is to be transformed into a caste. In fact, a tribe is a prospective caste.

The two names *caste* and *class* are often confounded with each other. They correspond neither in extent, in character, nor in natural tendencies. Each one among the castes which would belong to one and the same class is plainly distinguishable from its fellows. The class subserves political ambition. The caste obeys narrow scruples, traditional customs and local influence, which have generally no relation to class interests. More than all, the class clings to the safeguarding of an integrity which is the subject of deep concern and sensitiveness even with the humblest. It is the distant echo of the class struggles handed down by legend with which tradition resounds. By the reaction of principles on facts, two institutions have become fused together.

They are nonetheless essentially independent. The hierarchic division of the population into classes is universal. But the caste system is a unique institution. The Brahmanic ambition has taken advantage of it in order more securely to make its domination possible, but not obvious. A caste system is not necessarily the basis of theocracy. Its theory has confused the two sets of ideas. This is a fact of secondary importance. For the sake of historic development, they have to be carefully distinguished.

It is said that the Brahmans were the trustees and repositories to the civilization of South India after the decline of Buddhism. It was the Brahmans who prevented South

India from relapsing into savagery. Brahmanism in South India' stands for civilization, and Brahmans have guided human history and human thought for centuries. The concrete expression of this culture is found in :-

System in Castes
1. The worship of Shiva and Vishnu
2. Abstinence from animal food
3. Prohibition of animal sacrifice
4. Infant marriage
5. Prohibition of the marriage of widows
6. Sraddhas, the annual ceremony in honour of the dead ancestors.

These six factors have, by gradual adoption, contributed a great deal to the elevation of lower castes. The chief varieties in the formation of new castes are the following:-

1. *Functional caste.* This is composed of persons following the same occupation. Instances are numerous in the State. Functional castes have been described by E. A. Gait as aggregations of various tribes who have been drawn together by the bond of common occupation.
2. *Sectarian caste.* This is composed of persons united by a common belief.
3. *Tribal or racial basis of caste.* Gradual evolution of tribe into caste is an important factor in the development of caste system. Here the aborigines have contributed a great deal to it; and according to some authorities, their contributions were greater than those of the Aryans. Savage communities all over India, were and are even now divided into a number of tribes, and each living in a particular locality, maintained an attitude of enmity towards others in the vicinity. They became so far estranged that there was no intermarriage and inter-dining. But the Aryans after their immigration in India found that they had outgrown the stage of tribal exogamy and tribal endogamy. Before the advent of the Aryans, there were wide cultural differences—cultured and uncultured—and these have raised a wall of separation between the two types, and each avoided all intercourse with the other. These tribal and cultural divisions became

so strong that they could not be shaken or disturbed by the civilized Aryans, and these led to the formation of caste divisions, which with the caste regulations became more and more rigid.

4. Assimilation and survival which form the dynamics of caste, are also two important factors. By assimilation is meant that tendency which makes one community imitate the manners and customs of another community with which it comes in contact. Among some of the non-Brahman castes may be found some, who, by following the customs of the higher castes, became assimilated with them in course of time. It modifies the lower culture and converts it into a higher one.

5. Very often, a caste strikes out in a line for itself and in course of time revert to the original type. The Lingayats were originally a religious sect who revolted in the 12th century against the authority of the Brahmans, and rejected all caste distinctions. They have long deserted their principles and split up into functional and territorial groups modelled on the very caste system they sought to overthrow.

6. There are *national castes,* like those of the Mahrattas, based on actual or traditional sovereignty.

7. Differences in language and territorial divisions, which often result in migration, are the two main factors in the formation of new castes.

8. Castes have risen by fission owing to a change of custom by one portion of a caste, arising from some dispute about the question of food, social etiquette, or the adoption of a new custom such as widow marriage or the like the recent Census Reports afford numerous instances in all parts of India.

The sub-caste connotes no real difference of culture or occupation. Sub-castes are little known except within the caste itself. They consist of groups within the caste, which marry among them. They attend the communal feast held on the occasion of marriage, funerals and meetings of caste panchayats and the like. Among the non-Brahmans, instances are numerous, as among the Okkaligas, Reddies and Banajigas. Sometimes, the adoption of degrading occupation gives rise to a sub-caste within the caste. In Mysore, as in other parts of South India, a society originally homogeneous tends to be disintegrated according to the degree to which its members adopt Brahmanic usages, namely, the adoption of Brahmanic culture and refinement, as infant marriage, irrevocable widowhood, purchase of bridegroom, and abstinence from meat.

There are also other planes of cleavage, namely, linguistic barrier, difference in religious beliefs, means of livelihood, territorial division, racial distinction, all of which play conspicuous part in the formation of sub-castes as of castes. The *jus connubi* and *jus convivi*, which ramify through the divisions, are the expressions rather than the caste exclusiveness.

Distinction of caste is an easy matter, but the tendency to split a caste into innumerable sub-castes deserves mention. Religion is one of the factors. If we consider religious or philosophic belief, the difference between the monism of Sankara and the dualism of Sri Madhavacharya is seen to be as wide as that "between heaven and earth or between pole and pole." Between the two schools come the followers of Ramanuja. Their doctrines possess something in common with each of the other two; and a greater catholicity and tolerance might be expected to prevail among the Vaishnavas. And yet a mutual exclusiveness prevails amongst them. Persons holding widely different views may be allowed to express their theological difference though at first sight it may appear to be strange. But it is really so unaccountable that this difference of views should have so acted on its social customs as to crystallize it in varying set forms so ill-adapted to one another as to defy all attempts at the segmentation of the entire community. The three classes differ in their social habits, in the manner of wearing their clothes, in the mode of adorning their forehead, in their observances, such as temple festivals, household fasts and feasts, and in other ways even, to the form of household utensils. In spite of the differences, they have something in common. All men wear the sacred thread, and the prayers offered up thrice *(Sandhyavandanam)* are substantially the same. There is yet a curious difference, which finds its expression in relation to food. A Sri Vaishnava's mother and mother-in-law may partake of the food cooked by his wife, while neither will touch the meal prepared by the other. Among the Desasthas (followers of Madhva), a Telugu does not marry with a Mahratti nor a Saraswat with a Konkani. Here a racial difference can be traced. Locality is also a potent factor for the clean-cut groups. The idea of caste struck its roots very deeply into Hindu life, and its eradication is neither possible nor desirable. The total number of castes in Mysore varies according to the Census Reports from 1871 to 1931. The Census Report of 1871 gives the number as 101, while those of the next two are silent. The Census Report of 1901, pointing out certain difficulties, gives only a glossary of castes, some of which do not belong to the indigenous types. It is curious to mention that the Imperial Gazetteer of Mysore gives the number as 72. This number exactly tallies that that given in an old Malayalam work *(Jatinirnayam)*. The last two Census Reports limit the number to 34, which is far too low a figure. Unlike Malabar, Cochin, and Travancore, Mysore contains indigenous tribes and castes the number of which cannot be accurately determined. Mysore is connected with all parts of India, from which numerous castes have migrated. The process of migration is still going on.

The grouping of the tribes and castes, numbering 34, as mentioned above, though convenient for census purposes, is neither scientific nor satisfactory. Communities widely differing in language, religion, customs and manners, as also in racial traits, are lumped together under a common designation, based on occupation, which under the present political, social and economic conditions is constantly changing. The principle of social precedence adopted by Herbert Risley thirty years ago is now out of date. Further, the caste names themselves are being modified at the request of a large majority of the members of various castes, who hold annual conferences to discuss matters relating to caste and form resolutions for social elevation. Further, some of the sub-castes are liable to be treated as castes. In these circumstances, an alphabetical arrangement is the safest course for purposes of treatment. Nevertheless, a classification based on the evolution of material culture is tentatively attempted.

There has been of late, a tendency in various castes to claim for themselves some new names preference to those, which they have long possessed. It is perhaps due to the presumption of some innate superiority based on the acquisition of wealth or other considerations. Satanis desire to be known as "Venkitapur Brahmans," "Vishnu Brahmans or Prapanna Vaishnava Brahmans." Some among the Nayindas (Barbers) wished to be called " Nayee Brahmans." Similarly, "Devanga Dharma Prakasika " would like to have their community separately shown from Neygi. Panchalas fight hard to be called "Viswakarma Brahmans." A community in the Nagamangala Taluk long known as "Tirukuladevaru" wishes itself to be known as "Kani- kanna." Some Lingayats in Krishnarajapetta and others wish to be called "Virasaivas." A certain journalist of the *Kurubar community* suggested that " Kurubar" should be henceforth called "Arya Kshatriyas." The Holeyas and Madigas have been already named Adi Karnatakas. "Komatis come under the name of Vaisyas, and disclaim like liberality to Madigas and 'volpine intelligence.' Under Government sanction, Lambani, Besta, and Golla, are to be henceforth called Banjara, Gangakula, and Yadava."

From the foregoing account, it may be seen that the caste system existed in the embryonic stage during the Vedic period, and that its beginnings are found in the *Brahmanas* and the *Puranas.* The latter with the traces of the dim past furnish contemporary evidence of successive modifications. Since then, it has developed through ages under the influence of circumstances, which combined to form endogamous groups. Among the circumstances may be mentioned—Contact of races, of culture, and civilization; the composition and formation of powerful guilds; the influence of Hinduism in the attraction and assimilation of diverse elements; and the influence of a sacerdotal order able and willing to consolidate and regulate the multifarious groups. In fact, the caste system did not spring fully developed into existence, nor was it an artificial product of a man or body of men working consciously to that end. It was a natural growth, the result of a process of evolution. The process is still in continuation even up to the present day.

References

Srinivas, *Caste in India*, 1962.

Majumdar, R.C., *Panchayats in India.*

Rose, *Tribes and Castes.*

Srivastava. A.L., *Attitude Towads Harijans*, 1970.

Dube, S.C., Indian Villages.

O'Malley, L.S.S., *Indian Castes, Customs,* 1932.

Taya Zinbin, *In a Tanjore village.*

AICC Papers in NMML.

Morton, Robert K., *Social Theory and Social Structure.*

Five Year Plans, relevant extracts.

Oscar, Lewis, *Village Life in Northern India.*

Mukerjee, *Radhakumud, Local government in Ancient India,* Oxford Clarendon Press, 1919.

Harijan Welfare in U.P. published by Harijan Welfare Directorate, UP, Lucknow.

Harijan (Journal).

Young India (Journal).

4

Castes in India their Mechanism, Genesis and Development

Many have witnessed local, national or international expositions of material objects that make up the sum total of human civilization. But few can entertain the idea of there being such a thing as an exposition of human institutions. Exhibition of human institutions is a strange idea; some might call it the wildest of ideas. Subtler minds and abler pens have been brought to the task of unraveling the mysteries of caste but it still remains in the domain of the "unexplained", not to say of the "un-understood."

The caste problem is a vast one, both theoretically and practically. Practically, it is an institution that portends tremendous consequences. It is a local problem, but one capable of much wider mischief, for "as long as caste in India does exist, Hindus will hardly intermarry or have any social intercourse with outsiders; and if Hindus migrate to other regions on earth, Indian caste would become a world problem." Theoretically, it has defied great many scholars who have taken upon themselves, as a labour of love, to dig into its origin.

Theory of Ethnologists

According to well-known ethnologists, the population of

India is a mixture of Aryans, Dravidians, Mongolians and Scythians. All these stocks of people came into India from various directions and with various cultures, centuries ago, when they were in a tribal state. They all in turn elbowed their entry into the country by fighting with their predecessors and after a stomachful of it settled down as peaceful neighbours. Through constant contact and mutual intercourse they evolved a common culture that superseded their distinctive cultures. It may be granted that there has not been a thorough amalgamation of the various stocks that make up the people of India, and to a traveller from within the boundaries of India, the East presents a marked contrast in physique and even in colour to the West, as does the South to the North. But amalgamation can never be the sole criterion of homogeneity as predicated of any people. Ethnically all people are heterogeneous. It is the unity of culture that is the basis of homogeneity. Taking this for granted, I venture to say that there is no country that can rival the Indian Peninsula with respect to the unity of its culture. It has not only a geographic unity, but it has over and above all a deeper and a much more fundamental unity—the indubitable cultural unity that covers the land from end to end. But it is because of this homogeneity that caste becomes a problem so difficult to be explained. If the Hindu Society were a mere federation of mutually exclusive units, the matter would be simple enough. But caste is a parceling of an already homogeneous unit, and the explanation of the genesis of caste is the explanation of this process of parceling.

Before launching into our field of inquiry, it is better to advise ourselves regarding the nature of a caste. I will therefore draw upon a few of the best students of caste for their definitions of it :

1. Senart, a French authority, defines a caste as "a close corporation, in theory at any rate rigorously hereditary: equipped with a certain traditional and independent organization, including, a chief and a council, meeting on occasion in assemblies of more or less plenary authority and joining together at certain festivals: bound

together by common occupations, which relate more particularly to marriage and to food and to questions of ceremonial pollution, and ruling its members by the exercise of jurisdiction, the extent of which varies, but which succeeds in making the authority of the community more felt by the sanction of certain penalties and, above all, by final irrevocable exclusion from the group".

2. Nesfield defines caste as "a class of the community which disowns any connection with any other class and can neither intermarry nor eat nor drink with any but persons of their own community".

3. According to H. Risley, "a caste may be defined as a collection of families or groups of families bearing a common name which usually denotes or is associated with occupation, claiming common descent from a mythical ancestor, human or divine, professing to follow the same professional callings and are regarded by those who are competent to give an opinion as forming a single homogeneous community".

4. Dr. Kelkar defines caste as "a social group having two characteristics:
   (i) membership is confined to those who are born of members and includes all persons so born;
   (ii) the members are forbidden by an inexorable social law to marry outside the group."

To review these definitions is of great importance for our purpose. It will be noticed that taken individually the definitions of three of the writers include too much or too little: none is complete or correct by itself and all have missed the central point in the mechanism of the caste as an isolated unit by Itself, and not as a group within, and with definite relations to, the system of caste as a whole. Yet collectively all them are complementary to one another, each one emphasizing what has been obscured in other. By way of criticism, therefore, I will take only those points common to all castes in each of the above definitions, which are regarded as peculiarities of caste and evaluate them as such.

Theory of Senart

To start with Senart, he draws attention to the "idea of pollution" as a characteristic of caste. With regard to this point it may; be safely said that it is by no means a peculiarity of caste as such. It usually originates in priestly ceremonialism and is a particular case of the general belief in purity. Consequently its necessary connection with caste may be completely denied without damaging the working of caste. The "idea of pollution" has been attached to the institution of caste, only because the caste that enjoys the highest rank is the priestly caste: while we know that priest and purity are old associates. We may therefore conclude that the "idea of pollution" is a characteristic of caste only in so far as caste has a religious flavuor. Nesfield in his way dwells on the absence of messing with those outside the caste as one of its characteristics. In spite of the newness of the point we must say that Nesfield has mistaken the effect for the cause. Caste, being a self-enclosed unit naturally limits social intercourse, including messing etc. to members within it. Consequently this absence of messing with outsiders is not due to positive prohibition, but is a natural result of caste, i.e., exclusiveness. No doubt this absence of messing originally due to exclusiveness, acquired the prohibitory character of a religious injunction, but it may be regarded as a later growth. H. Risley makes no new point deserving of special attention.

We now pass on to the definition of Dr. Kelkar who has done much for the elucidation of the subject. Not only is he a native, but he has also brought a critical acumen and an open mind to bear on his study of caste. His definition merits consideration, for he has defined caste in its relation to a system of castes, and has concentrated his attention only on those characteristics which are absolutely necessary for the existence of a caste within a system, rightly excluding all others as being secondary or derivative in character. With respect to his definition it must, however, be said that in it there is a slight confusion of thought, lucid and clear as otherwise it is. He speaks of Prohibition of Intermarriage and Membership by Autogeny as the two characteristics of caste. These are but two aspects of one and the same thing, and not two different things as Dr. Kelkar supposes them to be. If you prohibit intermarriage the result is that you limit membership to those born within the group. Thus, the two are the obverse and the reverse sides of the same medal.

This critical evaluation of the various characteristics of caste leave no doubt that prohibition, or rather the absence of intermarriage—endogamy, to be concise—is the only one that can be called the essence of caste when rightly understood. But some may deny this on abstract anthropological grounds, for there exist endogamous groups without giving rise to the problem of Caste. In a general way this may be true, as endogamous societies, culturally different, making their abode in localities more or less removed, and having little to do with each other are a physical reality. The Negroes and the Whites and the various tribal groups that go by name of American Indians in the United States may be cited as more or less appropriate illustrations in support of this view. But we must not confuse matters, for in India the situation is different. As pointed out before, the people of India form a homogeneous whole. The various races of India occupying definite territories have more or less fused into one another and do possess cultural unity, which is the only criterion of a homogeneous population. Given this homogeneity as a basis, caste becomes a problem altogether new in character and wholly absent in the situation constituted by the mere propinquity of endogamous social or tribal groups. Caste in India means an artificial chopping off of the population into fixed and definite units, each one prevented from fusing into another through the custom of endogamy. Thus, the conclusion is inevitable that endogamy is the only characteristic that is peculiar to caste, and if we succeed in showing how endogamy is maintained, we shall practically have proved the genesis and also the mechanism of caste.

It may not also be out of place of emphasize at this moment that no civilized society of today presents more survivals of primitive times than does the Indian society. Its religion is essentially primitive and its tribal code, in

spite of the advance of time and civilization, operates in all
its pristine vigour even today. One of these primitive
survivals is the custom of exogamy. The prevalence of
exogamy in the primitive world is a fact too well-known to
need any' explanation. With the growth of history, however,
exogamy has lost its efficacy, and excepting the nearest
blood-kin's, there is usually no social bar restricting the
field of marriage. But regarding the people of India the law
of exogamy is a positive injunction even today. Indian
society still savors the clan system, even though there are
no clans; and this can be easily seen from the law of
matrimony which centers round the principle of exogamy,
for it is not that *Sapindas* (blood-kin's) cannot marry, but a
marriage even between Sagotras (of the same class) is
regarded as a sacrilege.

Various Gotras

Nothing is therefore more important than the fact that
endogamy is foreign to the people of India. The various
Gotras of India are and have been exogamous: so are the
other groups with totemic organization. It is no exaggeration
to say that with people of India exogamy is a creed and none
dare infringe it, so much so that in spite of the endogamy
of the castes within them, exogamy is strictly observed and
that there are more rigorous penalties for violating exogamy
than there are for violating endogamy. You will therefore
readily see that with exogamy as the rule there could be no
caste, for exogamy means fusion. But we have castes
consequently in the final analysis creation of castes, so far
as India is concerned, means the superposition of endogamy
on exogamy. However, in an originally exogamous
population an easy working out of endogamy (which is
equivalent to the creation of caste) is a grave problem, and
it is in the consideration of the means utilized for the
preservation of endogamy against exogamy that we may
hope to find the solution of our problem.

Thus, the superposition of endogamy on exogamy means
the creation of caste. But this is not an easy affair. Let us
take an imaginary group that desires to make itself into a
caste and analyze what means it will have to adopt to make

itself endogamous. If a group desires to make itself endogamous a formal injunction against intermarriage with outside groups will be of no avail, especially if prior to the introduction of endogamy, exogamy had been the rule in all-matrimonial relations. Again, there is a tendency in all groups lying in close contact with one another to assimilate and amalgamate, and thus consolidate into a homogeneous society. If this tendency is to be strongly counteracted in the interest of caste formation, it is absolutely necessary to circumscribe a circle outside which people should not contract marriages.

Nevertheless, this encircling to prevent marriages from without creates problems from within, which are not very easy of solution. Roughly speaking in a normal group the two sexes are more or less evenly distributed, and generally speaking there is equality between those of the same age. The equality is, however, never quite realized in actual societies. At the same time to the group that is desirous of making itself into a caste the maintenance of equality between the sexes becomes the ultimate goal, for without it endogamy can no longer subsist. In other words, if endogamy is to be preserved conjugal rights from within have to be provided for, otherwise members of the group will be driven out of the circle to take care of themselves in any way they can. But in order that the conjugal rights be provided for from within, it is absolutely necessary to maintain a numerical equality between the marriageable units of the two sexes within the group desirous of making itself into a caste. It is only through the maintenance of such equality that the necessary endogamy of the group can be kept intact, and a very large disparity is sure to break it.

The problem of caste, then, ultimately resolves itself into one of repairing the disparity between the marriage-able units of the two sexes within it. Left to nature, the much needed parity between the units can be realized only when a couple dies simultaneously. But this is a rare contingency. The husband may die before the wife and create a surplus woman, who must be disposed of, else through intermarriage she will violate the endogamy of the group.

In like manner the husband may survive his wife and be surplus man, whom the group, while it may sympathize wise with him for the sad bereavement, has to dispose of, else he will marry outside the caste and will break the endogamy. Thus, both the surplus man and the surplus woman constitute a menace to the caste if not taken care of, for not finding suitable partners inside their prescribed circle (and left to themselves they cannot find any for if the matter be not regulated there can only be just enough pairs to go round) very likely they will transgress the boundary, marry outside and import offspring that is foreign to the caste.

Status of Women

Let us see what our imaginary group is likely to do with this surplus man and surplus woman. We will first take up the case of the surplus woman.

She can be disposed of in two different ways so as to preserve the endogamy of the caste. First, burn her on the funeral pyre of her deceased husband and get rid of her. This, however, is rather an impracticable way of solving too problem of sex disparity. In some cases it may work, in others it may not. Consequently, every surplus woman cannot thus be disposed of, because it is an easy solution but a hard realization. And so the surplus woman (=widow), if not disposed of, remains in the group: but in her very existence lies a double danger. She may marry outside the caste and violate endogamy or she may marry within the caste and through competition encroach upon the chances of marriage that must be reserved for the potential brides in the caste. She is, therefore, a menace in any case, and something must be done to her if she cannot be burned along with her deceased husband.

The second remedy is to enforce widowhood on her for the rest of her life. So far as the objective results are concerned, burning is a better solution than enforcing widowhood. Burning the widow eliminates all the three evils that a surplus woman is fraught with. Being dead and gone she creates no problem of remarriage either inside or outside the caste. But compulsory widowhood is superior to burning because it is more practicable. Besides being comparatively humane it also guards against the evils of remarriage as does burning; but it fails to guard the morals of the group. No doubt under compulsory widowhood the woman remains, and just because she is deprived of her natural right of being a legitimate wife in future, the incentive to immoral conduct is increased. But this is by no means an insuperable difficulty. She can be degraded to a condition in which she is no longer a source of allurement.

The problem of surplus man (widower) is much more important, and much more difficult than that of the surplus woman in a group that desires to make itself into a caste. From time immemorial man as compared with woman has had the upper hand. He is a dominant figure in every group and of the two sexes has greater prestige. With this traditional superiority of man over woman his wishes have always been consulted. Woman, on the other hand, has been an easy prey to all kinds of iniquitous injunctions, religious, social or economic. But man, as a maker of injunctions is most often above them all. Such being the case, you cannot accord the same kind of treatment to a surplus man as you can to a surplus woman in a caste.

The project of burning him with his deceased wife is hazardous in two ways: first of all it cannot be done, simply because he is a man. Secondly, if done, a sturdy soul is lost to the caste. There remain then only two solutions, which can conveniently dispose of him.

Important as he is to the group, endogamy is still more important, and the solution must assure both these ends. Under these circumstances he may be forced or induced, after the manner of the widow, to remain a widower for the rest of his life. This solution is not altogether difficult, for without any compulsion some are so disposed as to enjoy self-imposed celibacy, or even to take a further step of their own accord and renounce the world and its joys. But, given human nature as it is, this solution can hardly be expected to be realized. On the other hand, as is very likely to be the case, if the surplus man remains in the group as an active participator in-group activities, he is a danger to the morals of the group. Looked at from different point of view celibacy, though easy in cases where it succeeds, is not so advantageous even then to the material prospects of the caste. If he observes genuine celibacy and renounces the world, he would not be a menace to the preservation of caste endogamy or caste morals as he undoubtedly would be if he remained a secular person. But as an ascetic celibate he is as good as burned, so far as the material well being of his caste is concerned. A caste, in order that it may be large enough to afford a vigorous communal life, must be maintained at a certain numerical strength. But to hope for this and to proclaim celibacy is the same as trying to cure atrophy by bleeding.

Celibacy

Imposing celibacy on the surplus man in the group, therefore, fails both theoretically and practically. It is in the interest of the caste to keep him as a *Grahastha* (one who raises a family), to use a Sanskrit technical term. But the problem is to provide him with a wife from within the caste. At the outset this is not possible, for the ruling ratio in a caste has to be one man to one woman and none can have two chances of marriage, for in a caste thoroughly self-enclosed there are always just enough marriageable women to go round for the marriageable men. Under these circumstances the surplus man can be provided with a wife only by recruiting a bride from the ranks of those not yet marriageable in order to tie him down to the group. This is certainly the best of the possible solutions in the case of the surplus man. This keeps him within the caste. By this means numerical depletion through constant outflow is guarded against, and by this endogamy and morals are preserved.

It will not be seen that the four means by which numerical disparity between the two sexes is conveniently maintained are: (1) burning the widow with her deceased husband; (2) compulsory widowhood— a milder burning; (3) imposing celibacy on the widower and (4) wedding him to a girl not yet marriageable. Though, burning the widow and imposing celibacy on the widower are of doubtful service to the group in its endeavour to preserve its endogamy, all of them operate as means. But means, as forces, when liberated or set in motion create an end. What then is the end that these means create? They create and perpetuate endogamy, while caste and endogamy, according to our analysis of the various definitions of caste, are one and the same thing. Thus the existence of these means is identical with caste and caste involves these means.

This, in my opinion is the general mechanism of a caste in a system of castes. Let us now turn from these high generalities to the castes in Hindu society and inquire into their mechanism. I need hardly premise that there are great many pitfalls in the path of those who try to unfold the past, and caste in India to be sure is a very ancient institution. This is especially true where there exist no authentic or written records or where the people like the Hindus, are so constituted that to them writing history is a folly, for the world is an illusion. But institutions do live, though for a long time they may remain unrecorded and as often as not customs and morals are like fossils that tell their own history. If this is true, our task will be amply rewarded if we scrutinize the solution the Hindus arrived at to meet the problems of the surplus man and surplus woman.

Complex though it be in its general working the Hindu society, even to a superficial observer, presents three singular uxorial customs, namely:

(i) *Sati* or the burning of the widow on the funeral pyre of her deceased husband.

(ii) Enforced widowhood by which a widow is not allowed to remarry.

(iii) Girl marriage.

In addition, one also notes a great hankering after *Sannyasa* (renunciation) on the part of the widower, but this may in some cases be due purely to psychic disposition.

Origin of Customs

So far as I know, no scientific explanation of the origin of these customs is forthcoming even today. We have plenty of philosophy to tell us why these customs were honoured, but nothing to tell us the causes of their origin and existence. Sati has been honoured because it is a "proof of the perfect unity of body and soul" between husband and wife and of "devotion beyond the grave" because it embodied the ideal of wifehood, which is well expressed by Uma when she said "Devotion of her Lord is woman's honour, it is her eternal heaven: and O Maheshvara," she adds with a most touching human cry, "I desire not paradise itself if thou are not satisfied with me?" Why compulsory widowhood is honoured I know not, nor have yet met with anyone who sang in praise of it, though there are a great many who adhere to it. The eulogy in honour of girl marriage is reported by Dr. Kelkar to be as follows: "A really faithful man or woman ought not to feel affection for a woman or a man other than the one with whom he or she is united. Such purity is compulsory not only after marriage but even before marriage, for that is the only correct ideal of chastity. No maiden could be considered pure if she feels love for a man other than the one to whom she might be married. As she does not know to whom she is going to be married, she must not feel affection for any man at all before marriage. If she does so, it is a sin. So it is better for a girl to know whom she has to love before any sexual consciousness has been awakened in her.

This high-flown and ingenious sophistry indicates why these institutions were honoured, but does not tell us why they were practiced. My own interpretation is that they were honoured because they were practiced. Any one lightly acquainted with rise of individualism in the 18th century will appreciate my remark. At all times, it is the movement that is most important; and the philosophies grow around it long afterwards to justify it and give it a moral support. These customs were so highly eulogized prove that they needed eulogy for their prevalence. Regarding the question as to why they arose, they were needed to create the structure of caste and the philosophies in honour of them were intended to popularize them, or to gild the pill, for they must have been so abominable and shocking to the moral sense of the unsophisticated that they needed a great deal of sweetening. These customs are essentially of the nature of means, though they are represented as ideals. But this should not blind us from understanding the results that flow from them. One might safely say that idealization of means is necessary and in this particular case was perhaps motivated to endow them with greater efficacy. Calling a means an end does no harm, except that it disguises its real character; but it does not deprive it of its real nature that of a means. Whether regarded as ends or as means, *sati*, enforced widowhood and girl marriage are customs that were primarily intended to solve the problem of the surplus man and surplus woman in a caste and to maintain its endogamy. Strict endogamy could not be preserved without these customs, while caste without endogamy is a fake.

Having explained the mechanism of the creation and preservation of caste in India, the further question as to its genesis naturally arises. The question of origin is always an annoying question and in the study of caste it is sadly neglected; some have connived at it, while others have dodged it. Some are puzzled as to whether there could be such a thing as the origin of caste and suggest that "if we cannot control our fondness for the word 'origin' we should better use the plural form, viz. 'origins of caste'.

The atomistic conception of individuals in a society so greatly popularized is the greatest humbug. To say that individuals make up society is trivial; society is always composed of classes. It may be an exaggeration to assert the theory of class-conflict, but the existence of definite classes in a society is a fact. Their basis may differ. They may be economic or intellectual or social, but an individual in a society is always a member of a class. This is a universal fact and early Hindu society could not have been an exception to this rule, and, as a matter of fact, we know it was not. If we bear this generalization in mind, our study of the genesis of caste would be very much facilitated, for we have only to determine what was the class that made itself into a caste, for class and caste, so to say, are next door neighbours, and it is only a span that separates the two. A caste is an enclosed class.

The study of the origin of caste must furnish us with an answer to the is the class that raised this "enclosure" around itself? The question may seem 100 inquisitorial, but it is pertinent, and an answer to this will serve us to elucidate the mastery of the growth and development of castes all over India. Unfortunately, a direct answer to this question is not within my power. I can answer it only indirectly. I said just above that the customs in question were current in the Hindu society. To be true to facts it is necessary to qualify the statement, as it connotes universality of their prevalence. These customs in all their strictness are obtainable only in one caste, namely the Brahmins, who occupy the highest place in the social hierarchy of the Hindu society and as their prevalence in non-Brahmin castes is derivative of their observance is neither strict nor complete. This important fact can serve as a basis of an important observation. If the prevalence of these customs in the non-Brahmin castes is derivative, as can be shown very easily, then it needs no argument to prove that class is the father of the institution of caste. Why the Brahmin class should have enclosed itself into a caste is a different question, which may be left as an employment for another occasion. But the strict observance of these customs and the social superiority arrogated by the priestly class in all ancient civilizations are sufficient to prove that they were the originators of this "unnatural institution" founded and maintained through these unnatural means.

Growth of Caste System

I now come to the part regarding the question of the growth and spread of the caste system all over India. The question is how did the institution of caste spread among the rest or the non-Brahmin population of the country? The question of the spread of the castes all over India has suffered a worse fate than the question of genesis. And the main cause as it seems to me, is that the two questions of spread and of origin are not separated. This is because of the common belief among scholars that the caste system has either been imposed upon the docile population of India by a law-giver as a divine dispensation, or that it has grown according to some law of social growth peculiar to the Indian people.

Every country has its law-giver, who arises as an incarnation (*avatar*) in times of emergency to set right a sinning humanity and give it the laws of justice and morality. Manu, the law-giver of India, if he did exist was certainly an audacious person. If the story that he gave the law of caste be credited, then Manu must have been a dare-devil fellow and the humanity that accepted his dispensation must be a humanity quite different from the one we are acquainted with. It is unimaginable that the law of caste was given. It is hardly an exaggeration to say that Manu could not have outlived his law, for what is that class that can submit to be degraded to the status of brutes by the pen of a man, and suffer him to raise another class to the pinnacle? Unless he was a tyrant who held all the population in subjection it cannot be imagined that he could have been allowed to dispense his patronage in this grossly unjust manner, as may be easily seen by a mere glance at his "Institutes". I may seem hard on Manu but I am sure my force is not strong enough to kill his ghost. He lives, like a disembodied spirit and is appealed to, and I am afraid will yet live long. One thing I want to impress upon you is that Manu did not give the law of caste and that he could not do so. Caste existed long before Manu. He was an upholder of it and therefore philosophized about it, but certainly he did not and could not ordain present order of Hindu society. His work ended with the codification of existing caste rules and the preaching of caste Dharma. The spread and growth of the caste system is too gigantic, a task to be achieved by the power or cunning of an individual or of a class. Similar in argument is the theory that the Brahmins created the caste. The Brahmins may have been guilty of many things, but the imposing of the caste system on the non-Brahmin population was beyond their mettle. They may have helped the process by their glib philosophy, but they certainly could not have pushed their scheme beyond their own confines. To fashion society after one's own pattern? How glorious? How hard? One can take pleasure and eulogize its furtherance, but cannot further it very far. The vehemence of my attack may seem to be unnecessary. There is a strong belief in the mind of orthodox Hindus that the Hindu society was somehow moulded into the framework of the caste system and that it is an organization consciously created by the *Shastras*. Not only does this belief exist, but is being justified on the ground that it cannot but be good, because it is ordained by the *Shastras* and the *Shastras* cannot be wrong. Preaching did not make the caste system neither will it unmake it. My aim is to show the falsity of the attitude that has exalted religious sanction to the position of a scientific explanation.

Thus, the great man theory does not help us very far in solving the spread of castes in India. Western scholars, probably not much given to, hero-worship, have attempted other explanations. The nuclei, round which have "formed" the various castes in India, are, according to them:

(1) occupation
(2) survivals of tribal organizations etc
(3) the rise of new belief
(4) cross-breeding and
(5) migration

The question may be asked whether these nuclei do not exist in other societies and whether they are peculiar to India. If they are not peculiar to India, but are common to the world, why is it that they did not "form" caste on other parts of this planet? Is it because those parts are holier than the land of the Vedas, or that the professors are mistaken?

In spite of the high theoretic value claimed by the several authors for their respective theories based on one or other of the above nuclei, one regrets to say that on close examination they are nothing more than filling illustrations- what Matthew Arnold means by "the grand name without the grand thing in it". Such are the various theories of caste advanced by Denzil Ibbetson, Nesfield, Senart and Sir H. Risley. To criticize them in a lump would be to say that they are a disguised from of the Petitio Principii of formal logic. To illustrate: Nesfield says that "function and function only... was the foundation upon which the whole system of castes in India was built up". But he may rightly be reminded that he does not very much advance our thought by making the above statement, which practically amounts to saying that castes in India are functional or occupational, which is a very poor discovery? We have yet to know from Nesfield why is it that an occupational group turned into an occupational caste?

Without stopping to criticize those theories that explain the caste system as a natural phenomenon occurring in obedience to the law of disintegration, as explained by Herbert Spencer in his formula of evolution, or as natural as "the structural differentiation within an organism"—to employ the phraseology of orthodox apologists—, or as an early attempt to test the laws of eugenics—as all belonging to the same class of fallacy which regards the caste system as inevitable, or as being consciously imposed in anticipation of these laws on a helpless and humble population.

Composition of Hindu Society

We shall be well advised to recall at the outset that the Hindu society, in common with other societies, was composed of classes and the earliest known are :

(1) the Brahmins or the priestly class;

(2) the Kshatriya, or the military class;

(3) the Vaishya, or the merchant class;

(4) the Shudra, or the artisan and menial class.

Particular attention has to be paid to the fact that this was essentially a class system, in which individuals, when qualified, could change their class, and therefore classes did change their personnel. At some time in the history of the Hindus, the priestly class socially detached itself from the rest of the body of people and through a closed-door policy became a caste by itself. The other classes being subject to the law of social division of labour underwent differentiation, some into large, others into very minute groups. The Vaishya and Shudra classes were the original inchoate plasm, which formed the sources of the numerous castes of today. As the military occupation does not very easily lend itself to very minute sub-division, the Kshatriya class could have differentiated into soldiers and administrators.

The sub-division of a society is quite natural. But the unnatural thing about these sub-divisions is that they have lost the open door character of the class system and have become self-enclosed units called castes. The question is: were they compelled to close their doors and become endogamous, or did they close them of their own accord? The one is a physiological interpretation and the other is mechanistic, but they are complementary and both are necessary to explain the phenomena of caste-formation in its entirety.

Endogamy or the closed-door system, was a fashion in the Hindu society, and as it had originated from the Brahmin Caste it was whole-heartedly imitated by all the non-Brahmin sub-divisions or classes, who, in their turn, became endogamous castes. It is "the infection of imitation" that caught all these sub-divisions on their onward march of differentiation and has turned them into castes. The propensity to imitate is a deep-seated one in the human mind and need not be deemed an inadequate explanation for the formation of the various castes in India. It is so deep-seated that Wallter Bagehot argues that, "We must not think of... imitation as voluntary, or even conscious. On the contrary it has its seat mainly in very obscure parts, of the mind, whose notions, so far from being consciously produced, are hardly felt to exist; so far from being conceived beforehand, are not even felt at the time. The main seat of the imitative part of our nature is our belief, and the causes predisposing us to believe this or disinclining us to believe that are among the obscurest parts of our nature. But as to the imitative nature of credulity there can be no doubt." This propensity to imitate has been made the subject of a scientific study by Gabriel Tarde, who, lays down three laws of imitation. One of this three laws is that imitation flows from the higher to the lower or, to quote his own word, "Given the opportunity, a nobility will always and everywhere imitates its leaders, its kings or sovereigns, and the people likewise, given the opportunity, its nobility." Another of Tarde's laws of imitation is : that the extent or the intensity of imitation varies inversely in proportion to distance, or in is own words "The thing that is most imitated is the most superior one of those that are nearest. In fact, the influence of the model's example is efficacious inversely to its distance as well as directly to its superiority. Distance is understood here in its sociological meaning. However, distant in space a stranger may be he is close by, from this point of view, if we have numerous and daily relations with him and if we have every facility to satisfy our desire to imitate him. This law of imitation of the nearest of the least distant, explains the gradual and consecutive character of the spread of an example that has been set by the higher social ranks".

In order to prove my thesis-which really needs no proof-that some castes were formed by imitation, the best way, it seems to me, is to find out whether or not the vital conditions for the formation, of castes by imitation exist in the Hindu society. The conditions for imitation, according to this standard authority are: (1) that the source of imitation must enjoy prestige in the group and (2) that there must be "numerous- and daily relations" among members of a group. That these conditions were: present in India there is little reason to doubt. The Brahmin is a semi-god and very nearly a demi-god. He sets up a mode and moulds rest. His prestige is unquestionable and is the fountainhead of bliss and good. Can such a being, idolized by scriptures and venerated by the priest-ridden multitude, fail to project his personality on the suppliant humanity? Why, if the story be true, he is believed to be the very end of creation. Such a creature is worthy of more than mere imitation, but at least of imitation; and if he lives in an endogamous enclosure, would not the rest follow his example? Frail humanity! Be it embodied in grave philosopher or a frivolous housemaid, it succumbs. It cannot be otherwise. Imitation is easy and invention is difficult. Yet another way of demonstrating the play of imitation in the formation of castes is to understand the attitude of non-Brahmin classes towards those customs which supported the structure of caste in its nascent days until, in the course of history, it became embedded in the Hindu mind and hangs there to this day without any support—for now it needs no prop but belief—like weed on the surface of a pond. In a way, but only in a way. The status of a caste in the life of Hindu society varies directly with the extent of the observance of the customs of *Sati* enforced widowhood, and girl marriage. But observance of the customs varies directly with the distance.

Those castes that are nearest to the Brahmins have imitated all the three customs and insist on the strict observance thereof. Those that are less near have imitated enforced widowhood and girl marriage; others, a little further off, have only girl- marriage and those furthest off have imitated only the belief in caste principle.

Doubts Among Researchers

While summarising the chapter let us clear some doubts which occur in the minds of researchers of caste system : European students of caste have unduly emphasized the role of colour in the caste system. Themselves impregnated by colour prejudices, they very readily imagined it to be the chief factor in the caste problem. But nothing can be farther from the truth, and Dr. Kelkar is correct when he insists that "All the princes whether they belonged to the so-called Aryan race, or the so-called Dravidian race, were Aryans. Whether a tribe or a family was racially Aryan or Dravidian was a question which never troubled the people of India, until foreign scholars came in and began to draw the line. The colour of the skin had long ceased to be a matter of importance." "Again they have mistaken mere descriptions for explanation and fought over them as though they were theories of origin. There are occupational, religious castes. It is true, but it by no means an explanation of the origin of caste. We have yet to find out why occupational groups are caste; but this question has never even been raised. Lastly, they have taken caste very lightly as though a breath had made it. On the contrary, caste, as I have explained is almost impossible to re-sustained: for the difficulties that it involves are tremendous. It is true that caste rests on belief, but before belief comes to be the foundation of an institution, the institution itself needs to be perpetuated and fortified. My study of the caste problem involves four main points : (1) that in spite of the composite make-up of the Hindu population, there is a deep cultural unity; (2) that caste is a parceling into bits of a larger cultural unit; (3) that there was one caste to start with and (4) that classes have become castes through imitation and excommunication.

Peculiar interest attaches to the problem of caste in India today as persistent attempts are being made to do away with this unnatural institution. Such attempts at reform, however, have aroused a great deal of controversy regarding its origin as to whether it is due to the conscious command of a Supreme Authority, or is an unconscious growth in the life of a human society under peculiar circumstances. Those who hold the latter view will, I hope find some food for thought in the standpoint adopted in this paper. Apart from its practical importance the subject of caste is an all absorbing problem and the interest aroused in me regarding its theoretic foundations has moved me to put before you some of the conclusions, which seem to me well-founded, and the grounds upon which they may be supported. I am not, however so presumptuous as to think them in any way final, or anything more than a contribution to a discussion of the subject. It seems to me that the car has been shunted on wrong lines, and the primary object of the paper is to indicate what is regard to be the right path of investigation, with a view to arrive at a serviceable truth. We must, however, guard against approaching the subject with a bias sentiment must be outlawed from the domain of science and things should be judged from an objective standpoint. For myself I shall find as much pleasure in a positive destruction of my own ideology, as in a rational disagreement on a topic which, notwithstanding many learned disquisition's is likely to remain controversial forever. To conclude, while I have ambitions to advance a theory of caste, if it can be shown to be untenable I shall be equally willing to give it up.

References

Sorokin, P.A., *Social and Cultural Mobility*, 1959.
Harijan Social Welfare Office, Jaunpur : A Report.
Majumdar, R.C., *Panchayats in India*.
Srikant, L.M., Report of the Commissioner for Scheduled Castes and Scheduled Tribes for 1953.
Srimat Bhagavat, Part II, Gita Press, Gorakhpur.

Dube, S.C., *Indian Village.*
Taya Zinkin, *In a Tanjore Village.*
Ketkar, S.V., *History of Caste in India,* New Delhi, 1995.
Morton, Robert K., *Social Theory and Social Structure.*
Ghurye, G.S., *Caste and Occupations,* Bombay, 1961.
Singh, R.D., *Social Change in a U.P. Village.*
Miller, S.M., Comparative Social Mobility.
Indian Annual Register, relevant volumes
AICC Papers.

5

Annihilation of Caste

The path of social reform like the path to heaven at any rate in India, is strewn with many difficulties. Social reform in India has few friends and many critics. The critics fall into two distinct classes. One class consists of political reformers and the other of the socialists.

It was at one time recognized that without social efficiency no permanent progress in the other fields of activity was possible, that owing to mischief wrought by the evil customs, Hindu society was not in a state of efficiency and that ceaseless effort must be made to eradicate these evils. It was due to the recognition of this fact that the birth of the Indian National Congress was accompanied by the foundation of the Social Conference. While the Congress was concerned with defining the weak points in the political organization of the country, the Social Conference was engaged in removing the weak points in the social organization of Hindu society. For some time the Congress and the Conference worked as two wings of one common activity and they held their annual sessions in the same pandal. But soon the two wings developed into two parties, a Political Reform Party and a Social Reform Party, between whom there raged a fierce controversy. The Political Reform Party supported the Indian National Congress and Social Reform Party supported the Social Conference. The two bodies thus, become two hostile camps. The point at issue was whether social reform should precede political reform. For a decade the forces were evenly balanced and the battle was fought without victory to either side. It was, however, evident that the fortunes of the Social Conference were ebbing fast. The gentlemen who presided over the sessions of the Social Conference lamented that the majority of the educated Hindus were for political advancement and indifferent to social reform and that while the number of those who attended the Congress was very large and the number who did not attend but who sympathized with it even larger, the number of those who attended the Social Conference was very much smaller. This indifference, this thinning of its ranks was soon followed by active hostility from the politicians. Under the leadership of the late Mr. Tilak, the courtesy with which the Congress allowed the Social Conference the use of its pandal was withdrawn and the spirit of enmity went to such a pitch that when the Social Conference desired to erect its own pandal a threat to burn the pandal was held out by its opponents. Thus, in course of time the party in favour of political reform won and the Social Conference vanished and was forgotten.

Views of W.C. Bonnerji

The speech, delivered by Mr. W.C. Bonnerji in 1892 at Allahabad as President of the eighth session of the Congress sounds like a funeral oration at the death of the Social Conference and is so typical of the Congress attitude that I venture to quote from it the following extract Mr. Bonnerji said: "for one have no patience with those who say we shall not be fit for political reform until we reform our social system. I fail to see any connection between the two... Are we not fit (for political reform) because our widows remain unmarried and our girls are given marriage earlier than in other countries? because our wives and daughters do not drive about with us visiting our friends? because we do not send our daughters to Oxford and Cambridge?" I have stated the case of political reform as put by Mr. Bonnerji.

There were many who are happy that the victory went to me Congress. But those who believe in the importance of social reform may ask, is the argument such as that of Mr. Bonnerji final? Does it prove that the victory went to those who were in the right? Does it prove conclusively that social reform has no bearing on political reform? It will help us to understand the matter if I stale the other side of the case. I will draw upon the treatment of the untouchables for my facts.

Rules for Untouchables

Under the rule of the Peshwas in the Maratha country the untouchable was not allowed to use the public streets if a Hindu was coming along lest, he should pollute the Hindu by his shadow. The untouchable was required to have a black thread either on his wrist or in his neck as a sign or a mark to prevent the Hindus from getting themselves polluted by his touch through mistake. In Poona, the capital of the Peshwa, the untouchable was required to carry, strung from his waist, a broom to sweep away from behind the dust he treated on lest a Hindu walking on the same should be polluted. In Poona, the untouchable was required to carry an earthen pot, hung in his neck wherever he went, for holding his spit lest his spit falling on earth should pollute a Hindu who might unknowingly happen to tread on it. Let me take more recent facts. The tyranny practiced by the Hindus upon the Balais, an untouchable community in Central India, will serve my purpose. You will find a report of this in the *Times of India* of 4th January 1928. The correspondent of the *Times of India* reported that high caste Hindus, viz. Kalotas, Rajputs and Brahmins including the Patels and Patwaris of villages of Kanaria. Bicholi-Hafsi, Bicholi-Mardana and of about 15 other villages in the Indore district (of the Indore State) informed the Balais of (their respective village that if they wished to live among them they must conform 10 the following rules:

1. Balais must not wear gold-lace-bordered *pugrees*.
2. They must not wear *dhotis* with coloured or fancy borders.
3. They must convey intimation of the death of any Hindu to relatives of the deceased no matter how far away these relatives may be living.

4. In all Hindu marriages Balais must play music before the processions and during the marriage.

5. Balai women must not wear gold or silver ornaments; they must not wear fancy gowns or jackets.

6. Balai women must attend all cases of confinement of Hindu women.

7. Balais must render services without demanding remuneration and must accept whatever a Hindu is pleased to give.

8. If the Balais do not agree to abide by these terms they must clear out of the villages. The Balais refused to comply; and the Hindu element proceeded against them. Balais were not allowed to get water from the village wells; they were not allowed to let go their cattle to graze. Balais were prohibited from passing through land owned by a Hindu, so that if the field of Balai was surrounded by field owned by Hindus, the Balai could have no access to his own field. The Hindus also let their cattle graze down the fields of Balais. The Ballais submitted petitions to the Darbar against these prosecutions; but as they could get no timely relief, and the oppression continued, hundreds of Balais with their wives and children were obliged to abandon their homes in which their ancestors lived for generations and to migrate to adjoining State, viz. to villages in Dhar, Dewas, Bagli, Bhopal, Gwalior and other States, what happened to them in their new homes may for the present be left out of our consideration. The incident at Kavitha in Gujarat happened only last year. The Hindus of Kavitha ordered the untouchables not to insist upon sending their children to the common village school maintained by Government. What sufferings the untouchables of Kavitha had to undergo for daring to exercise a civic right against the wishes of the Hindus is too well-known to need detailed description. Another instance occurred in the village of Zanu in the Ahmedabad district of Gujarat. In November 1935 some untouchable women of well-to-do families started fetching water in metal pots. The Hindus looked upon the use of metal pots by untouchables as an affront to their dignity and assaulted

untouchable women for their impudence. A most recent
event is reported from the village Chakwara in Jaipur
State. It seems from the reports that have appeared in
the newspapers that an untouchable of Chakwara who
had returned from a pilgrimage had arranged to give a
dinner to his fellow untouchables of the villages as an
act of religious piety. The host desired to treat the guests
to a sumptuous meal and the items served included *ghee*
(butter) also. But while the assembly of untouchables
was engaged in partaking of the food, the Hindus in
their hundreds, armed with *lathis,* rushed to the scene,
despoiled the food and belaboured the untouchables who
left the food they were served with and ran away for
their lives and why was this murderous assault
committed on defenceless untouchables? The reason
given is that the untouchables host was impudent
enough to serve *ghee* and his untouchable guests were
foolish enough to taste it. *Ghee* is undoubtedly a luxury
for the rich. But no one would think that consumption
of *ghee* was a mark of high social status. The Hindus of
Chakwara thought otherwise and in righteous
indignation avenged themselves for the wrong done to
them by the untouchables, who insulted them by treating
ghee as an item of their food which they ought to have
known could not be theirs, consistently with the dignity
of the Hindus. This means that an untouchable must
not use *ghee* even if he can afford to buy it, since it is
an act of arrogance towards the Hindus. This happened
on or about the 1st of April 1936.

Having stated the facts, let me now state the case for
social reform. In doing this, I will follow Mr. Bonnerji, as
nearly as I can and ask the, political-minded Hindus. "Are
you fit for political power even though you do not allow a
large class of your own countrymen like the untouchables
to use public school? Are you fit for political power even
though you do not allow them the use of public wells? Are
you fit for political power even though you do not allow them
the use of public streets? Are you fit for political power even
though you do not allow them to wear what apparel or
ornaments they like? Are you fit for political power even

though you do not allow them to eat any food they like? I can ask a string of such questions. But these will suffice. I wonder what would have been the reply of Mr. Bonnerji. I am sure no sensible man will have the courage to give an affirmative answer. Every Congressman who repeats the dogma of Mill that one country is; not fit to rule another must admit that one class is not fit to rule another class.

Social Reform Party

How it is then the Social Reform Party lost the battle? To understand this correctly it is necessary, to take note of the kind of social reform which the reformers were agitating for. In this connection it is necessary to make distinction between social reform in the sense of the reform of the Hindu family and social reform in the sense of the recognition and reconstruction of the Hindu society. The former has relation to widow remarriage, child marriage etc., while the latter relates to the abolition of the caste system. The Social Conference was a body which mainly concerned itself with the reform of the high caste Hindu family. It consisted mostly of enlightened high caste Hindus who did not feel the necessity for agitating for the abolition of caste or had not the courage to agitate for it. They felt quite naturally a greater urge to remove such evils as enforced widowhood, child marriages etc., evils which prevailed among them and which were personally felt by them. They did not stand up for the reform of the Hindu society: The battle that was fought centred round the question of the reform of the family. It did not relate to the social reform in the sense of the break-up of the caste system. It was never put in issue by the reformers. That is the reason why the Social Reform Party lost.

I am aware that this argument cannot alter the fact that political reform did in fact gain precedence over social reform. But the argument has this much value if not more. It explains why social reforms lost the battle. It also helps us to understand how limited was the victory which the Political Reform Party obtained over the Social Reform Party and that the view that social reform need not precede political reform is a view which may stand only when by social reform is meant the reform of the family. That political reform cannot with impunity take precedence over social reform in the sense of reconstruction of society is a thesis which, I am sure, cannot be controverted. That the makers of political constitutions must take account of social forces is a fact which is recognized by no less a person than Ferdinand Lassalle, the friend and co-worker of Karl Marx. In addressing a Prussian audience in 1862 Lassalle said:

"The constitutional questions are in the first instance not questions of right but questions of might. The actual constitution of a country has its existence only in the actual condition of force which exists in the country: hence political constitutions have value and permanence only when they accurately express those conditions of forces which exist in practice within a society".

Communal Award

But it is not necessary to go to Prussia. There is evidence at home. What is the significance of the Communal Award with its allocation of political power in defined proportions to diverse classes and communities? In my view, its significance lies in this that political constitution must take note of social organization. It shows that the politicians who denied that the social problem in India had any bearing on the political problem were forced to reckon with the social problem in devising the constitution. The Communal Award is so to say the nemesis following upon the indifference and neglect of social reform. It is a victory for the Social Reform Party which shows that though defeated they were in the right in insisting upon the importance of social reform. Many, I know, will not accept this finding. The view is current, and it is pleasant to believe in it, that the Communal Award is unnatural and that it is the result of an unholy alliance between the minorities and the bureaucracy. I do not wish to rely on the Communal Award as a piece of evidence to support my contention if it is said that it is not good evidence. Let us turn to Ireland. What does the history of Irish Home Rule show? It is well-known that in the course of the negotiations between the representatives of Ulster and Southern Ireland, Redmond, the representative of Southern

Ireland, in order to bring Ulster in a Home Rule Constitution common to the whole of Ireland said to the representatives of Ulster: "Ask any political safeguards you like and you shall have them. "What was the reply that Ulstermen gave? Their reply was "Damn your safeguards, we don't want to be ruled by you on any terms. "People who blame the minorities in India ought to consider what would have happened to the political aspirations of the majority if the minorities had taken the attitude which Ulster took. Judged by the attitude of Ulster to Irish Home Rule, is it nothing that the minorities agreed to be ruled by the majority which has not shown much sense of statesmanship provided same safeguards were devised for them? But this is only incidental.

The main question is why did Ulster like this attitude? The only answer I can give is that there was a social problem between Ulster and Southern Ireland the problem between Catholics and Protestants, essentially a problem of caste. That Home Rule in Ireland would be Home Rule was the way in which the Ulstermen had framed their answer. But that is only another way of stating that it was the social problem of Caste between the Catholics and Protestants, which prevented the solution of the political problem. This evidence again is sure to be challenged. It will be urged that here too the hand of the Imperialist was at work. But my resources are not exhausted. I will give evidence from the *History of Rome*. Here no one can say that any evil genius as at work. Any one who has studied the History of Rome will know that the Republican Constitution of Rome bore marks having strong resemblance to the Communal Award. When the kingship in Rome was abolished, the kingly power or the Imperium was divided between the Consuls and the Pontifex Maximus. In the Consuls was vested the secular authority of the King, while the latter took over the religious authority of King. The Republican Constitution had provided, that of the *two Consuls* one was to be Patrician and the other Plebian. The same constitution had also provided that, of the Priests under the Pontifex Maximus, half were to be Plebians and the other half Patricians. Why is it that the Republican Constitution of Rome had these provisions which, as I said, resemble so strongly the provisions which, as I said resemble so strongly the provisions of the Communal Award? The only answer one can get is the Constitution of Republican Rome had to take account of the social division between the Patricians and the Plebians, who formed two distinct castes. To sum up, let political reformers turn to any direction they like, they will find that in the making of a constitution, they cannot ignore the problem arising out of the prevailing social order.

The illustrations which I have in support of the proposition that social and religious problems have a bearing on political constitutions seem to be too particular. Perhaps they are. But it should not be supposed that the bearing of the one on the other is limited. On the other hand one can say that generally speaking, History bears out the proposition that political revolutions have always been preceded by social and religious revolutions. The religious Reformation started by Luther was the precursor of the political emancipation of the European people. In England Puritanism led to the establishment of political liberty. Puritanism founded the new world. It was Puritanism which won the war of American Independence and Puritanism was a religious movement. The same is true of the Muslim Empire. Before the Arabs became a political power they had undergone a thorough religious revolution started by the Prophet Mohammad. Even Indian History supports the same conclusion. The political revolution led by Chandragupta was preceded by the religious and social revolution of Buddha. The political revolution led by Shivaji was preceded by the religious and social reform brought about by the saints of Maharashtra. The political revolution of the Sikhs was preceded by the religious and social revolution led by Guru Nanak. It is unnecessary to add more illustrations. These will suffice to show that the emancipation of the mind and the soul is a necessary preliminary for the political expansion or the people.

Socialists and their Role

Let me now turn to the Socialists. Can the Socialists ignore the problem arising out of the social order? The Socialists of India following their fellows in Europe are seeking to apply the economic interpretation of history to the facts of India. They propound that man is an economic creature, that his activities and aspirations are bound by economic facts, that property is the only source of power. They, therefore, preach that political and social reforms are but gigantic illusions and that economic reform by equalization of property must have precedence over every other kind of reform. One may join issue on every one of those premises on which rests the Socialists' case for economic reform having priority over every other kind of reform. One may contend that economic motive is not the only motive by which man is actuated. That economic power is the only kind of power no student of human, society can accept that the social status of an individual by itself often becomes a source of power and authority is made clear by the sway which the Mahatmas have held over the common man. Why do millionaires in India obey penniless Sadhus and Fakirs? Why do millions of paupers in India sell their trifling trinkets which constitute their only wealth and go to Benaras and Mecca? That, religion is the source of power is illustrated by the history of India where the priest holds a sway over the common man often greater than the magistrate and where everything, even such things as strikes and elections, so easily take a religious turn and can so easily be given a religious twist. Take the case of the Plebians of Rome as a further illustration of the power of religion over man. It throws great light on this point the Plebs had fought for a share in the supreme executive under the Roman Republic and had secured the appointment of a Plebian Consul elected by a separate electorate constituted by the *Commitia Centuriata*, which was an assembly of Plebians. They wanted a Consul of their own because they felt that the Patrician Consuls used to discriminate against the Plebians in carrying on the administration. They had apparently obtained a great gain because under the Republican Constitution of Rome one Consul had the power of vetoing an act of the other Consul. But did they in fact gain anything? The answer to this question must be in the negative. The Plebians never could get a Plebian Consul who could be said to be a strong man and who could act independently of the Patrician Consul. In the ordinary course of things the Plebians should have got a strong Plebian Consul in view of the fact that his election was to be by a separate electorate of Plebians. The question is why did they fail in getting a strong Plebian to officiate as their Consul? The answer to this question reveals the dominion which religion exercises over the minds of men. It was an accepted creed of the whole Roman populus that no official could enter upon the duties of his office unless the Oracle of Delphi declared that he was acceptable to the Goddess. The priests who were in charge of the temple of the Goddess of Delphi were all patricians. Whenever therefore the Plebians elected a Consul who was known to be a strong party man opposed to the Patricians or "communal" to use the term that is current in India, the Oracle invariably declared that he was not acceptable to the Goddess.

This is how the Plebians were cheated out of their rights. But what is worthy of note is that the Plebians permitted themselves to be thus cheated because they too like the Patricians, held firmly the belief that the approval of the Goddess was a condition precedent to the taking charge by an official of his duties and that election by the people was not enough. If the Plebians had contended that election was enough and that the approval by the Goddess was not necessary they would have derived the fullest benefit from the political right which they had obtained. But they did not. They agreed to elect another less suitable to themselves but more suitable to the Goddess, which in fact meant more amenable to the patricians. Rather than give up religion, the Plebians give up material gain for which they had fought so hard. Does this not show that religion can be a source of power as great as money if not greater? The fallacy of the socialists lies in supposing that because in the present stage of European society property as a source of power is predominant, that the same is true of India or that the same was true of Europe in the past Religion, social status and property are all sources of power and authority, which one man has to control the liberty of another. One is predominant at one stage, the other is predominant at another stage. That is the only difference. If liberty is the Ideal, if liberty means the destruction of the dominion which one man holds over another then obviously it cannot be insisted upon that economic reform must be the one kind of reform worthy of pursuit. If the source of power and dominion is at any given time or in any given society, social and religious, then social reform and religious reform must bc accepted as the necessary sort of reform.

One can thus attack the doctrine of Economic Interpretation of History adopted by the Socialists of India. But I recognize that economic interpretation of history is not necessary for the validity of the Socialist contention that equalization of property is the only real reform and that it must precede everything else. However, can you have economic reform without first bringing about a reform of the social order? The Socialists of India do not seem to have considered this question. A Socialist said, "I do not believe that we can build up a free society in India so long as there is a trace of this ill-treatment and suppression of one class by another. Believing as I do in a socialist ideal, inevitably I believe in perfect equality in the treatment of various classes and groups. I think that Socialism offers the only true remedy for this as well as other problem." Now the question is : Is it enough for a Socialist to say, "I believe in perfect equality in the treatment of the various classes?" To say that such a belief is enough is to disclose a complete lack of understanding of what is involved in Socialism. If Socialism is a practical programme and is not merely an ideal, distant and far off, the question for a Socialist is not whether he believes in equality. The question for him is whether he minds one class ill-treating and suppressing another class as a matter of system, as a matter of principle and thus allow tyranny and oppression to continue to divide one class from another. Let me analyze the factors that are involved in the realization of Socialism in order to explain fully the point. Now it is obvious that the economic reform contemplated by the Socialists cannot come about unless there is a revolution resulting in the seizure of power. That seizure of power must be by a proletariat. The first question is: Will the proletariat of India combine to bring about this revolution? What will move men to such an action? It seems to me that other things being equal the only thing that will move one man to take such an action is the feeling that other man with whom he is acting are actuated by feeling of equality and fraternity and above all of justice.

Men will not join in a revolution for the equalization of property unless they know that after the revolution is achieved they will be treated equally and that there will be no discrimination of caste and creed. The assurance of a socialist leading the revolution that he does not believe in caste will not suffice. The assurance must be the assurance proceeding from much deeper foundation, namely, the mental attitude of the compatriots towards one another in their spirit of personal equality and fraternity. Can it be said that the proletariat of India, poor as it is recognizes no such distinctions except that of the rich and the poor? Can it be said that the poor in India recognize no such distinctions of caste or creed, high or low? If the fact is that they do, what unity of front can be expected from such a proletariat in its action against the rich? How can there be a revolution if the proletariat cannot present a united front? Suppose for the sake of argument that by some freak of fortune a revolution does take place and the Socialists come in power, will they not have to deal with the problems created by the particular social order prevalent in India? I can't see how a Socialist State in India can function for a second without having to grapple with the problems created by the prejudices which make Indian people observe the distinctions of high and low, clean and unclean. If Socialists are not be content with the mouthing of fine phrases, if the Socialists wish to make Socialism a definite reality then they must recognize that the problem of social reform is fundamental and that for them there is no escape from it. That, the social order prevalent in India is a matter which a Socialist must deal with, that unless he does so he cannot achieve his revolution and that if he does achieve it as a result of good fortune will have to grapple with it if he wishes to realize his ideal, is a proposition which in my opinion is incontrovertible. He will be compelled to take account of caste after revolution if he does not take account of it before revolution. This is only another way of saying that, turn in any direction you like, caste is the monster that crosses your path. You cannot have political reform, you cannot have economic reform, unless you kill this monster.

Defenders of Caste

It is a pity that caste even today has its defenders. The defenses are many. It is defended on the ground that the caste system is but another name for division of labour is a necessary feature of every civilized society then it is argued that there is nothing wrong in the caste system. Now the first thing is to be urged against this view is that caste system is not merely division of labour. It is also a division of labourers. Civilized society undoubtedly needs division of labour. But in no civilized society is division of labour accompanied by this unnatural division of labourers into water-tight compartments. Caste system is not merely a division of labourers which is quite different from division of labour—it is an heirarchy in which the divisions of labourers are graded one above the other. In no other country is the division of labour accompanied by this gradation of labourers. There is also a third point of criticism against this view of the caste system. This division of labour is not spontaneous, it is not based on natural aptitudes. Social and individual efficiency requires us to develop the capacity of an individual to the point of competency to choose and to make his own career. This principle is violated in the caste system in so far as it involves an attempt to appoint tasks to individuals in advance, selected not on the basis of trained original capacities, but on that of the social status of the parent. Looked at from another point of view this stratification of occupations which is the result of the caste system is positively pernicious. Industry is never static. It undergoes rapid and abrupt changes. With such changes an individual must be free to change his occupation. Without such freedom to adjust himself to changing circumstances it would be impossible for him to gain his livelihood. Now the caste system will not allow Hindus to take to occupations where they are wanted if they do not belong to them by heredity. If a Hindu is seen to starve rather than take to new occupations not assigned to his caste, the reason is to be found in the caste system. By not permitting readjustment of occupations, caste becomes a direct cause of much of the unemployment we see in the country. As a form of division of labour the caste system suffers from another serious defect. The division of labour brought about by the caste system is not a division based on choice. Individual sentiment, individual preference has no place in it. It is based on the dogma of predestination. Considerations of social efficiency would compel us to recognize that the greatest evil in the industrial system is not so much poverty and the suffering that it involves as the fact that so many persons have calling which make no appeal to those who are engaged in them. Such calling constantly provoke one to aversion, ill-will and the desire to evade. There are many occupations in India, which on account of the fact that they are regarded as degraded by the Hindus provide those who are engaged them to aversion. There is a constant desire to evade and escape from such occupations which arises solely because of the slighting effect which they produce upon those who follow them owing to the slight and stigma cast upon them by the Hindu religion. What efficiency can there be in a system under which neither men's hearts nor their minds are in their work? As an economic organization caste is therefore harmful institution, inasmuch as, it involves the subordination of man natural powers and inclinations to the exigencies of social rules.

Some have dug a biological trench in defence of the caste system. It is said that the object of caste was to preserve purity of race and purity of blood. Now ethnologists are of opinion that men of pure race exist nowhere and that there has been a mixture of all races in all parts of the world. Especially is this the case with the people of India. Mr. D.R. Bhandarkar in his paper on Foreign Elements in the Hindu Population has stated that "There is hardly a class or caste in India which has not a foreign strain in it. There is an admixture of alien blood not only among the warrior classes—the Rajputs and the Marathas—but also among the Brahmins who are under the happy delusion that they are free from all foreign elements. "The caste system cannot be said to have grown as a means of preventing the admixture of races or as a means of maintaining purity of blood. As a matter of fact caste system came into being long after the different races of India had commingled in blood and culture. To hold that distinctions of castes or really distinctions of race and to treat different castes as though they were so many different races is a gross perversion of facts. What racial affinity is there between the Brahmin of the Punjab and the Brahmin of Madras? What racial affinity is there between the untouchable of Bengal and the untouchable of Madras? What racial difference is there between the Brahmin of the Punjab and the *Chamar* of the Punjab? What racial difference is there between the Brahmin of Madras and the Pariah of Madras? The Brahmin of the Punjab is racially of the same stock as the *Chamar* of the Punjab and the Brahmin of Madras is of the same race as the Pariah of Madras. Caste system does not demarcate racial division. Caste system is a social division of people of the same race. Assuming it, however, to be a case of racial divisions one may ask: What harm could there be if a mixture of races and of blood was permitted to take place in India by inter-marriages between different castes? Men are no doubt divided from animals by so deep a distinction that recognize men and animals as two distinct species. But even scientists who believe in purity of races do not assert that the different races constitute different species of men. They are only varieties of one and the same species. As such they can interbreed and produce an offspring which is capable of breeding and which is not sterile. An immense lot of nonsense is talked about heredity and eugenics in defence of the caste system. Few would object to the caste system if it was in accord with he basic principle of eugenics because few can object to thc improvement of the race by judicious mating. But one fails to understand how the caste system secures judicious mating. Caste system is a negative thing. "It merely prohibits persons belonging to different castes from intermarrying. It is not a positive method of selecting which two among a given caste should marry. If caste is eugenic in origin then the origin of sub-castes must also be eugenic. But can any seriously maintain that the origin of sub-castes is eugenic?

I think it would be absurd to contend for such a proposition and for a very obvious reason. If caste means race then differences of sub-castes cannot mean differences of race because sub-castes become ex-hypothesia sub-divisions of one and the same race. Consequently the bar against intermarrying and inter-dining between sub-castes cannot be for the purpose of maintaining purity of race or of blood. If sub-castes cannot be eugenic in origin there cannot be any substance in the contention that caste is eugenic in origin. Again if caste is eugenic in origin one can understand the bar against intermarriage. But what is the purpose of the interdict placed on inter-dining between castes and sub-castes alike? Inter-dining cannot infect blood and therefore cannot be the cause either of the improvement or of deterioration of the race. This shows that caste has no scientific origin and that those who are attempting to give it an eugenic basis are trying to support by science what is grossly unscientific. Even today eugenics cannot become a practical possibility unless have definite knowledge regarding the laws of heredity. Prof. Bateson in his *Mendel's Principles of Heredity* says, "There is nothing in the descent of the higher mental qualities to suggest that they follow any single system of transmission. It is likely that both they and the more marked developments of physical powers result rather from the coincidence of numerous factors than from the possession of anyone genetic element. "To argue that the caste system was eugenic in its conception is to attribute to the forefathers of present-day Hindus a knowledge of heredity which even the modern scientists do not possess. A tree should be judged by the fruits it yields. If caste is eugenic what sort of a race of men it should have produced? Physically speaking the Hindus are a C3 people. They are a race of pygmies and *dwarfs* stunted in structure and wanting in stamina. It is a nation 9/10ths of which is declared to be unfit for military service. This shows that the caste system does not embody the eugenics of modern scientists. It is a social system which embodies the arrogance and selfishness of a perverse section of the Hindus who were superior enough in social status to set it in fashion and who had authority to force it on their inferiors.

Caste does not result in economic efficiency. Caste cannot and has not improved. The caste has however done one thing. It has completely disorganized and demoralized the Hindus.

Hindu Society

The first and foremost thing that must be recognized is that Hindu society is a myth. The name Hindu is itself a foreign name. It was given by the Mohammedans to the natives for the purpose of distinguishing themselves. It does not feel the necessity of a common name because they had no conception of their having constituted a community. Hindu society as such does not exist it is only a collection of castes. Each caste is conscious of its existence. Its survival is the be all and end all of its existence. Castes do not even form a federation. A caste has no feeling that it is affiliated to other castes except when there is a Hindu-Muslim riot. On all other occasions each caste endeavours to segregate itself and to distinguish itself from other castes. Each caste not only dines among itself and marries among itself but each caste prescribes its own distinctive dress. What other explanation can there be of the innumerable styles of dress worn by the men and women of India which so amuse the tourists? Indeed the ideal Hindu must be like a rat living in his own hole refusing to have any contact with other. There is an utter lack among the Hindus of what the sociologists call "consciousness of kind." There is no Hindu consciousness of kind. In every Hindu the consciousness that exists is the consciousness of his caste. That is the reason why the Hindus cannot be said to form a society or a nation. There are however many Indians whose patriotism does not permit them to admit that Indians are not a nation, that they are only an amorphous mass of people. They have insisted that underlying the apparent diversity there is a fundamental unity which marks the life of the Hindus in as much as there is a similarity of habits and customs, beliefs and thoughts there is. But one cannot accept the conclusion that therefore, the Hindus constitute a society. To do so is to misunderstand the essentials which go to make up a society. Men do not become a society by living in physical proximity any more than a man ceases to be a member of his society by living so many miles away from other men. Secondly similarity in habits and customs, beliefs and thoughts is not enough to constitute men into society. Things may be passed physically from one to another like bricks. In the same way habits and customs, beliefs and thought of one group may be taken over by another group and there may thus appear a similarity between the two. Culture spreads by diffusion and that is why one finds similarity between various primitive tribes in the matter of their habits and customs, beliefs and thoughts, although they do not live in proximity. But no one could say that because there was this similarity the primitive tribes constituted one society. This is because similarly in certain things is not enough to constitute a society. Men constitute a society because they have things, which they possess in common. To have similar thing is totally different from possessing things in common. And the only way by which men can come to possess things in common with one another is by being in communication with one another. This is merely another way of saying that society continues to exist by communication indeed in communication. To make it concrete, it is not enough if men act in a way which agrees with the acts of others. Parallel activity even if similar, is not sufficient to bind men into a society. This is proved by the fact that the festivals observed by the different castes amongst the Hindus are the same. Yet these parallel performances of similar festivals by the different casts have not bound them into one integral whole. For that purpose what is necessary is for a man to share and participate in a common activity so that the same emotions are aroused in him that animate the others. Making the individual a sharer or partner in the associated activity so that he feels its success as his success, its failure as his failure is the real thing that binds men and makes a society of them. The caste system prevents common activity and by preventing common activity it has prevented the Hindus from becoming a society with a unified life and a consciousness of its own being.

The Hindus often complain of the isolation and exclusiveness of a gang or a clique and blame them for antisocial spirit. But they, conveniently forget that this anti-social spirit is the worst feature of their own caste system. One caste enjoys singing a hymn of hate against another caste as much as the Germans did in singing their hymn of hate against the English during the *last* war. The literature of the Hindus is full of caste genealogies in which an attempt is made to give a noble origin to one caste and an ignoble origin to other castes. The Sahyadrikhand is a notorious instance of this class of literature. This anti-social spirit is not confined to caste alone. It has gone deeper and has poisoned the mutual relations of the sub-castes as well. In my province the Golak Brahmins. Deorukha Brahmins, Karada Brahmins, Palshe Brahmins and Chitpavan Brahmins, all claim to be sub-divisions of the Brahmin caste. But the anti-social spirit that prevails between them is quite as marked and quite as virulent as the anti-social spirit that prevails between them and other non-Brahmin castes. There is nothing strange in this. An anti-social spirit is found wherever one group has "interests of its own" which shut it out from full interaction with other groups, so that its prevailing purpose is protection of what it has got. This anti-social spirit, this spirit of protecting its own interests is as much a marked feature of the different castes in their isolation from one another as it is of nations in their isolation. The Brahmin's primary concern is to protect "his interest" against those of the non-Brahmins and the non-Brahmin primary concern is to protect their interest against those of the Brahmins. The Hindus, therefore, are not merely an assortment of castes but they are so many warring groups each living for itself and for its selfish ideal. There is another feature of caste which is deplorable. The ancestors of the present day English fought on one side or the other in the wars of the Roses and the Cromwellian War. But the descendants of those who fought on the one side do not bear any animosity—any grudge against the descendents of those who fought on the other side. The feud is forgotten. But the present-day non-Brahmins cannot forgive the present-day Brahmins for the insult their ancestors gave to Shivaji. The present-day Kayasthas will not forgive the present-day Brahmins for the infamy cast upon their forefathers by the forefathers of the latter. To what is this differences due? Obviously to the caste system. The existence of caste and caste consciousness has served to keep the memory of past feuds between castes green and has prevented solidarity.

The recent discussion about the excluded and partially included areas has served to draw attention to the position of what are called the aboriginal tribes in India. They number about 13 millions if not more. Apart from the questions whether their exclusion from the new Constitution is proper or improper, the fact still remains that these aborigines have remained in their primitive uncivilized state in a land which boasts of a civilization thousands of years old. Not only are they not civilized but some of them follow pursuits which have led to their being classified as criminals. Thirteen millions of people living in the midst of civilization are still in a savage state and are leading the life of heredity criminals!! But the Hindus have never felt ashamed of it. This phenomenon which in my view is quite unparalleled. What is the cause of this shameful state of affairs? Why has no attempt been made to civilize these aborigines and to lead them to take to a more honourable way of making a living? The Hindus will probably seek to account for this savage State of the aborigines by attributing to them congenital stupidity. They will probably not admit that the aborigines have remained savages because they had made no effort to civilize them, to give them medical aid, to reform them, to make them good citizens. But supposing a Hindu wished to do what the Christian missionary is doing for these aborigines, could he have done it? I submit not. Civilizing the aborigines means adopting them as your own, living in their midst, and cultivating fellow-feeling, in short loving them. How is it possible for a Hindu to do this? His whole life is one anxious effort to preserve his caste. Caste is his precious possession which he must save at any cost. He cannot consent to lose it by establishing contact with the aborigines the remnants of the hateful Anaryas of the Vedic days. Not that a Hindu could not be taught the sense of duty to fallen humanity, but the trouble is that no amount of sense of duty can enable him to overcome his duty to preserve his caste. Caste is, therefore, the real explanation as to why the Hindus has let the savage remain a savage in the midst of his civilization without blushing or without feeling any sense of remorse or repentance. Hindu has not realized that these aborigines are a source of potential danger. If these savages remain savages they may not do any harm to the Hindus. But if they are reclaimed by non-Hindus and converted to their faiths they will swell the ranks of the enemies of the Hindus. If this happens the Hindu will have to thank himself and his caste system.

Humanitarian Cause

Not only has the Hindu made no effort for the humanitarian cause of civilizing the savages but the higher-caste Hindus have deliberately prevented the lower castes who are within the pale of Hinduism from rising to the cultural level of the higher castes. I will give two instances, one of the Sonars and the other of the Pathare Prabhus. Both are communities quite well-known in Maharashtra. Like the rest of the communities desiring to raise their status these two communities were at one time endeavouring to adopt some of the ways and habits of the Brahmins. The Sonars were styling themselves Daivadnya Brahmans and were wearing their *dhotis* with folds on and using the word namaskar for salutation. Both, the folded way of wearing the *dhoti* and the *namaskar* were special to the Brahmins. The Brahmins did not like this imitation and this attempt by Sonars to pass off as Brahmins. Under the authority of the Peshwas the Brahmins successfully put down this attempt on the part of the Sonars to adopt ways of the Brahmins. They even got the President of the Councils of East India Company's settlement in Bombay to issue a prohibitory order against the Sonars residing in Bombay. At one time the Pathare Prabhus had widow-remarriage as a custom of their caste. This custom of widow-remarriage was later on looked upon as a mark of social inferiority by some members of the caste especially because it was contrary to the custom prevalent among the Brahmins. With the object of raising status of their community some Pathare Prabhus sought to stop this practice of widow-remarriage that was prevalent in their caste. The community was divided into two camps, one for and the other against the innovation. The Peshwas took the side of those in favour of widow-remarriage and thus virtually prohibited the Pathare Prabhus from following the ways of the Brahmins. The Hindus criticize the Mohammedans for having spread their religion by the use of the sword. They also redicule Christianity on the score of the inquisition. But really speaking who is better and more worthy of our respect—the Mohammedans and Christians who attempted to thrust down the throats of unwilling persons what they regarded as necessary for their salvation or the Hindu who would not spread the light, who would endeavour to keep others in darkness, who would not consent to share his intellectual and social inheritance with those who are ready and willing to make it a part of their own make-up?

Whether the Hindu religion was or was not a missionary religion has been a controversial issue. Some hold the view that it was never a missionary religion. Others hold that it was. That the Hindu religion was once a missionary religion must be admitted. It could not have spread over the face of India. If it was not a missionary religion. That today it is not a missionary religion is also a fact which must be accepted. The question therefore is not whether or not the Hindu religion was a missionary religion. The real question is why did the Hindu religion cease to be a missionary religion? My answer is this Hindu religion ceased to be a missionary religion when the caste system grew up among the Hindus. Caste is inconsistent with conversion. Inculcation of beliefs and dogmas is not the only problem that is involved in conversion. To find a place for the convert in the social life of the community is another and a much more important problem that arises in connection with conversion. That problem is where to place the convert in what caste? It is a problem which must baffle every Hindu wishing to make aliens converts to his religion. Unlike the club the membership of a caste is not open to all and sundry. The law of caste confines its membership to person born in the caste. Castes are autonomous and there is no authority anywhere to compel a caste to admit a new-comer to its social life. Hindu society being a collection of castes and each caste being a close corporation there is no place for a convert. Thus it is the caste which has prevented the Hindus from expanding and from absorbing other religious communities. So long as caste remain; Hindu religion cannot be made a missionary religion and *Shudhi* will be both a folly and a futility.

Shudhi and Hindus

The reasons which have made *Shudhi* impossible for Hindus are also responsible for making *Sanghatan* impossible. The idea underlying *Sanghatan* is to remove from the mind of the Hindu that timidity and cowardice which so painfully make him off from the Mohammedan and the Sikh and which have led him to adopt the low ways of treachery and cunning for protecting himself. The question naturally arises : From where does the Sikh or the Mohammedan derive his strength which makes him brave and fearless? I am sure it is not due to relative superiority of physical strength, diet or drill. It is due to strength arising out of the feeling that all Sikhs will come to the rescue of a Sikh when he is in danger and that all Mohammedans will rush to save a Muslim if he is attacked. The Hindu can derive no such strength. He cannot feel assured that his fellows will come to his help. Being one and fated to be alone he remains powerless, develops timidity and cowardice and in a fight surrenders or runs away. The Sikh as well as the Muslim stands fearless and gives battle because he knows that though one he will not be alone. The presence of this belief in the one helps him to hold out and the absence of it in the other makes him to give way. If you pursue this matter further and ask what is it that enables the Sikh and the Mohammedan to feel so assured and why is the Hindu filled with such despair in the matter of help and assistance you will find that the reasons for this difference lie in the defference in their associated mode of living. The associated mode of life practiced by the Sikhs and the Mohammedans produces fellow-feeling. The associated mode of life of the Hindus does not. Among Sikhs and Muslims there is a social cement which makes them Bhais. Among Hindus there is no such cement and one Hindu does not regard another Hindus as his *Bhai*. This explains why a Sikh says and feels that one Sikh, or one *Khalsa* is equal to sava lakh men. This explains why one Mohammedan is equal to a crowd of Hindus. This difference is undoubtedly a difference due to caste. So long as caste remains there will be no *Sanghatan* and so long as there is no *Sanghatan* the Hindu will remain week and meek. The Hindus claim to be a very tolerant people. In my opinion this is a mistake. On many occasions they can be intolerant and if on some occasions they are tolerant that is because they are too weak to oppose or too indifferent to oppose. This indifference of the Hindus has become so much a part of their nature that a Hindu will quite meekly tolerate an insult as well as a wrong. You see amongst them to use the words of Morris. "The great treading down the little, the strong beating down the weak, cruel men fearing not, kind men daring not and wise men caring not." With the Hindu Gods all forbearing it is not difficult to imagine the pitiable condition of the wronged and the oppressed among the Hindus. Indifferentism is the worst kind of disease that can infect a people. Why is the Hindu so indifferent? In my opinion this indifferentism is the result of caste system which has made *Sanghatan* and co-operation even for a good cause impossible.

The assertion by the individual of his own opinions and beliefs, his own independence and interest as over against group standards, group authority and group interests is the beginning of all reform. But whether the reform will continue depends upon what scope the group affords for such individual assertion. If the group is tolerant and fair-minded in dealing with such individuals they will continue to assert and in the end succeed in converting their fellows. On the other hand if the group is intolerant and does not bother about the means it adopts to stifle such individuals they will perish and the reform will die out. Now a caste has an unquestioned right to excommunicate any man who is guilty of breaking the rules of the caste and when it is realized that excommunication involves a complete cesser of social intercourse it will be agreed that as a form of punishment there is really little to choose between excommunication and death. No wonder individual Hindus have not had the courage to assert their independence by breaking the barriers of caste. It is true that man cannot get on with his fellows. But it is also true that he cannot do without them. He would like to have the society of his fellows on his terms. If he cannot get it on his terms then he will be ready to have it on any terms even amounting to complete surrender. This is because he cannot do without society. A caste is ever ready to take advantage of the helplessness of a man and insist upon complete conformity to its code in letter and in spirit. A caste can easily organize itself into a conspiracy to make the life of a reformer a hell and if a conspiracy is a crime I do not understand why such a nefarious act as an attempt to excommunicate a person for daring to act contrary to the rules of caste should not be made an offence punishable in law. But as it is, even law gives each caste an autonomy to regulate its membership and punish dissenters with excommunication. Caste in the hands of the orthodox has been a powerful weapon for persecuting the reforms and for killing all reform.

Ethics of Hindus

The effect of caste on the ethics of the Hindus is simply deplorable. Caste has killed public spirit. Caste has destroyed the sense of public charity. Caste has made public opinion impossible. A Hindu's public is his caste. His responsibility is only to his caste. His loyalty is restricted only to his caste. Virtue has become caste-ridden and morality has become caste-bound. There is no sympathy to the deserving. There is no appreciation of the meritorious. There is no charity to the needy. Suffering as such calls for no response. There is charity but it begins with the caste and ends with the caste. There is sympathy but not for men of other caste. Would a Hindu acknowledge and follow the leadership of a great and good man? The case of a Mahatma apart, the answer must be that he will follow a leader only if he is a man of his caste. A Brahmin will follow a leader only if he is a Brahmin, a Kayastha if he is a Kayastha and so on. The capacity to appreciate merits in a man apart from his caste does not exist in a Hindu. There is appreciation of virtue but only when the man is a fellow caste-man. The whole morality is as bad as tribal morality. My caste-man, right or wrong; my caste-man, good or bad. It is not a case of standing by virtue and not standing by vice. It is a case of standing or not standing by the caste. Have not Hindus committed treason against their country in the interests of their caste?

I would not be surprised if some of you have grown weary listening to this tiresome tale of the sad effects which caste has produced. There is nothing new in it. I will therefore turn to the constructive side of the problem. What is your ideal society if you do not want caste is a question that is bound to be asked of you. If you ask me, my ideal would be a society based on Liberty, Equality and Fraternity. And why not? What objection can there be to Fraternity? I cannot imagine any. An ideal society should be mobile, should be full of channels for conveying a change taking place in one part to other parts. In an *ideal* society there should be many interests consciously communicated and shared. There should be varied and free points of contact with other modes of association. In other words there must be social endosmosis. This is fraternity, which is only another name for democracy. Democracy is not merely a form of government. It is primarily a mode of associated living, of conjoint communicated experience. It is essentially an attitude of respect and reverence towards fellowmen. Any objection to Liberty? Few object to liberty in the sense of a right to free movement, in the sense of a right to life and limb. There is no objection to liberty in the sense of a right to property, tools and materials as being necessary for earning a living to keep the body in due state of health. Why not allow liberty to benefit by an effective and competent use of a person's powers? The supporters of caste who would allow liberty in the sense of a right to life, limb and property, would not readily consent to liberty in this sense, inasmuch as it involves liberty to choose one's profession. But to object to this kind of liberty perpetuate slavery. For slavery does not merely mean a legalized form of subjection. It means a state of society in which some men are forced to accept from other the purposes which control their conduct. This condition obtains even where there is not slavery in the legal sense. It is found where, as in the caste system, some persons are compelled to carry on certain prescribed callings which are not of their choice. Any objection of equality? This has obviously been the most contentious part of the slogan of the French Revolution. The objections to equality may be sound and one may have to admit that all men are not equal. But what of that? Equality may be a fiction but nonetheless one must accept it as the governing principle. A man's power is dependent upon (1) physical heredity, (2) social inheritance or endowment in the form of parental care, education, accumulation of scientific knowledge, everything which enables him to be more; efficient than the savage, and finally, (3) on his own efforts. In all these three respects men are undoubtedly unequal. But the question is, shall we treat them as unequal because they are unequal? This, is a question which the opponents of equality must answer.

From the standpoint of the individualist it may be just to treat men unequally so far as their efforts are unequal. It may be desirable to give as much incentive as possible to the full development of everyone's powers. But what would happen if men were treated unequally as they are, in the first two respects? It is obvious that those individuals also in whose favour; there is birth, education, family name, business connections and inherited wealth would be selected in the race. But selection under such circumstances would not be a selection of the able. It would be the selection of the privileged. The reason therefore, which forces that in the third respect we should treat men unequally demands that in first two respects we should treat men as equally as possible. On the other hand it can be urged that if it is good for the social body to get the most out of its members, it can get most out of them only by making them equal as far as possible at the very start of the race. That is one reason why we cannot escape equality. But there is another why reason why we must accept equality. A statesman is concerned with vast numbers of people. He has neither the time nor the knowledge to draw fine distinctions and to treat equitably, i.e., according to need or according to capacity. However, desirable or reasonable an equitable treatment of men may be humanity is not capable of assortment and classification. The statesman, therefore, must follow some rough and ready rule and that rough and ready rule is to treat all men alike not because they are alike but because classification and assortment is impossible. The doctrine of equality is glaringly fallacious but taking all in all it is the only way a statesman can proceed in politics which is a severely practical affair and which demands a severely practical test.

Role of Reformers

But there is a set of reformers who hold out a different ideal. They go by the name of the Arya Samajists and their ideal of social organization is what is called *Chaturvarnya* or the division of society into four classes instead of the four thousand castes that we have in India. To make it more attractive and to disarm opposition the protagonists of *Chaturvarnya* take great care to point out, that their *Chaturvarnya* is based not on birth but on *Guna* (worth). At the outset, I must confess that notwithstanding the worth-basis of this *Chaturvarnya*, it is an ideal to which I cannot reconcile myself. In the first place, if under the *Chaturvarnya* of the Arya Samajists an individual is to take his place in the Hindu society according to his worth. I do not understand why the Arya Samajists insist upon labelling men as Brahmin, Kshatriya, Vaishya and Shudra. A learned man would be honoured without his being labelled a Brahmin. A soldier would be respected without his being designated a Kshatriya. If Europe society honours its soldiers and its servants without giving them permanent labels, why should Hindu society find it difficult to do so is a question, which Arya Samajists have not cared to consider. There is another objection to the continuance of these labels. All reform consists in a change in the notions, sentiment and mental attitudes of the people towards men and things. It is common experience that certain names become associated with certain notions and sentiments, which determine a person's attitude towards men and things. The names, Brahmin, Kshatriya, Vaishya and Shudra are names which are associated with a definite and fixed notion in the mind of every Hindu. That notion is that of a hierarchy based on birth. So long as these names continue, Hindus will continue to think of the Brahmin, Kshatriya, Vaishya and Shudra as hierarchical divisions of high and low, based on birth, and act accordingly. The Hindu must be made to unlearn all this. But how can this happen if the old labels remain and continue to recall to his mind old notions. If new notions are to be inculcated in the minds of people it is necessary to give them new names. To continue the old name is to make the reform futile. To allow this *Chaturvarnya*, based on worth to be designated by such stinking labels of Brahmin, Kshatriya, Vaishya, Shudra, indicative of social divisions based on birth, is a snare.

To me this *Chaturvarnya* with its old labels, is utterly repellent and my whole being rebels against it. But I do not wish to rest my objection to *Chaturvarnya* on mere grounds of sentiments. There are more solid grounds on which I rely for my opposition to it. A close examination of this ideal has convinced me that as a system of social organization, *Chaturvarnya* is impracticable, harmful and has turned out to be a miserable failure. From a practical point of view, the system of *Chaturvarnya* raises several difficulties which its protagonists do not seem to have taken into account. The principle underlying caste is fundamentally different from the principle underlying *varna*. Not only are they fundamentally different but they are also fundamentally opposed. The former is based on worth. How are you going to compel people who have acquired a higher status based on birth without reference to their worth to vacate that status? How are you going to compel people to recognize the status due to a man in accordance with his worth, who is occupying a lower status based on his birth? For this you must first break up the caste system, in order to be able to establish the *varna* system. How are you going to reduce the four thousand castes, based on birth, to the four *varnas* based on worth? This is the first difficulty which the protagonists of the *Chaturvarnya* must grapple with. There is a second difficulty which the *Protagonists* of *Chaturvarnya* must grapple with, if they wish to make the establishment of Chaturvarnya a success.

Chaturvarnya pre-supposes that you can classify people into four definite classes. Is this possible? In this respect, the ideal of *Chaturvarnya* has, as you will see, a close affinity to the Platonic ideal. To Plato, men fell by nature into three classes. In some individuals, he believed mere appetites dominated. He assigned them to the labouring and trading classes. Others revealed to him that over and above appetites, they have a courageous disposition. He classed them as defenders in war and guardians of internal peace. Other showed a capacity to grasp the universal reason underlying things. He made them the law-givers of the people. The criticism to which Plato's Republic is subject, is also the criticism which must apply to the system of *Chaturvarnya*, in so far as it proceeds upon the possibility of an accurate classification of men into four distinct classes. The chief criticism against Plato is that his idea of lumping of individuals into a few sharply marked-off classes is a very superficial view of man and his powers. Plato had no perception of the uniqueness of every individual, of his incommensurability with others of each individual forming a class of his own. He had no recognition of the infinite diversity of active tendencies and combination of tendencies of which an individual is capable. To him there were types of faculties or powers in the individual constitution. All this is demonstrably wrong. Modern science has shown that lumping together of individuals into a few sharply marked-off classes is a superficial view of man not worthy of serious consideration. Consequently, the utilization of the qualities of individuals is incompatible with their stratification by classes, since the qualities of individuals are so variable. *Chaturvarnya* must fail for the very reason for which Plato's Republic must fail, namely, that it is not possible to pigeon men into holes, according as he belongs to one class or the other. That it is impossible to accurately classify people into four definite classes is proved by the fact that the original four classes have now become four thousand castes.

There is a third difficulty in the way of the establishment of system of *Chaturvarnya*. How are you going to maintain the system of *Chaturvarnya*, supposing it was established? One important requirement for the successful working of *Chaturvarnya* is the maintenance of the penal system which could maintain it by its sanction. The system of *Chaturvarnya* must perpetually face the problem the transgressor. Unless there is a penalty attached to the of transgression, men will not keep to their respective classes. The whole system will break down, being contrary to human nature. *Chaturvarnya* cannot subsist by its own inherent goodness. It must be enforced by law. That without penal sanction the ideal of *Chaturvarnya* cannot be realized, is proved by the story in the *Ramayana* of Rama killing Shambuka. Some people seem to blame Rama because he want only and without reason killed Shambuka. But to blame Rama for killing Shambuka is to misunderstand the whole situation. *Ram Raj* was a *Raj*-based on *Chaturvarnya*. As a king, Rama was bound to maintain *Chaturvarnya*. It was his duty therefore to kill Shambuka, the Shudra, who had transgressed his class and wanted to be a Brahmin. This is the reason why Rama killed Shambuka. But this also shows that penal sanction is necessary for the maintenance of *Chaturvarnya*. Not only penal sanction is necessary, but penalty of death is necessary. That is why Rama did not inflict on Shambuka a lesser punishment. That is why *Manusmriti* prescribes such heavy sentences as cutting off the tongue or pouring of molten lead in the ears of the Shudra, who recites or hear the Veda. The supporters of *Chaturvarnya* must give an assurance that they could successfully classify men and they could induce modern society in the twentieth century to reforge the penal sanctions of *Manusmriti.*

The protagonists of *Chaturvarnya* do not seem to have consider what is to happen to women in their system. Are they also to be divided into four classes, Brahmin, Kshatriya, Vaishya and Shudra? or are they to be allowed to take the status of their husbands. If the status of the woman is to be the consequence of marriage what become of the underlying principle of *Chaturvarnya*, namely, that the status of person should be based upon the worth of that person? If they are to be classified according to their worth is their classification to be nominal or real? If it is to be nominal then it is useless and then the protagonists of *Chaturvarnya* must admit that their system does not apply to women. If it is real, are the protagonists of *Chaturvarnya* prepared to follow the logical consequences of applying it to women? They must be prepared to have women priests and women soldiers. Hindu society has grown accustomed to women teachers and women teachers and women butchers. But he would be bold person, who would say that it will allow women priests women soldiers. But that will be the logical outcome of applying *Chaturvarnya* to women. Given these difficulties, I think no one except congenital idiot could hope and believe in a successful regeneration of the *Chaturvarnya*.

Assuming that *Chaturvarnya* is practicable, I contend that it is most vicious system. That the Brahmin should cultivate knowledge that the Kshatriya should bear arms, that the Vaishya should trade and that the Shudra should serve sounds as though it was a system of division of labour. Whether the theory was intended to state that the Shudra need not or that whether it was intended to lay down that be must not, is an interesting question. The defenders of *Chaturvarnya* give it the rust meaning. They say, why should the Shudra need trouble to acquire wealth, when the three *varnas* are there to support him? Why need the Shudra bother to take to education, when there is the Brahmin to whom he can go when the occasion for reading or writing arises? Why need the Shudra worry to arm himself because there is the Kshatriya to protect him? The theory of *Chaturvarnya*. understood in this sense, may be said to look upon the Shudra as the ward and the three *varnas* as his guardians. Thus interpreted, it is a simple, elevating and alluring theory. Assuming this to be the correct view of the underlying conception of *Chaturvarnya*, it seems to me that the system is neither fool-proof nor knave-proof. What is to happen, if the Brahmins, Vaishyas and Kshatriyas fail to pursue knowledge, to engage in economic enterprise and to be efficient soldiers, which are their respective functions? Contrary-wise, suppose that they discharge their functions but flout their duty to the Shudra or to one another what is to happen to the Shudra or for the matter of that of the Vaishya and Kshatriya when the person who is trying to take advantage of his ignorance is the Brahmin? Who is to defend the liberty of the Shudra and for the matter of that, of the Brahmin and the Vaishya when the person who is robbing him of it is the Kshatriya? Inter-dependence of one class on another is inevitable. Even dependence of one class upon another may sometimes become allowable. But why make one person depend upon another in the matter of his vital needs? Education everyone must have. Means of defence everyone must have. These are the paramount requirements of every man for his self-preservation.

How can the fact that his neighbour is educated and armed help a man who is uneducated and disarmed. The whole theory is absurd. These are the questions, which the defenders of *Chaturvarnya* do not seem to be bothered about. But they are very pertinent questions. Assuming their conception of *Chaturvarnya* that the relationship between the different classes is that of ward and guardian is the real conception underlying *Chaturvarnya*. It must be admitted that it makes no provision to safeguard the interests of the ward from the misdeeds of the guardian. Whether the relationship of guardian and ward was the real underlying conception, on which *Chaturvarnya* was based, there is no doubt that in practice the relation was that of master and servants. The three classes, Brahmins, Kshatriyas and Vaishyas although not very happy in their mutual relationship managed to work by compromise. The Brahmin flattered the Kshatriya and both let the Vaishya live in order to be able to live upon him. But the three agreed to beat down the Shudra. He was not allowed to acquire wealth lest he should be independent of the three *varnas*. He was prohibited from bearing arms lest he should have means to rebel against their authority. That this is how the Shudra were treated by the Tryavarnibs is evidenced by the laws of Manu. There is no code of laws more infamous regarding social rights than the Laws of Manu. Any instance from anywhere of social injustice must pale before it. Why have the mass of people tolerated the evils to which they have been subjected? There have been social revolutions in other countries of the world. Why have were not been social revolutions in India is a question which has incessantly troubled me. There is only one answer, which I can give and it is that the lower classes of Hindus have been completely disabled for direct action on account of this wretched system of *Chaturvarnya*. They could not bear arms and without arms they could not rebel. They were all ploughmen or rather condemned to be ploughmen and they never were allowed to convert their ploughshare into swords. They had no bayonets and therefore everyone who chose could and did sit upon them. On account of the *Chaturvarnya*, they could receive no education. They could neither think out nor know the way to their salvation. They were condemned to be lowly and not knowing the way of escape and not having the means of escape, they became reconciled to eternal servitude, which they accepted as their inescapable fate. It is true that even in Europe the strong has not shrunk from the exploitation, nay the spoliation of the weak. But in Europe, the strong have never contrived to make the weak helpless against exploitation so shamelessly as was the case among the Hindus. Social war has been raging between the strong and the weak far more violently in Europe than it has ever been in India, the weak in Europe has had in his freedom of military service his physical weapon, in suffering his political weapon and in education his moral weapon. These weapons for emancipation were never withheld by the strong from the weak in Europe. All these weapons were, however, denied to the masses in India by *Chaturvarnya*. Their cannot be a more degrading system of social organization than *Chaturvarnya*. It is the system which deadens, paralyses and cripples the people from helpful activity. This no exaggeration. History bears ample evidence, there is only one period in Indian history which is period of freedom, greatness and glory. That is the period of the Maurya Empire. At all other times the country suffered from defeat and darkness. But the Maurya period was a period when *Chaturvamya* was completely annihilated, when the Shudra, who constituted the mass of the people, came into their own and became the rulers of the country. The period of defeat and darkness is the period when *Chaturvarnya* flourished to the damnation of the greater pan of the people of the country.

Chaturvarnya is not new. It is as old as the Vedas. That is one of the reasons why we are asked by the Arya Samajists to consider its claims. Judging from the past as a system of social organization, it has been tried and it has failed. How many times have the Brahmins annihilated seed of the Kshatriyas. How many times have the Kshatriyas annihilated the Brahmins! The *Mahabharata* and the *Puranas* are full of incidents of the strife between the Brahmins and the Kshatriyas. They even quarrelled over such petty questions as to who should salute first, as to who should give way first, the Brahmins or the Kshatriyas, when the two met in the street not only was the Brahmin, an eyesore to the Kshatriya and the Kshatriya an eyesore to the Brahmin, it seems that the Kshatriyas had become tyrannical and the masses, disarmed as they were under the system of *Chaturvarnya*, were praying Almighty God for relief from their tyranny. The Bhagwat tells us very definitely that Krishna had taken *Avtar* for one sacred purpose and that was to annihilate the Kshatriyas. With these instances of rivalry and enmity between the different Varnas before us. I do not understand how any one can hold out *Chaturvarnya* as a ideal to be aimed at or as a pattern, on which the Hindu society should be remodelled.

I have dealt with those, who are without you and whose hostility to your ideal is quite open. There appear to be others, who are neither without you nor with you. I was hesitating whether I should deal with their point of view. But on further consideration I have come to the conclusion that I must and that for two reasons. Firstly, their attitude to the problem of caste is not merely an attitude of neutrality, but is an attitude of armed neutrality. Secondly, they probably represent a considerable body of people. Of these, there is one set, which finds nothing neither peculiar nor odious in the caste system of the Hindus. Such Hindus cite the case of Muslims, Sikhs and Christians and find comfort in the fact that they too have castes amongst them. In considering this question you must at the outset bear in mind that nowhere is human society one single whole. It is always plural. In the world of action, the individual is one limit and society the other. Between them lie all sorts of associative arrangements of lesser and larger scope, families, friendship, co-operative associations, business combines, political parties, bands of thieves and robbers. These small groups are usually firmly welded together and are often as exclusive as castes. They have a narrow and intensive code, which is often anti-social. This is true of every society, in Europe as well as in Asia. The question to be asked in determining whether a given society is an ideal society; is not whether there are groups in it, because groups exist in all societies. The questions to be asked in determining what is an ideal society are how numerous and varied are the interests which are consciously shared by the groups? How full and free is the inter play with other forms of associations? Are the forces that separate groups and classes more numerous than the forces that unite? What social significance is attached to this group life? Is its exclusiveness a mallet of custom and convenience or is it a matter *of religion*? It is in the light of these questions that one must decide whether caste among non-Hindus is the same as caste among Hindus. If we apply these considerations to castes among Mohammedan, Sikhs and Christians on the one hand and to castes among Hindus on the other you will find that caste among non-Hindus is fundamentally different from caste among Hindus. First, the ties, which consciously make the Hindus, hold together, are non-existent, while among non-Hindus there are many that holds them together. The strength of a society depends upon the presence of points of contact, possibilities of interaction between different groups, which exist in it. These are what Carlyle calls "organic filaments", i.e., the elastic thread which help to bring the disintegrating elements together and to reunite them. There is no integrating force among the Hindus to counteract the disintegration caused by caste. While among the non-Hindus there are plenty of these organic filaments which bind them together. Again it must be borne in mind that although there are castes among non-Hindus as there are among Hindus, caste has not the same social significance for non-Hindus as it has for Hindus.

Mohammedan or a Sikh, who is? He tells one that he is a Mohammedan or a Sikh as the case may be. He does not tell one his caste although he has one and one are satisfied with his answer. When he tells One that he is a Muslim, One do not proceed to ask him whether he is a Shiya or Suni; Sheikh or Saiyad; *Khatik* or *Pinjari*. When he tells One he is a Sikh. One does not ask him whether he is Jat or

Roda; Mazbi or Ramdas. But one are not satisfied if a person tells One that he is a Hindu. One feel bound to inquire into his caste. Why? Because so essential is caste in the case of a Hindu that without knowing it One do not feel sure what sort of a being he is. That caste has not the same significance among non-Hindus as it has among Hindus is clear if One take into consideration the consequences, which follow breach of caste. There may be castes among Sikhs and Mohammedans but the Sikhs and the Moharmmedan will not outcast a Sikh or a Mohammedan if, he broke his caste. Indeed the very idea of excommunication is foreign to the Sikhs and the Mohammedans. But with the Hindus the case is entirely different. He is sure to be outcasted if he broke caste. This shows the difference in the social significance of caste to Hindus and Non-Hindus. This is the second point of difference. Caste among the non-Hindus caste is only a practice, not a sacred institution. They did not originate it. With them it is only a survival. They do not regard caste as a religious dogma. Religion compels the Hindus to treat isolation and segregation of caste as a virtue. Religion does not compel the non-Hindus to take the same attitude towards caste. If Hindus wish to break caste, their religion will come in their way. But it will not be so in the case of Non-Hindus. It is therefore, a dangerous delusion to take comfort in the mere existence of caste among Non-Hindus, without caring to know what place caste occupies in their life and whether there are other "organic filaments", which subordinate the feeling of caste to the feeling of community. The sooner the Hindus are cured of this delusion the better.

Hindus and Problems

The other set denies that caste presents any problem at all for the Hindus to consider. Such Hindus seek comfort in the view that the Hindus have survived and take this as a proof of their fitness to survive. This point of view is well expressed by Dr. S. Radhakrishnan in his *Hindu View of Life*. Referring to Hinduism he says, "The civilisation itself has not been a shortlived one. Its historic records date back for over four thousand years and even then it had reached a stage of civilization which has continued its unbroken though at times slow and static, course until the present day. It has stood the stress and strain of more than four or five millenniums of spiritual thought and experience. Though peoples of different races and cultures have been pouring into India from the dawn of History, Hinduism has been able to maintain its supremacy and even the proselytizing creeds backed by political power have not been able to coerce the large majority of Hindus to their views. The Hindu culture possesses some vitality; which seems to be denied to some other more forceful currents. It is no more necessary to dissect Hinduism than to open a tree to see whether the sap still runs. The name of Dr. Radhakrishnan is big enough to invest with profundity whatever he says and impress the minds of his readers. But one must not hesitate to speak out my mind. It seems that the question is not whether a community, lives or dies; the question is on what plane does it live. There are different modes of survival. But all are not equally honourable. For an individual as well as for a society, there is a gulf between merely living and living worthily. To fight in a battle and to live in glory is one mode. To beat a retreat, to surrender and to live the life of a captive is also a mode of survival. It is useless for a Hindu to lake comfort in the fact that he and his people have survived. What he must consider is what is the quality of their survival. If he does that, I am sure he will cease to take pride in the mere fact of survival. A Hindu's life has been a life of continuous defeat and what appears to him to be life everlasting is not living everlastingly but is really a life which is perishing everlastingly. It is a mode of survival of which every right-minded Hindu, who is not afraid to own up the truth will feel ashamed.

There is no doubt in my opinion, that unless one change the social order one can achieve little by way of progress. One cannot mobilize the community either for defence or for offence. One cannot build anything on the foundations of caste. One cannot build up a nation, one cannot build up a morality. Anything that one will build on the foundations of caste will crack and will never be a whole.

The only question that remains to be considered is How to bring about the reform of the Hindu social order? How to abolish caste? This is a question of supreme importance. There is a view that in the reform of caste, the first step take, is to abolish sub-castes. This view is based upon the supposition that there is a greater similarity in manners and status between sub-castes than there is between castes. I think, this is an erroneous supposition. The Brahmins of Northern and Central India are socially of lower grade, as compared with the Brahmins of the Deccan and Southern India. The former are only cooks and water-carriers while the latter occupy a high social position. On the other hand, in Northern India, the Vaishyas and Kshatriyas are intellectually and socially on a par with the Brahmins of the Deccan and Southern India. Again, in the matter of food there is no similarity between the Brahmins of the Deccan and southern India, who are vegetarians and the Brahmins of Kashmir and Bengal who are non-vegetarians. On the other hand, the Brahmins of the Deccan and Southern India have more in common so far as food is concerned with such non-Brahmins as the Gujaratis, Marwaris, Banias and Jains. There is no doubt that from the standpoint of making the transit from one caste to another easy, the fusion of the Kayasthas of Northern India and the other non-Brahmins of Southern India with the non-Brahmins of Southern India with non-Brahmins of the Deccan and the Dravid country is more practicable than the fusion of the Brahmins of the South with the Brahmins of the North. But assuming that the fusion of sub-castes is possible, what guarantee is there that the abolition of sub-castes will necessarily lead to the abolition of castes? On the contrary, it may happen that the process may stop with the abolition of sub-castes. In that case, the abolition of sub-castes will only help to strengthen the castes and make them more powerful and therefore more mischievous. This remedy is therefore neither practicable nor effective and may easily prove to be a wrong remedy. Another plan of action for the abolition of caste is to begin with inter-caste dinners. This also, in my opinion, is an inadequate remedy. There are many castes which allow intercaste dining. But it is a common experience that inter-dining has not succeeded in killing the spirit of caste and the consciousness of caste. I am convinced that the remedy is inter-marriage. Fusion of blood can alone create the feeling of being kith and kin and unless this feeling of kinship, of being kindred, becomes paramount in the separatist feeling; the feeling of being aliencreated by caste will not vanish. Among the Hindus inter-marriage must necessarily be a factor of greater force in social life than it need be in the life of the non-Hindus. Where society is already well-knit by other ties, marriage is an ordinary incident of life. But where society cut asunder, marriage as a binding force becomes a matter of urgent necessity. The real remedy for breaking caste is inter-marriage. Nothing else will serve as the solvent of caste. One *Jat-Pat-Todak Mandal* has adopted this line of attack. It is direct and frontal attack, and I congratulate one upon a correct diagnosis and more upon One having shown the courage to tell the Hindus what is really wrong with them. Political tyranny is nothing compared to social tyranny and a reformer who defies society, is a much more courageous man than a politician, who defies government. One are right in holding that caste will cease to be an operative force only when inter-dining and inter-marriage have become matters of common exercise. One have located the source of the disease. But is One option the right prescription for the disease? Ask yourself this question; Why is it that average majority of Hindus do not inter-dine and do not inter-marry? Why is it that the cause is not popular? There can be only one answer to this question and it is that inter-dining and inter-marriage are repugnant to the beliefs and dogmas which the Hindus regard as sacred. Caste is not a physical object like a wall of bricks or a line of barbed wire which prevents the Hindus from co-mingling and which has, therefore, to be pulled down. Caste is a notion, it is a state of the mind. The destruction of caste does not therefore mean the destruction of a physical barrier. It means a notional change. Caste may be bad. Caste may lead to conduct so gross as to be called man's inhumanity to man. All the same it must be recognized that the Hindus observe caste not because they are inhuman or wrong headed. They observe caste because they are deeply religious. People are not wrong in observing caste. In my view, what is wrong is their religion which has inculcated this notion of caste. If this is correct, then obviously the enemy One must grapple with, is not the people who observe caste but the *Shastras* which teach them this religion of caste. Criticizing and ridiculing people for not inter-dining or inter-marriages, is a futile method of achieving the desired end. The real remedy is to destroy the belief in the sanctity of the *Shastras*. How can one expect to succeed if one allows the *Shastras* to continue to mould the beliefs and opinions of the people? Not to question the authority of the *Shastras*, to permit the people to believe in their sanctity and their sanctions and to blame them and to criticize them for their acts as being irrational and inhuman is a incongruous way of carrying on social reform. Reformers working for the removal of untouchability including Mahatma Gandhi do not seem to realize that the acts of the people are merely the results of their beliefs inculcated upon their minds by the *Shastras* and that people will not change their conduct until they cease to believe in the sanctity of the *Shastras* on which their conduct is founded. No wonder that such efforts have not produced any results. One also seem to be erring in the same way as the reformers working in the cause of removing untouchability. To agitate for and to organise inter-caste dinners and inter-caste marriages is like forced feeding brought about by artificial means.

It is no use seeking refuge in quibbles. It is no use telling people that the *Shastras* do not say what they are believed to say grammatically read or logically interpreted. What matters is how the Shastras have been understood by the people. One must take the stand that Buddha took. One must take the stand which Guru Nanak Dev took. One must not only discuss the Shastras One must deny their authority as did Gautam Buddha and Guru Nanak Dev. One must have courage to tell the Hindus, that what is wrong with them is their religion—the religion which has produced in them this notion of the sacredness of caste. Will One show that courage?

Chances of Success

What are the chances of success? Social reforms fall

into different species. There is a species of reform which does not relate to the religious notion of people but is purely secular in character. There is also a species of reform which relates to the religious notions of people. Of such a species of reform there are two varieties. In one, the reform accords with the principles of the religion and merely invite people who have departed from it, to revert to them and to follow them. The second is a reform which not only touches the religious principles but is diametrically opposed to those principles and invite people to depart from and to discard with authority and to act contrary to those principles. Caste is the natural outcome of certain religious beliefs which have the sanction of the *Shastras* which are believed to contain the command of divinely inspired sages who were endowed with a supernatural wisdom and whose commands, therefore, cannot be disobeyed without committing sin. The destruction of caste is a reform which falls under the third category. To ask people to give up caste is, to ask them to go contrary to their fundamental religious notions. It is obvious that the first and second species of reform are easy. But the third is a stupendous task, well-nigh impossible. The Hindus hold to the sacredness of the social order. Caste has a divine basis One must therefore destroy the sacredness and divinity with which caste has become invested.

The Brahmins form the vanguard of the movement for political reform and in some cases also of economic reform. But they are not to be found even as camp-followers in the army raised to break down the barricades of caste. Is there any hope of the Brahmins ever taking up a lead in the future in this matter? I say no. One may ask why? One may argue that there is no reason why Brahmins should continue to shun the social reform. One may argue that the Brahmins know that the bane of Hindu society is caste and as an enlightened class could not expected to be indifferent to its consequences. One may argue that there are secular Brahmins and priestly Brahmins and if the latter do not take up the cudgels on behalf of those who want to break caste, the former will. All this of course sounds very plausible. But in all this it is forgotten that the break up of the caste system is bound to affect adversely the Brahmin caste. Having regard to this, it is reasonable to expect that the Brahmins will ever consent to lead a movement the ultimate result of which is to destroy the power and prestige of the Brahmins caste? Is it reasonable to expect the secular Brahmins and priestly Brahmins. Both are kith and kin. They are two arms of the same body and one bound to fight for the existence of the other. I am reminded of some very pregnant remarks made by Prof. Dicey in his English constitution.

Speaking of the actual limitation on the legislative supremacy of parliament, Dicey says: "The actual exercise of authority by any sovereign whatever and notably by parliament, is bounded or controlled by two limitations. Of these the one is an external and the other is an internal limitation. The external limit to the real power of a sovereign consists in the possibility or certainty that his subjects or a large number of them will disobey or resist his laws. The internal limit to the exercise of sovereignty arises from the nature of the sovereign power itself. Even a despot exercises his powers in accordance with his character, which is itself moulded by the circumstances under which he lives, including under that head the moral feelings of the time and the society to which he belongs. The Sultan could not, if he could, change the religion of the Mohammedan world, but even if he could do so, it is in the very highest degree improbable that the head of Mohammedanism should wish to overthrow the religion of Mohammed; the internal check on the exercise of the Sultan's power is at least as strong as the external limitation. People sometimes ask the idle question, why the Pope does not introduce this or that reform? The true answer is that a revolutionist is not the kind of man who becomes a Pope and that a man who becomes a Pope has no wish to be a revolutionist. I think these remarks apply equally to the Brahman of India and one can say with equal truth that if a man who becomes a Pope has no wish to become a revolutionary, a man who is born a Brahmin has much less desire to become a revolutionary.

Some may say that it is a matter of small concern

whether the Brahmins come forward to lead the movement against caste or whether they do not take this view to ignore the part played by the intellectual class in the community. Whether one accepts the theory of the great man as the maker of history or whether one does not, this much one will have to concede that in every country the intellectual class is the most influential class, if not the governing class. The intellectual class is the class which can foresee, it is the class which can advise and give lead. In no country does the mass of the people live the life of intelligent thought and action. It is largely imitative and follows the intellectual class. There is no exaggeration in saying that the entire destiny of a country depends upon its intellectual class. If the intellectual class is honest, independent and disinterested it can be trusted to take the initiative and give a proper lead when a crisis arises. It is true that intellect by itself is no virtue. It is only a means and use of means depends upon the ends which an intellectual person pursues. An intellectual man can be a good man but he can easily be bad. Similarly an intellectual class may be a band or high—souled persons, ready to help, ready to emancipate erring humanity or it may easily be a gang of crooks or a body of advocates of a narrow clique from which it draws its support. One may think it a pity that the intellectual class in India is simply another name for the Brahmin caste. One may regret that the two are one that the existence of the intellectual class should share the interest and the aspirations of that Brahmin caste. Which has regarded itself the custodian of the interest of that caste, rather than of the interests of the country. All this may be very regrettable. But the fact remains, that the Brahmins form the intellectual class of the Hindus. It is not only an intellectual class but it is a class which is held in great reverence by the rest of the Hindus. The Hindus are taught that the Brahmins are *Bhudevas* (Gods on earth). The Hindus are taught that Brahmins alone can be their teachers. Manu says, "If it be asked how it should be with respect to points of the *Dharma* which have not been specially mentioned" the answer is that which Brahmins who are Shishthas propound shall doubtless have legal force.

When such an intellectual class, which holds the rest of the community in its grip, is opposed to the reform of caste, the chances of success in a movement for the break-up of the caste system appear to be very very remote.

The second reason, why I say the task is impossible, will be clear if one will bear in mind that the caste system has two aspects. In one of its aspects, it divides men into separate communities. In its second aspect it places these communities in a graded order one above the other in social status. Each caste takes its pride and its consolation in the fact that in the scale of castes it is above some other caste. As an outward mark of this gradation, there is also a gradation of social and religious rights technically spoken of an *Ashtadhikaras* and *Sanskars*. The higher the grade of a caste, the greater the number of these rights and the lower the grade the lesser their number. Now this gradation; this scaling of castes, makes it impossible to organise a common front against the caste system. If a caste claims the right to inter-dine and inter-marry with another caste placed above it, it is frozen instantly, it is told by mischief-mongers, and there are many Brahmans amongst such mischief mongers, that it will have to concede inter-dining and inter-marriage with castes below it. All are slaves of the caste system. But all the slaves are not equal in status. To excite the proletariat to bring about an economic revolution, Karl Marx told them: "You have nothing to lose except your chains;" But the artful way in which the social and some have less, makes the slogan of Karl Marx quite useless to excite the Hindus against the caste system. Castes form a graded system of sovereignties, high and low, which are jealous of their status and which know that if a general dissolution came, some of them stand to lose more of their prestige and power than others do. One cannot, therefore, have a general mobilization of the Hindus, to use a military expression, for an attack on the caste system.

Can one appeal to reason and ask the Hindus to discard Caste as being contrary to reason? That raises the question. Is a Hindu free to follow his reason? Manu has laid down three sanctions to which every Hindu must conform in the matter of his behaviour. Here there is no place for reason to play its part. A Hindu must follow either *Veda, Smriti* or *Sadachar*. He cannot follow anything else. In the first place how are the texts of the *Vedas* and *Smritis* to be interpreted whenever any doubt arises regarding their meaning? On this important question the view of Manu is quite definite.

Vedas and Smritis

According to this rule, rationalism as a cannon of interpreting the *Vedas* and *Smritis*, is absolutely condemned. Thus, where a matter is covered by the *Veda* or the *Smriti*, a Hindu cannot resort to rational thinking. Even when there is a conflict between *Veda* and *Smritis* on matters on which they have given a positive injunction, the solution is not left to reason. When there is a conflict between two *Shrutis*, both are to be regarded as of equal authority. Either of them may be followed. No attempt is to be made to find out which of the two accords with reason. This is made clear by Manu "When there is a conflict between *Shruti* and *Smriti*, the *Shruti* must prevail." But here too, no attempt must be made to find out which of the two accords with reason.

Again, when there is a conflict between two *Smritis*, the *Manu—Smriti* must prevail, but no attempt is to be made to find out which of the two accords with reason.

It is, therefore, clear that in any matter on which the *Shrutis* and *Smritis* have given a positive direction, a Hindu is not free to use his reasoning faculty. He must abide by their directions. The caste and *varna* are matters which are dealt with by the *Vedas* and the *Smritis* and consequently, appeal to reason can have no effect on a Hindu. So far as caste and *varna* are concerned, not only the Shastras do not permit the Hindu to use his reason in the decision of the question, but they have taken care to see that no occasion is left to examine in a rational way the foundations of his belief in caste and *varna*. It must be a source of silent amusement to many a non-Hindu to find hundreds and thousands of Hindus breaking caste on certain occasions, such as railway journey and foreign travel and yet endeavouring to maintain caste for the rest of their lives. The explanation of this phenomenon discloses another fetter on the reasoning faculties of the Hindus. Man's life is generally habitual and unreflective. Reflective thought, in the sense of active, persistent and careful consideration of any belief is supposed form or knowledge in the light of the grounds that support and further conclusions to which it tends, is quite rare and arises only in a situation which presents a dilemma—a crisis. Railway journey and foreign travels are really occasions of crisis in the life of a Hindu and it is natural to expect a Hindu to ask himself why he should maintain caste at all, if he cannot maintain it at all times. But he does not breaks caste at one step and proceeds to observe it at the next without raising any question. The reason for this astonishing conduct is to be found in the rule of the *Shastras,* which directs him to maintain caste as far as possible and to undergo *prayaschita* when he cannot. By this theory of *prayaschita,* the *Shastras* by following a spirit of compromise have given, caste a perpetual lease of life and have smothered reflective thought which would have otherwise led to the destruction of the notion of caste.

There have been many who have worked in the cause of the abolition of caste and untouchability. Of those, who can be mentioned, Ramanuja, Kabir and others stand out prominently. Can you appeal to the acts of these reformers and exhort the Hindus to follow them ?   It is true that Manu has included *Sadachar* as one of the sanctions along with *Shruti* and *Smriti.* Indeed, *Sadachar* has been given a higher place than *Shastras.*

According to this, *Sadachar,* whether, it is *Dharma* or *Adharma* in accordance with *Shastras* or contrary to *Shastras,* must be followed. But what is the meaning of *Sadachar?* If any one were to suppose that *Sadachar* means right or good acts, i.e., acts of good and righteous men he would find himself greatly mistaken. *Sadachar* does not mean good acts or acts of good men. It means ancient custom good or bad.

Sadachar and Good Acts

As though to warn people against the view that *Sadachar* means good acts or acts of good men and fearing that people might understand it that way and follow the acts of good men, the *Smritis* have commanded the Hindus is unmistakable terms not to follow even Gods in their good deeds, if they are contrary to *Shruti, Smriti* and *Sadachar.* This may sound to be most extraordinary, most perverse, but the fact remains that is an injunction, issued to the Hindus by their *Shastras.* Reason and morality are the two most powerful weapons in the armoury of a reformer. To deprive him of the use of these weapons is to disable him for action. How are we going to break up caste if people are not free to consider whether it accords with reason? How is one going to break up caste if people are not free to consider whether it accords with morality? The wall built around caste is impregnable and the material, of which it is built contains none of the combustible stuff of reason and morality. Add to this the fact that inside this wall stands the army of Brahmins, who form the intellectual class, Brahmins who are the natural leaders of the Hindus, Brahmins who are there not as mere mercenary soldiers but as any army fighting for its homeland and one will get, an idea why we think that breaking-up of caste amongst the Hindus is well-nigh impossible. At any rate it would take ages before a breach is made. But whether the doing of the deed takes time or whether it can be done quickly, one must not forget that if we wish to bring about a breach in the system then we have got to apply the dynamite to the *Vedas* and the *Shastras*, which deny any part to reason, to *Vedas* and *Shastras*, which deny any part to morality. One must destroy the Religion of the *Shrutis* and the *Smritis*. Nothing else will avail. This is my considered view of the matter.

Some may not understand what I mean by destruction of Religion; some may find the idea revolting to them and some may find it revolutionary. Let me therefore explain my position. I do not know whether we draw distinction between principle and rules. But I do not only I make a distinction but I say that this distinction is real and important. Rules are practical; they are habitual ways of doing things according to prescription. But principles are intellectual; they are useful methods of judging things. Rules seek to tell an agent just what course of action to pursue. Principles do not prescribe a specific course of action. Rules like cooking recipes do tell just what to do and how to do it. A principle, such as that of justice, supplies a main head by reference to which he is to consider the bearings of his desires and purposes, it guides him in his thinking by suggesting to him the important consideration which he should bear in mind. This difference between rules and principles makes the acts done in pursuit of them different in quality and in content. Doing what is said to be good by virtue of a rule and doing good in the light of a principle are two different things. The principle may be wrong but the act is conscious and responsible. The rule may be right but the act is mechanical. A religious act may not be a correct act but must at least be a responsible act to permit of this responsibility. Religion must mainly be a matter of principles only. It cannot be a matter of rules. The moment it degenerates into rules it ceases to be religion as it kills responsibility which is the essence of a truly religious act what is this Hindu religion? Is it a set of principles or is it a code of rules? Now the Hindu religion, as contained in the *Vedas* and the *Smritis*, is nothing but a mass of sacrificial, social, political and sanitary rules and regulations all mixed up. What is called religion by the Hindus is nothing but a multitude of commands and prohibitions. Religion in the sense of spiritual principles truly universal applicable to all races to all countries to all times is not to be found in them and if it is it does not form the governing part of a Hindu's life. That for a Hindu *Dharma* means commands and prohibitions is clear from the way the word *Dharma* is used in *Vedas* and the *Smritis* and understood by the commentators. The word *Dharma* as used in the Vedas in most cases means religious ordinances or rites. Even Jaimini in his *Purva Mimansa* defines *Dharma* as a "desirable goal or result that is indicated by injunctive (Vedic) passages". To put it in plain language, what the Hindus call religion is really Law or at best legalized' class-ethics. Frankly, I refuse to call this code of ordinances, religion. The first evil of such a code of ordinances, misrepresented the people as religion is that it tends to deprive moral life of freedom and spontaneity and to reduce it (for the conscientious as any rate) to a more or less anxious and survial conformity to externally imposed rules. Under it, there is no loyalty to ideals there is only conformity to commands. But the worst evil of this code of ordinances is that the laws it contains must be the same yesterday, today and forever. They are iniquitous in that they are not the same for one class as for another. But this iniquity is made perpetual in that they are prescribed to be the same for all generations. The objectionable part of such a scheme is not that they are made by certain persons called Prophets or Law-givers. The objectionable part is that this code has been invested with the character of finality and fixity. Happiness notoriously varies with the conditions and circumstances of a person, as well as with the conditions of different people and epochs. That being me case, how can humanity endure this code of eternal laws, without being cramped and without being crippled? I have, therefore, no hesitation in saying that such a religion must be destroyed and I say, there is nothing religious in working for the destruction of such a religion. Indeed I hold that it is your bounded duty to tear the mask, to remove the misrepresentation mat as caused by misnaming this law as Religion. This is an essential step for all of us. Once one clears the minds of the people of this misconception and enable them to realize that what they are told as religion is not religion but that it is really Law, One will be in a position to urge for its amendment or abolition. So long as people look upon it as Religion they will not be ready; for a change, because the idea of religion is generally speaking not associated with the idea of change. But the idea of law is associated with the idea of change and when people come to know that what is called religion is really law, old and archaic,they will be ready for a change, for people know and accept that a law can be changed.

Necessity of Religion

While I condemn a Religion of Rules, I must not be understood to hold the opinion that there is no necessity for a religion. On the contrary, I agree with Burke when he says that, "True religion is the foundation of society, the basis on which all true civil government rests, and both their sanction." Consequently, when I urge that these ancient rules of life be annulled, I am anxious that its place shall be taken by a religion of Principles, which alone can claim to being a true religion. Indeed, I am so convinced of the necessity of religion that I feel I ought to tell one in outline what I regard as necessary items in this religious reform. The following in my opinion should be the cardinal items in the reform:

(1) There should be one and only one standard book of Hindu Religion, acceptable to all Hindus and recognized by all Hindus. This, of course, means that all other books of Hindu religion such as *Vedas, Shastras* and *Puranas,* which are treated as sacred and authoritative, must by law cease to be so and the preaching of any doctrine, religious or social contained in these books should be panelized.

(2) It should be better if priesthood among Hindus if was abolished. But as this seems to be impossible. The priesthood must at least cease to be hereditary. Every person who professes to be a Hindu must be eligible for being a priest. It should be provided by law that no Hindu shall be entitled to be priest unless he has passed an examination prescribed by the State and holds a *sanad* from the stale permitting him to practise.

(3) No ceremony performed by a priest who does not hold a *sanad* shall be deemed to be valid in law and it should be made penal for a person who has no *sanad* to officiate as a priest.

(4) A priest should be the servant of the State and should be subject to the disciplinary action by the State in the matter of his morals, beliefs, and worship, in addition to his being subject along with other citizens the ordinary law of the land.

(5) The number of priest should be limited by law according to the requirements of the State as is done in the case of the I.C.S. To some, this may sound radical. But to my mind there is nothing revolutionary in this. Every profession in India is regulated. Engineers must show proficiency. Doctor must show proficiency. Lawyers must show proficiency before they are allowed to practise their professions. During the whole of their career they must not only obey the law of the land civil as well as criminal;

but they must also obey the special code of morals prescribed by their respective professions. The priest is the only profession where proficiency is not required. The profession of a Hindu priest is the only profession which is not subject to any code. Mentally a priest may be an idiot, physically a priest may be suffering from a foul disease such as syphilis or gonorrhea, morally he may be a wreck. But he is fit to officiate at solemn ceremonies, to enter the sanctum sanctorum of Hindu temple and worship the Hindu God. All this becomes possible among the Hindus because for a priest it is enough to be born in priestly caste. The whole thing is abominable and is due to the fact that the priestly class among Hindus is subject neither to law nor morality. It recognize no duties. It knows only of rights and privilege. It is a pest which divinity seems to have let loose on the masses for the mental and moral degradation. The priestly class must be brought under control by some such legislation as I have outlined above. It will prevent it from doing mischief and from misguiding people. It will demonstrate it by throwing it open to every one. It will certainly help to kill the Brahminism and will also help to kill caste, which is nothing but Brahminism incarnate. Brahminism is the poison which has spoiled Hinduism. One will succeed in saving Hinduism if we will kill Brahminism. There should be no opposition to this reform from any quarter. It should be welcomed even by the Arya Samajists, because this is merely an application of their own doctrine of *guna-karma.*

Whether we do that or we do not we must give a new doctrinal basis to other religion—a basis that will be in consonance with Liberty, Equality and Fraternity, in short with Democracy. I am no authority on the subject. But I am told that for such religious principles as will be in consonance with Liberty, Equality and Fraternity it may not be necessary for us to borrow from foreign sources and that one could draw for such principles on the Upanishads. Whether we could do so without a complete remoulding, a considerable scraping and chipping off the ore they contain, is more than I can say. This means a complete change in the fundamental notions of life. It means a complete change in the values of life. If means a complete change in outlook and in attitude towards men and things. It means conversion; but if we do not like the word, I will say, it means new life. But a new life cannot enter a body that is dead. New life can enter only in a new body. The old body must die before a new body can come into existence and a new life can enter into it. To put it simply, the old must cease to be operative before the new can begin to enliven and to pulsate. This is what I meant when I said one must discard the authority of the *Shastras* and destroy the religion of the *Shastras*.

Beliefs and Morals

In the first place, the Hindus must consider whether it is sufficient to take the placid view of the anthropologist that there is nothing to be said about the beliefs, morals and outlooks on life, which obtain among the different peoples of the world except that they often differ, or whether it is not necessary to make an attempt to find out what kind of morality, beliefs, habits and outlook have worked best and have enabled those who possessed them to flourish, to go strong, to people the earth and to have dominion over it. As is observed by Prof. Carver: "Morality and religion, as the organised expression of moral approval, and disapproval, must be regarded as factors in the struggle for existence as truly as are weapons for offence and defence, teeth and claws, horns and hoofs, furs and feathers. The social group, community, tribe or nation, which develops an unworkable scheme of morality or within which those social acts which weaken it and unfit it for survival, habitually create the sentiment of approval, while those which would strengthen and enable it to be expanded habitually create the sentiment of disapproval, will eventually be eliminated. It is its habits of approval or disapproval (these are the results of religion and morality) that handicap it, as really as the possession of two wings on one side with none on the other will handicap the colony of flies. It would be as futile in the one case as in the other to argue that one system is just as good as another". Morality and religion therefore, are not mere matters of likes and dislikes. One may dislike exceedingly a scheme of morality, which, if universally practised within a nation would make that nation the strongest nation on the face of the earth. Yet in spite of one's dislike such a nation will become strong. One may, like exceedingly a scheme of morality and an ideal of justice, which if universally practised within a nation, would make it unable to hold its own in the struggle with other nations. Yet in spite of one's admiration this nation will eventually disappear. The Hindus must, therefore, examine their religion and their morality in terms of the survival value.

Secondly, the Hindus must consider whether they, should conserve the whole of their social heritage or select what is helpful and transmit it to future generations only that much and no more. Prof. John Dewey said society gets encumbered with what is trivial, with dead wood from the past and with what is positively perverse. As a society becomes more enlightened, it realizes that it is responsible not to conserve and transmit the whole of its existing achievements but only such as make for a better future society. "Even Burke, in spite of the vehemence with which he opposed the principle of change embodies in the French Revolution, was compelled to admit that a State without the means of some change is without the means of its conservation. Without such means it might even risk the loss of that part of the constitution which it wished the most religiously to reserve." What Burke said of a State applies equally to a society.

Thirdly, the Hindus must consider whether they must not cease to worship the past as supplying its ideals. The beneful effect of this worship of the past are best summed up by Prof. Dewey when he says: "An individual can live only in the present. The present is not just something which comes after the past; much less something produced by it. It is what life is in leaving the past behind it. The study of past products will not help us to understand the present. A knowledge of the past and its heritage is of great significance when it enters into the present, but not otherwise. And the mistake of making the records and remains of the past the main material of education is that it tends to make the past a rival of the present and the present a more or less futile imitation of the past". The principle, which makes little of the present act of living and growing, naturally looks upon the present as empty and upon the future as remote. Such a principle is inimical to progress and is hindrance to a strong and a steady current of life.

Fourthly, the Hindus must consider whether the time has not come for them to recognise that there is nothing fixed, nothing eternal, nothing *sanatan* that everything is changing, that change is the law of life for individuals as well as for society. In a changing society, there must be a constant revolution of old values and the Hindus must realize that if there must be standards to measure the acts of men there must also be a readiness to revise those standards.

References

Ketkar, S.V., *History of Caste in India,* New Delhi, 1995.

Blunt, E.A.H., *The Caste System of Northern India.*

Rapson, E.J., The Cambridge History of India, Vol. 1 Ancient India.

History of the Marathas, Vol.I and II.

Memo of Central India, Vol. II.

Wilson, *Rig Veda,* XL III.

Burnett and Hopkins, *Ordinances of Manu.*

Central Provinces Gazetteer, Calcutta, 1908.

Rajputana Gazetteer, Calcutta, 1908.

Vedic Index, I.

Vedic Index, II.

Talke, J., *Islam in Bengal,* 1914.

Indian Annual Register, relevant volumes.

AICC Papers.

The Collected Works of Mahatma Gandhi.

6

The Social Reforms

The institution of caste, with its corollary-untouchability is a peculiar and complex social phenomenon. Its roots are buried deep in dim and distant antiquity and therefore, it has not been possible for scholars to be unanimous about the origin and growth of this unique system. The broad outlines, however, are clear and there is general agreement about them. The division of society into classes or guilds, though to some extent hereditary in character, was unavoidable in the early stages of the evolution of society. Certain features of the caste system are thus as old as primitive society itself.

Endogamy was, to a certain extent, a tribal characteristic. Primitive nations in embryo used to be divided into an infinite number of tribes, which usually bore an intense hatred towards each other and did not inter-marry even though they might have lived in contiguous areas and spoken the same language.

Idea of Pollution

Inter-dining, or the practice of distributing food only to one's own kith and kin, did not start from any idea of pollution; it was because of the need to preserve scarce food which had been collected with great endeavour. When the Aryans entered India, they had outgrown the stage of tribal endogamy. Among them there were only three divisions conforming to the three primitive functional divisions of priest, warrior and artisan. *Varna* in this trivarnic society indicated a particular social function and a distinct level of culture and way of living. The clash between the Aryan invaders and the aboriginal inhabitants of India accentuated not only the cultural but even the occupational and functional divisions. A fourth caste, the Shudras, came into being, society became *chaturvarnic*. The sages sang of its eternal nature. Men gradually came to believe that the order was divinely ordained.

The conquered aborigines, or the broken men, were deprived of all claim for a place in the divinely ordained social order and on the communal land. They were forced to live outside the village, and occupations regarded as low and contemptible were assigned to them. They were the ancestors of the untouchables (now a distinct number of castes and were known as the *Asparshyas* or the *Panchama*. They were attached to the Hindu society and yet they did not belong to it, having been assigned no place in the social hierarchy of caste in the *chaturvarnya*.

While the process of conquest and settlement was in progress, various other factors were making their impact felt on the social organization of the age. There was migration as a result of this process.

Customs were changing. Some aboriginal tribes submitted to the Aryans and even accepted their faith. Others continued in their persistent hostility. The colour-conscious Aryans, who regarded themselves as culturally superior, were anxious to maintain the purity of their blood. Under the impact of these forces the *trivarnic* society became *Chaturvarnic*, and the latter split into a large number of castes and sub-castes within the framework of this fourfold system of society.

Priestly Class

The priestly class or the Brahmins were the intellectual and spiritual leaders. It was believed that learning and spiritual knowledge were esoteric virtues and their cultivation needed exclusive attention. Manual labour, therefore, became taboo for the Brahmins. It also became taboo for the Kshatriyas, with whom the Brahmins shared power and who were their rivals and equals. The aristocratic order of the Kshatriyas could not be sustained by mere force. So the Brahmins framed elaborate rules laying down not only the status and grade of the various social and cultural groups but also prescribing distinct rituals and ceremonies for each.

The original idea of *varna*, as indicating a particular social function and a distinct level of culture, gave way to the idea of a divinely ordained division of society. The doctrines of transmigration, *karma*, and the theory of *maya* or illusion were brought to the aid of the social system and made to sustain an iniquitous and undemocratic social order, imposed by a powerful and influential minority on the majority of the population.

It appears that in Europe, strong territorial governments brought about a change not only from tribalism to territorialism, but also the imposition of a national or credal religion led to the abolition of tribal differences. In India, until the fifth century BC there appears to have been no strong territorial power which could weld divergent tribalism into a "semblance of a nation". The Hindu religion was more cosmopolitan than national, with the baffling conception that it was an eternal religion and that the other religions were only derived from it or were its corrupt forms. Hinduism believed implicitly in the division of all humanity into four *varnas*.

These beliefs and the peculiar social organizations that Hindus evolved, facilitated the absorption of a major part of foreign invaders into the Hindu caste system. By the time the Muslim conquest started, the stratification of the caste system had been completed. Rules and regulations regarding the life and conduct of the various castes had been elaborated until they covered all aspects of life. There was no equality before law. The inequality resulting from caste was supposed to be ordained by God, and the law-makers, therefore, prescribed without any compunction different kinds or punishments and taxes for men belonging to different *varnas*.

Theory of Karma

With the aid of religion, the theories of transmigration and of *karma*, a complete mental conditioning of the people had been achieved. This conditioning had eliminated all sense of revolt from the minds of the majority, which had to toil not only for its own upkeep, but for the upkeep of the exploiting upper castes. Even the untouchables believed that if they carried on with their duties in this life, which were ordained by Providence, uncomplainingly, willingly and obediently they would probably be born in a higher group in their next birth.

Islam and Christianity, however were different. They came as the religions of the conquerors and the rulers. They were vigorous and proselytising. Hinduism, on the other hand, is non-proselytising. Both Islam and Christianity proclaimed the inherent equality of man and boasted of the feeling of brotherhood among their followers. It was not, therefore, possible for the Hindu religion to absorb the Mohammedans or the Christians as it had done such invading tribes as the Huns, the Shakas, the Yueh-chihs and other nomadic tribes which had entered India from the North-West.

The impact of these two religions led to a thought-ferment which gave rise to a number of protestant movements, which aimed to achieve social equality and to do away with the predominance of the Brahmins. There had been earlier revolts against the Brahminical system, against the theory of the inherent inequality of man and the system of elaborate rituals and ceremonials which helped the Brahmins to maintain their firm grip on the social order.

Protest and Revolt

There has been no such period in history when there was no protest or revolt against this system. In this sense Buddha was the first great social revolutionary who successfully challenged, for a period of time, the supremacy of the Brahmins and preached a simple religion which stressed righteousness of conduct. The social bases, however, which could sustain the revolutionary thoughts propounded by the Buddha, were not yet ready or organized.

Brahminism, therefore, succeeded in establishing its hold again. It could do so partly because it assimilated the teachings of the Buddha into the Hindu religion and started emphasizing righteous conduct, thereby giving the Buddha a high place in the Hindu pantheon. It also succeeded because the edifice which Buddhism had erected, had started tottering because of some of its inherent contradictions.

The later movements of revolt and reform were led by saints such as Ramananda, Kabir, Ravidas (Raidas), Eknath, Tukaram, Chaitanya, Guru Nanak and many others. None of these reformers had aimed at the formation of a sect. The inequalities in the Hindu social system which were said to be divinely ordained, the exploitations and persecutions which were sought to be justified by the theory of *karma* and transmigration of soul and the denial of the light of knowledge about God to various sections of the community filled their souls with anguish; they sought to reform the people of the country and inculcate in them a new belief in the equality of all men before God. But the people had been living for so long in psychological cages and had become so acquiescent to prevalent Brahminical beliefs that the efforts of these saint-reformers invariably ended in the formation of new sects some of which leaned heavily on the traditional Hindu thought.

Many of these sects exist even today, but they have lost their old dynamism. Many others are not distinguishable from the Hindu religion commonly practiced by the people. Considerable thought and research should be devoted to finding out why these reformers could not succeed in liberating the masses, who had become prisoners of theological doctrines that were anti-social and pernicious in the extreme.

The Rituals

It is noteworthy that many of these sects took to rituals and ceremonials as mystic as those that the Brahmins had evolved. The underlying motive behind this was a pathetic desire to emulate the Brahmins. These sects, which were like small rivulets taking off from the main Hindu stream, became dry and sterile after a time, or again merged into the main channel. They however, gave their adherents a new sense of confidence and solace and enabled them to withstand the temptations which the Islamic democracy offered. In this sense, these sects acted as a prop to Brahminical Hinduism and saved Hinduism from large-scale disintegration.

Notwithstanding these reform movements, a large number of those belonging to the Shudras or the untouchables were attracted towards Sikhism, Islam and Christianity. They could not, however, be free from the taint of caste even under Sikhism and Christianity and the strange and amazing phenomenon of untouchable Sikhs and untouchable Christians is unique and peculiar to India—a reminder of the grip which caste has on the public mind. It also demonstrates that the effect of the Hindu social order on Islam and Christianity was not inconsiderable.

Those who maintain that it is because of this peculiar system that the Hindus were able to withstand the pressure of Islam and Christianity and save their religion and their community from disintegration forget one crucial fact. They forget that this peculiarity was also a source of weakness and it limited the achievements of the community. All achievements of India and all her successes were confined only to the upper castes. The masses constituting the lower classes were made to work for the advancement of society but were excluded from being partners in the process of history-making. They were deliberately kept outside history. Thus, they were outside creative national endeavour.

Role of Upper Caste

The upper castes could do such a thing because they were socially powerful, and could commander the vast majority of the lower castes to work for them as dictated. But the fact remains that a large section of the population was not allowed to make a creative contribution to the moulding of the destiny of the people and the country. This was one of the major weaknesses of Indian society. It led to degradation not only of the lower castes but of the upper classes as well and caused, in the words of Pandit Nehru, "a petrification which became a dominant feature of India's economy and life."

Given a larger cohesion and higher loyalty, there would have been, perhaps, no Muslim conquest. The fact therefore, that Indian society was moribund for a long period, that the feudal system continued to be a drag till recent times, and that the spirit of adventure and inventiveness which brought about the industrial revolution in the west were lacking in India, should not surprise anybody.

Perhaps the reason why the earlier reformers failed was that they made a direct attack on the prevalent Hindu thought structure. Society was not made to appreciate or imbibe the new values which underlay the reform movements. Though the conception and practice of caste, was based on the aristocratic idea and is opposed to democratic concepts, it did give the society of those times a certain static equilibrium within the boundaries laid by the caste system, the people were free to move and do as they pleased; but such freedom was, naturally, strictly limited.

It was under this system that the self-sufficient economy of the Indian villages evolved and withstood the onslaught of revolutions, invasions, ravages of internal wars and conflicts. The village could change hands but there would be no change in its internal life or its economy. The mass of the villagers, irrespective of who the ruler was, were to remain serfs and slaves. Politics was not for them. The prosperity of the weaver, carpenter, tanner, barber, washerman and others depended on their daily labour without being much affected by the varying fortunes in the political scene.

Advent of British Rule

This static equilibrium was shattered by the advent of British rule. Indian village economy and its more or less self-sufficient character received a killing blow when machine-made or mill-made commodities started competing with hand-made products. When industrial regions started expanding, the progressively pauperized agricultural worker or peasantry and even the artisans were drawn to these industrial centres. The methods of imperialistic exploitation dictated that the village should produce nothing except the primary commodities which could be used as raw materials by the manufacturing industries. The advent of industrial life and the effects of industrialization helped to reduce the rigours of the caste system in the urban areas, but the villages remained conservative and faithful to the Hindu system of thought.

In this context when we talk of the Hindu system of thought, or Hindu thought-structure, we have to remember that the Hindu thought-structure itself is very complex. There are different and often conflicting strands of thought in Hindu philosophy. There is the humanist and democratic assertion that man is the measure of everything, that all men are born free and equal, that the human personality is divine and unique. Such thought currents in the composite Hindu thought-structure would justify the stand that Hinduism is the most liberal of religions. Different strands of the same composite thought-structure provide inspiration and support to the diehard *Sanatanists*, who sincerely believe that the *chaturvarnya* is divinely ordained. Hinduism is not faith or religion. It is a fellowship of faiths and religions.

The original and basic functional theory underlying the four *varnas* has had a long life. It's grip on the mass mind, is still very strong. But the impact of the conditions of modern life has been gradually weakening its hold. There can   be no two opinions that the theory has ceased to have any validity either in the context of democratic theory and belief or in the context of India's socio-economic needs. The thinking section of the community is united in holding that the sooner this tenacious relic of the past is given a decent burial the better it would be for Indian society.

But though there is an agreement about the end, there is considerable divergence about the means to be employed. There are the theoretical democrats and fervent nationalists who would like to cease mentioning caste. They believe that if people did not talk of caste, if they came out of the psychological cage and breathed in a free atmosphere where human beings are treated on their own intrinsic merit and not on the basis of caste labels, there would be an end to the problem of caste and untouchability.

Then, there are those who give more importance to the solidarity of the nation and less to the individuals who compose it collectively. They feel that by making caste the basis of ameliorative measures, we create vested interests in an institution against which we profess to be battling and thus unwittingly give caste a new lease of life. The only criteria for ameliorative measures, they maintain, should be backwardness—social or economic—and not caste.

There are still others who think that the problem is largely and mainly economic and that its social, cultural and other aspects will take care of themselves if the economic problem is rightly tackled. They think that it is only by a process of sublimation that the energy and the cohesiveness of caste may be directed to national unity and overall cooperative endeavour.

Persons having such views are opposed to special safeguards such as reservations or concessions, as they believe that reservations, safeguards and concessions would perpetuate caste feelings and caste loyalties and would retard progress towards higher loyalties and larger social cohesion. These very well-meaning people unwittingly arrogate to themselves, the role of benevolent guardians of the backward communities and feel that they should repay the moral debt which they owe to the submerged millions in a manner which they consider to be most conducive to the good of the nation.

The Conviction

It is not the intellectual conviction alone, about caste being a pernicious and inhuman institution that matters. Professing such convictions is not of any value. It is the behaviour towards such castes, which counts, and the behaviour even of the educated is determined mostly by certain prejudices which occupy a significant place in the Hindu thought structure. The original prejudice of treating occupational manual labour with contempt, and associating those engaged in such labour with lowliness, persists. Social prestige is still attached to the man who does not work with his hands.

The force of inherited habit and ideas about endogamy and the hierarchy of the caste system mostly determine the behaviour of the upper caste intellectual, his convictions not withstanding. These prejudices are a part of the social

fabric. They have sunk deep into the very recesses of our
being. Hence it is that we find such a glaring discrepancy
between profession and practice. It is for this reason that
do not find many emancipated minds even amongst the so-
called intellectuals.

How is this discrepancy between the professed belief and
the prevalent practice to be overcome? How are the backward
communities to be assured that, even if no reservations or
safeguards are provided for them, their interest would be
safe in the hands of the well-meaning intellectuals of the
upper caste? The upper caste which, in spite of its best
intentions and intellectual beliefs, is still unable to rise above
caste prejudices and practices. That is the crucial problem
which should be sincerely and seriously considered.

The problem does not pose itself as a negative result of
the eradication of caste and untouchability. Personally, the
problem appears as a positive one of changing the way of
thinking of our people and of bringing about a change in
the age-old Hindu thought pattern and thought structure.
The problem is one of completing the process or renaissance
and reform which was begun by several prominent saints
but which never ran its full course.

One can recall that phase in the development of Europe
which is known as the Renaissance. It did not only bring
about a change in the intellectual and moral attitude of the
people. It also provided a new socio-economic basis which
could sustain these new ideas. Under its impact and
inspiration, the European nations entered upon a fresh
stage-of vital action. It stimulated creative activity greatly,
not only in the intellectual sphere but in other spheres as
well.

How did this happen? It freed man from the thraldom of
theology and led to a vivid recognition of the godliness in
man. It was this new idea of the intrinsic worth of man and
of human life that really worked the miracle. At the
sametime, it did not imply a break with the past. It developed
what was original in medieval ideas and emphasised through
man's fresh endeavour after spiritual freedom—the
continuity of history and the identity of human nature. It
shattered the narrow mental barriers imposed by medieval

orthodoxy. This recovery of freedom for the human spirit, after a long period of bondage to oppressive religious and political orthodoxy paved the way for the emergence of modern states. Not only the economic life and the thought structure, but also the religious beliefs were affected and religion itself underwent a great change.

In India, unfortunately, this movement never ran its full course. Buddha failed because he was a reformer who was too advanced for his times. The reforms initiated by other saints failed because their followers became segregated and ended, not in obliterating caste, but in creating a new one of their followers. Thus the whole idea behind such reforms, of securing greater recognition and respect for the individual human personality was defeated.

The last and the most powerful blow to the old system was given by Mahatma Gandhi. He moved firmly, aggressively, persistently and yet cautiously. He did not start by challenging the basic assumptions behind the four-fold division of Indian society and yet succeeded, to a considerable extent, in shaking the very foundations of the system. The work begun by him has to be carried on. It has to be realised that the real end of man's journey is freedom. Anything which restrains or injures human dignity, restrains freedom. It is to be realised that the question of the eradication of untouchability and caste is but the negative aspect of the issue of the expansion of human spirit and of its attaining freedom.

It is also to be realized that ideas of dignity and the inviolability of the individual will not find full play within the framework of the existing system of Hindu thought, because as long as this system of thought continues, the behaviour of Hindus is likely to be influenced by it.

It is a great coercive force. Though invisible, it subjugates the Hindu to a state of complete acquiescence. Under its grip, he does not challenge the environment. He accepts it and gives up the highest of virtues and the only abiding human value and privilege to be free. This spirit of willing and voluntary servitude is the first hurdle which a reform movement has to negotiate. The feeling of seeking security and recognition within the confines of the caste arises from a sense of helplessness—the psychology of a child seeking parental support.

The effect of this system is so pernicious and all-pervasive that the majority of the population of this country, which is composed of the backward communities, thinks more of aping the customs and manners of the upper castes, and less of breaking the shackles. There are innumerable instances or men belonging to the lower communities taking surnames which are supposed to be dignified, or of discouraging the re-marriage of widows, as it is believed that these are tokens of social advancement. If the untouchables practise untouchability within their own communities to such a surprising extent it can be explained by the fact that it is a sincere but poor imitation of the Brahmins, the Brahmins who constitute the most heterogeneous collection of minute and independent sub-divisions that ever bore a common designation.

The urgency of the problem becomes apparent once it is realized that Indian nationalism arose amidst such peculiarly powerful social institutions as customs and cultural traditions and that the prevalent social and mental framework is, therefore, essentially unsuitable for its development or for the development of democracy.

Harijan Sevak Sangh

Gandhi's constructive programme was devoted to social reform and development of the backward communities. His aim was to regenerate a new spirit, a new thinking and self-reliance amongst the Harijans. This kind of feeling, he believed, would greatly enhance their prestige and self-respect. They could raise their heads by becoming economically stronger by hard work and incessant labour. It was made clear at numerous meetings and through his writings that untouchability was a cruel and inhuman institution. It always violated human dignity by compelling untouchables to do work which was unclean and degrading. It was opined that untouchability was against the spirit of democracy which made no distinction among citizens of a free country. It also raises economic problems because the untouchables were the poorest section of Indian society. Their avenues of employment were strictly limited. They lived apart, in unhygienic surroundings, on the outskirts of villages and cities. Though they were Hindus and believed in and worshipped Hindu gods and goddesses, they were not allowed to enter Hindu temples. Public institutions like schools, hostels, etc., were closed to them.[1]

Harijans' Upliftment

To boost up the work for the upliftment of Harijans, Gandhi laid the foundation of the Harijan Sevak Sangh. Its main function was the removal of all such disabilities which hampered the progress and development of Harijans. As it consisted of dedicated workers it did remarkable work, so far so, Gandhi brought a Harijan family in the Ashram and he adopted their daughter as his own. He also offered his blessings on the eve of marriages which were celebrated between Harijans and Caste Hindus. A few such marriages were celebrated in his own Ashram. In an article on 'Task before Harijan Sevaks', Gandhi stated that the growing number of reformers should be active in the execution of various programmes and should not sit still. Rather they should demonstrate that change by their visible conduct. He was sure that the change to full self-reliance would never come unless all the workers realized that this was essentially a religious movement. He opined that propaganda among Caste Hindus could only be successfully carried out by influential persons with a remarkable capacity in them.[2]

'Though I have concurred in the policy of centralization I have always desired, as I have no doubt the Board too has desired, decentralization at the first opportunity. But that could only be done when the Provincial Boards were ready and able to raise their own funds, I would love nothing so much as that every village had its Harijan Board and was able to find its own funds. When that day comes, it will also be one of complete abolition of untouchability in every shape and form. For the present it has to be unfortunately admitted that the cause is still led by a handful of earnest reformers scattered all over the country.[3]

Ever since the inauguration of the Harijan Sevak Sangh, the central organization has been feeling, every properly, the provincial branches. But the time has certainly arrived for the branches to stand on their own and be self-sustained even though it may be at the sacrifice of a part of their programme. The work in each province, and for that matter in each district or taluka, should be an unequivocal demonstration of active Savarna support. For the chief mission of the Sangh is to touch the Savarna heart and change it. Supposing the central organization had collected from two or three reformers a crore of rupees, and with it established branches all over India to cover it with schools and hostels for Harijan boys and girls, it would not have hastened the day of the doom of untouchability. For the Savarna heart would remain as stony as ever. Supposing conversely that without cost of a single pice, by some stroke, of good fortune, the Savarna heart was changed and untouchability became a thing of the past, the whole object the Sangh would be fulfilled. For in that case every public school, place of worship and other institutions would be open to Harijans precisely on the same terms as to Caste Hindus. That day may be far off or much nearer than many people expect. Anyway that is the goal of the Harijan Sevak Sangh, and never the opening of separate schools, wells, temples and the like for Harijans and consequent perpetuation of untouchability. At present these things are undoubtedly done, but they are done only as a means to the end. They have become necessary because the Savarna heart is slow to change.

The growing number of reformers must not sit still and make protestations of removal of untouchability from themselves. They must demonstrate that change by their visible conduct. The spending of their purse for the Harijan cause is a tangible proof of the change and, therefore, an essential part of the programme. But immediately it becomes a corner confined to a few individuals who salve their conscience by liberal donations, it ceases to be a token in the manner indicated by me. Hence it becomes a matter of duty for the Central Board to invite the attention of the branches to this fundamental part of the programme and for the branches to appreciate it and prepare the way to becoming wholly self-reliant. Indeed the burden has been progressively thrown on provincial boards of financing their own institutions.

This change to full self-reliance will never come unless all the workers realize that this is essentially a religious movement. We are a nation spending lavishly for causes which the masses believe to be religious. One has only to go the places of pilgrimage to have an ocular demonstration of the fact. A study of the history of religious endowments will reveal the tragic story of fortunes being entrusted to them by credulous millions without ever caring to know-how they were spent. It is enough for people to believe that they pay their mite to a cause which in their opinion is religious. Harijan workers have a cause that is wholly religious in the best sense of the term. If they have a living faith in it, if they do not move mountains, they will at least get from their surroundings enough for the institutions in their charge.[4]

Gandhi's Reaction

Q. The Harijan Sevak Sangh is looked upon as a part of the Congress. But very few Congressmen are Harijan workers. Why?

A. The Sangh is not a part of the Congress. It was the outcome of the fast I undertook in 1932 when I was in jail. The meeting of Hindus drawn from every class, which was held under the Presidentship of Pandit Malaviyaji and which gave birth to Sangh, deliberately decided to keep the organization separate from the Congress and non-political. It was this quality of the Sangh that enabled Seth G.D. Birla to become its President and Shri Thakkar Bapa its Secretary. Nevertheless there are ought to be many Congressmen in the Sangh, because practically all reformers are drawn into the Congress fold. But it is true that there are plenty of non-Congress persons in the Sangh. It is also true that those Congressmen who are only interested in politics do not come into it. It is, therefore, sometimes wrongly thought that Congressmen do not take an interest in the Sangh. It is the duty of every Congressman to remove untouchability, root and branch, from his life.

Q. Harijan service has really developed into mere Harijan uplift. Practically no work is done among Caste Hindus for the removal of untouchability. What is the remedy for this?

A. Experience shows that propaganda among Caste Hindus can only be successfully carried out by influential persons whose words carries weight with the general public. Such persons are hard to find. But it is within the capacity of every Harijan worker to carry on mute propaganda. Our Caste Hindu workers are often satisfied with mere uplift work among the Harijans, which is not sufficient. Many workers, while they do not observe untouchability themselves, are unable even to convert their own families. How then can they influence the outside world? Moreover it is my confirmed opinion that every Harijan worker has to make a point to beg for even one pice for Harijans from those Caste Hindus with whom he comes in contact. If all devoted themselves, heart and soul, to this task, very good results would ensue.

Q. Should not the Sangh take upon itself the service of those Harijans who have been converted to Christianity or Islam and are yet treated as untouchables? Are we not out to remove untouchability root and branch and, therefore, help all who come under its sway?

A. This question has already been answered in the columns of Harijan but must bear repetition so long as it is raised. The moment untouchability is utterly banished from Hindu society it will, ipso facto, disappear from elsewhere too. Whatever the merits or demerits of the case, it is clear that our interference with converts will be the cause of strife with Muslims and Christians. Such converts have either broken off all contacts with, or they have been in their turn boycotted by Hindus. They have thrown in their lot with other sects whose leaders will not allow them to maintain their old contacts. Hence the Harijan Sevak Sangh quite rightly decided from its inception to confine its area of work to Harijans who had not left the Hindu fold. A convert, having left his original fold, is no longer guided or controlled by it.

Q. What should be the attitude of the Sangh, if Harijan boys wish to enlist in the army?

A. They should be allowed to do so. They may not be controlled by the Congress policy or Ahimsa. They must be given absolute freedom of choice.

Q. Harijans are of opinion that Caste Hindus who are sympathetic to their cause should not use those temples where they are not allowed entry.

A. They are right. It is the bounden duty of Harijan workers not to go where Harijans are not allowed and likewise to dissuade Caste Hindus.

Q. Harijans are legally entitled to send their children to many educational institutions as also to draw water from public wells. But public sentiment still militates against this being put into practice. Should Harijans resort to the law courts for justice in these matters or wait patiently until the Caste Hindus are converted?

A. Where there is no danger of violence being done to them, the Harijans should exercise their legal right and where necessary, resort to law courts. Harijan workers must continue agitation among Caste Hindus and not rest content with mere legal rights.

Q. Is it not essential to reform the insanitary methods employed by sweepers for cleaning latrines and scavenging?

A. It is not necessary. What is more, until this is done the condition of sweepers will remain pitiable. To this end it is the duty of Harijan workers and Caste Hindus to do sweepers' work themselves. No Caste Hindu will employ the methods used by sweepers. He will do the work scientifically. For example, he will never remove excreta in a basket or carry it on his head; he will cover excreta with dry earth and remove it in a metal vessel. He will avoid touching dirt with his hands as far as possible; he will clean the vessel with water and a rod; he will bathe immediately after doing the work; he will wear special clothes when scavenging. These reforms do not cost much. They require intelligence, hard work, and love of an ideal. We may not relegate sweepers' work to one particular class. Therefore, all should learn it the same way as cooking. Each person should be his own sweeper. If this ideal were to be put into practice in society, the miserable condition of sweepers would at once be rectified.[5]

Welfare Work

The Harijan Sevak Sangh was mainly concerned with the welfare work. The members were also advised to organise unions or even induce hartals, not from political motives or for such purposes, but for bettering the social or economic position of Harijans. 'The Harijan Sevak Sangh, however, being a non-political organization should never put expediency before its primary duty towards the Harijans.'

Q. The Communist Party as successfully organized sweepers' unions and helped them to secure their rights through hartals, etc. But the Harijan Sevak Sangh's activities are confined mostly to welfare work. It cannot, therefore, successfully compete with the Communists for popularity among the Harijans. Don't you think that in view of this, the Harijan Sevak Sangh ought to alter its policy and method of work?

A. We must be guided in our policy by our sense of right, not by the lure of winning cheap popularity. If the Harijan Sevak Sangh is convinced that it is working on the right line, it will keep on to it, regardless of what others might or might not do. Thus we may organize unions or even induce *hartals,* not from political motives or for such purposes, but for bettering the social or economic position of Harijans.

Q. The feeling is gaining ground among the Harijans that the Congress is showing more solicitude for Muslim demands than for the just rights of the Harijans. What have you to say to it?

A. The Congress being a political organization is likely to be more susceptible to political pressure, which the Muslims are in a far stronger position to exert than the Harijans. If it succumbs to that pressure, it will pay the price for it. The Harijan Sevak Sangh, however, being a non-political organization should never put expediency before its primary duty towards the Harijans.

Q. Would you advise the so-called Savarna Hindus to start, even under the present circumstances an agitation in selected places for securing elementary civic and social rights for the Harijans? Would you for this purpose advise the Harijan Sevak Sangh to organize Satyagraha against the Savarna Hindus if necessary?

A. I would not advise the Sangh as an organization to offer Satyagraha against the Savarna Hindus, but I would certainly not only advise but expect members of the Sangh in their individual capacity to organize such Satyagraha in their respective places. I shall certainly support any such move on their part if it is undertaken in the proper spirit. It is their duty.

Q. Would you, in the absence of popular governments in the provinces, advise the Sangh to carry on a vigorous and energetic programme of temple entry for Harijans?

A. I could. I understand it is being done even at present but at a rather slow pace. I would certainly like its tempo to be stepped up.

Q. Should not the Harijan Sevak Sangh try to secure for the Harijans political power by demanding due representation for them on Grama Panchayats, municipalities and Legislatures?

A. Certainly it ought to. No effort can be too great for it.

Q. Should not the Sangh give instructions in the essentials of Hindu religion in the Harijan hostels and in Harijan gatherings of adults?

A. It ought to be the primary duty of the Sangh to give to Harijan children and adults a grounding in the essentials of Hindu religion. If they were brought up in ignorance of these, they would not continue to remain in the Hindu fold, and the responsibility for it would rest on those who had failed to give them the necessary instructions.

Role of Sadhus

Gandhiji was asked to give his opinion on the recent work in the Gwalior State to enlist the services of the Sadhu community in the cause of Harijan uplift. He replied that he had grave doubts to the correctness or advisability of the step. It seemed to him to smack of politics. He would welcome the assistance of true Sadhus, if it was available. But he confessed, he looked in vain in the country for

Sadhus of his conception. Such Sadhus as he saw disappointed him. There might be here and there honourable exceptions and their help would be welcome. But he was frankly skeptical of the possibility of utilizing Sadhus as a body for their work. Even if they tried the experiment, he was afraid they would come to the parting of the ways before long.

Another friend asked whether a portion of the Kasturba Memorial Trust Fund ought not to be earmarked for Harijan sisters. Gandhiji's reply was that they could have the whole of it if they could show the capacity to utilize it. No special earmarking of a part was, therefore, necessary.

The questions and answers finished, Gandhiji addressed a few general remarks to those assembled to give his diagnosis of the relative sluggishness of the Harijan Sevak Sangh's activities and his remedy for the same. "I'am responsible for the policy of conducting Harijan uplift work through the agency of the Savarna Hindus. They had to do expiation. All of them, I argued to myself, could help with money even if they could not, owing to lack of necessary qualifications, render direct service. For instance, they might not be able themselves to do teaching work, but they could engage a competent teacher to give education to Harijan children. That would be one way of doing expiation. They would be able to penetrate Harijan society and help in its progress." He knew there were skeptical critics, who questioned whether this kind of work could lead to the eradication of untouchability. He himself was at one time among the doubters. But he had since realized his mstake. He owed a debt of gratitude in this respect to the late Shri Devdhar, at whose activity he had at one time looked askance and which he had even criticized. A year's experience, however, had cured him of his conceit and taught him humility. He realized that if he confined himself exclusively to doing propaganda among the Savarna Hindus with a view to their conversion, he might have to wait till the Greek Kalends and in the meantime the actual uplift work among the Harijans would remain hopelessly bogged. His own experience has since convinced him that if they could only have sufficient workers with the requisite purity and devotion and spirit of sacrifice to work among Harijans, untouchability would become a thing of the past, even if the Savarna Hindus were left severely alone. But that would mean that they must become Harijans at heart and live and labour among the Harijans as Harijans. "But can the members of the Harijan Sevak Sangh truthfully claim to have eradicated the last trace of untouchability from their on hearts? Are their professions altogether on a par with their practice?" he asked.

A member asked as to what his criterion was in that respect. "Are you married?" questioned Gandhiji in return. "I happen to be", replied the puzzled interlocutor. "Then have you an unmarried daughter?" resumed Gandhiji. "If you have, get for her a Harijan bridegroom not to satisfy her lust but in a purely religious spirit and I shall send you a wire of congratulations at my expense."

"You will now realize," continued Gandhiji, "why the Harijan Sevaks are unable to move the hearts of the Savarna Hindus. The reason is that they have not that fire of faith in their hearts, impatient hunger for service which is the first essential for an effective appeal. Let but a handful of Savarna Hindus go forth in that true missionary spirit and they will leaven the entire Hindu mass. Bus not even a whole army of missionaries so-called will produce any effect upon them." It needed a Malaviyaji to make such a missionary. He (Gandhiji) could not convert his own sister. And if he could not, argued he, how could he blame others? That would show how hard and thorny was that path. It was, however, open to them if they felt that had the necessary qualification, to try the experiment for themselves in their locality.

The reason for this partial failure, Gandhiji proceeded to explain, was also that the approach of most of the members of the Harijan Sevak Sangh to their mission was not unmixed with political motives. If they really wanted to penetrate the hearts of Savarna Hindus, they ought to be filled with a purely religious spirit. Mere dialectics was a poor weapon for this kind of work. As it was, they were too much weighed down by inertia, heedlessness and woodenness of mind.

"The other method is more fierce and not altogether

free from danger," continued Gandhiji. "It is the method of
fasting." He himself had before condemned fasting when it
seemed to him to be wrong or morally unjustified. But to
shirk a fast when there was a clear moral indication was a
dereliction from duty. Such a fast had to be based on
unadulterated Truth and Ahimsa.[6]

Harijan Board

The creation of Harijan Boards was suggested and the
qualifications of members were laid down. Only those who
were to show sincerity, deep interest and honesty of purpose
were to be enrolled as members.' The member should have
firm belief for the removal of untouchability from its roots.
He should serve the Harijans in numerous ways.

What should be the qualifications of members of Harijan
Boards and what should be the number constituting them
are the questions often asked. Only those will be included
who are eager to serve the cause and whose presence will
promote the usefulness of the Board to which they belong
and whose capacity for service will be increased by their
being members of a Board.

No one should allow himself or herself to be a member
of a Board unless he or she:

(1) believes in the uttermost removal of untouchability;
(2) pays something to the Board according to his or her
    capacity;
(3) does some definite Harijan service, e.g., having a Harijan
    in his or her home as a member of the family, or at least
    as a domestic servant, or his teaching a Harijan or
    Harijans, or paying a regular visit to Harijan quarters
    and cleaning them, or, if he or she is a doctor, treating
    Harijan patients free of charge, etc.;
(4) sends to the Board a diary containing a record of his or
    her service from month to month.

If some such conditions are observed, there need be no
restriction on the number of members. The more, the
merrier. Such Boards will meet to take notes, exchange
experiences and solve mutual difficulties. They will never
waste time in fruitless discussions.

There may be Advisory Committees attached to the
Boards. These will lay down for themselves some minimum

qualifications. Naturally the qualifications of Advisors will be less stringent than those of members of regular Boards.

What if members with the qualifications I have described cannot be found is the natural question arising from the bare mention of them. I must repeat the answer I have given often enough before now. The persons invited by the Central Board to form Sanghs in their on provinces will, in the absence of members having the necessary qualifications, perform the service through agents. "Act True" must be the motto of every Harijan Board, and there should never be any departure from the wholesome maxim.[7]

The sense of unanimity should prevail among the members of the Advisory Committee of Harijans. The factions and divisions should be avoided and 'Let there be no quarrels among you'.[8]

Gandhiji had suggested the formation of Advisory Committees of Harijans to assist Harijan Sevak Sangh Boards consisting of caste Hindus. When asked for guidance in this matter by a Harijan correspondent, Gandhiji replied:

'I should suggest the formation of compact, small representative Committees which would truly represent the opinion of local Harijans. They would frame rules for the conduct of their proceedings and formulate their expectations of Savarna Hindus and generally watch the proceedings of Harijan Boards. These Advisory Committees, wherever they are formed, would advise Harijan Boards of their existence and show their preparedness to help the latter. If the Boards are sincere in their desire to is charge their debt, that is, to serve Harijans, they will establish the friendliest contact with the Advisory Committees, and perfect co-operation and harmony will prevail. There may be friction in the beginning because of mutual suspicion. Harijan Boards, being naturally better organized and better off in every respect, will have to exercise tact in handling what may appear to be extravagant demands. Advisory Committees would endeavour to be considerate. The more considerate they are, the better able they will be to help themselves. From their ability to conduct themselves in a dignified manner, they will learn the art of asserting themselves if the occasion ever arises. For they should know that Savarna Hindus will never be able to discharge their debt except with the co-operation of Harijans. But the question of asserting themselves does not arise just yet, because the vast mass of Harijans have been rendered so completely helpless that they have no power of resisting injustice, even if they wanted to. Let me explain what I mean. Harijan Boards have three functions, to raise the economic, social and religious status of Harijans, or to put it in another way, to remove the difficulties that Savarna Hindus have for centuries put in the way of Harijans raising their heads in any department of life. Thus, the Harijan Boards have to provide wells, scholarships, boarding houses, schools and social amenities, wherever the need arises. In all these, the general body of Harijans simply take the help wherever it is offered. Advisory Committees can, therefore, help the cause and themselves by making useful suggestions to the Boards and also rendering such help as they themselves can to those whom they represent. Thus only will they acquire the power of asserting themselves. In short, Advisory Committees will best help the cause by taking up internal reform and causing an awakening among the Harijan masses, so that they may begin to realize that they are men and women entitled to the same rights as are enjoyed by the other members of the society to which they belong."[9]

At Rajahmundry a deputation of Harijans met Gandhiji and had a long talk with him. They agreed, among other things, that, as they had sufficient men among them who were enlightened and efficient, they should be entrusted with the reins of the Harijan Sevak Sangh. Caste Hindus, they said, might help in the work, but the office bearers should be all Harijans. Gandhiji gave them the following reply:

"One important question that you have raised is that the Harijan Sevak Sangh should be principally manned and managed by you. That shows that you have not followed the pages of the *Harijan*. That shows also that you have not understood the origin of the Board. The Board has been formed to enable Savarna Hindus to do repentance and reparation to you. It is thus a Board of Debtors, and you are the creditors. You owe nothing to the debtors, and therefore so far as this Board is concerned, the initiative has to come from the debtors. You have to certify whether the debtors discharge their obligation or not. What you have to do is to enable and help them to discharge their obligation; that is to say, you can tell them how they can discharge their obligation, you can tell them what, in your opinion, will satisfy the great body of Harijans. They may or may not accept your advice. If they do not, naturally they run the risk of incurring your displeasure. A debtor may go to a creditor and say to him, 'I have brought so much money, will you take it?' The creditor may say, 'Off you go; I want full payment or none.' Or the creditor may say, 'What you have brought is not part payment, but worse.' All these things you, creditors, can do. And so, when this Board was established and some Harijan friends wrote to me, I told them that Harijans should form themselves into Advisory Boards or Boards of Inspection. I want you to understand this distinction thoroughly. You will please see that there is no desire not to accept your advice or co-operation or help. I am only putting before you the true and logical position. This is a period of grace that God has given to Caste Hindus, and it is during this period of grace that they have to prove their sincerity. And I am moving heaven and earth and am going about from place to place, simply in order that this obligation on the part of Savarna Hindus may be fully discharged."

A member of the deputation then suggested that the Board should appoint Advisory Committees of Harijans of its own selection. Gandhiji, 'as a fellow Harijan by choice', showed them the danger underlying this suggestion and said, "Do not ask the Board to select a Committee of Harijans, but select your own Committee and say to the Board, you have selected these members and it should carry on correspondence with them. There is another danger in the suggestion. There may be factions and divisions among you. Different committees may be appointed by different factions. The Board may recognize all of them. But that will be unfortunate. Let there be no quarrels among you. Present a united front to the debtors. The debtors may put you against one another, though the Board, if it is worth its name, will not do that, the Congress has been able to present a united front. Today, the Congress is full of simple men like you and me. You should have a body of business-like men who will put down with a strong hand all quarrels among you. Then you will dominate the Board without being on it. Do not be easily satisfied. Tell the debtors you are not going to be satisfied with 5 shillings in the pound but that you must have 20 shillings in the pound. This is not a matter for bargaining".[10]

Harijan Day

The Mahatma recommended a 'Harijan Day' to be fixed under the auspices of the Harijan Sevak Sangh. It should be a day of sanitation and cleanliness. The poorest could do this by denying themselves a meal or a portion thereof. House to house collection was to be made by the members. The literature should be sold or given away as the exigency of the time might require.[11]

The fixing of a special day can only be warranted by extraordinary effort. In a sacred cause like the Harijan cause, a special day should be one of greater dedication, prayer and intensive work. I should divide the day somewhat after this style:

I should begin the day from 5 A.M. with prayer and set apart for the cause some money or cloth or grain according to my means. The poorest can do this by denying themselves a meal or meals or a portion thereof without feeling the slightest deprivation. Preferably donations in kind should be converted into cash. Where this is not possible, they should be given to the most deserving and needy Harijans.

The work of the family Bhangi, if there is any, should be wholly done by the family or at least shared with him. This will enable one to understand the nature of the service that the Bhangi performs and may also lead to an improved method of performing such services. Not many persons have any consideration for the 'knight of the broom' at the time of using the sanitary conveniences. If we had no untouchability in us and if we even occasionally shared the work with the Bhangis, we would have a different method of working the home sanitary system.

Having done these two things, we are ready for corporate effort for the day, which should open with house to house collection of donations in cash or kind. This work should be finished by a given hour. The donations should be handed to the local committee, which will in its turn, hand the collection to the superior committee till it reaches the headquaters of the province. Collectors should take with them a judicious selection of literature including leaflets, pamphlets books and even copies of *Harijan,* English or vernacular edition as may be required. The literature should be sold or given away as the exigency of the moment may require. But each committee should bear the cost of the literature ordered by it. If extra copies of the *Harijan* required, previous advice should be given to the publishers so as to enable them to print extra copies.

Harijan quarters should be visited in each place and they should be cleaned wherever necessary. Meetings of Harijan should be held and their wants noted. They should be advised as to the part they have to play in the removal of untouchability. Dr. Desmukh's authoritative opinion should be used in support of the plea for the giving up of carrioneating. Children can arrange meetings and excursions for Harijan children. Possibilities of inauguration of improved methods of sanitation should be explored. It is neither difficult nor expensive if the people will shoulder the burden willingly. In the end it means a visible addition to the health and wealth of the community.

The day should be wound-up by a general meeting of both Savarnas and Harijans to pass resolutions, pledging the meeting to the removal of untouchability and emphasizing the desirability of permissive legislation regarding temple entry.

Where public opinion is favourable, public wells and private temples should be opened to Harijans.

An accurate report of the work done should be sent to the Central Committee.[12]

Hardly has the great central organization of the Servants of Untouchables Society made the commencement, when complaints against it and the provincial organizations have cropped up. They come chiefly and naturally from Harijans.

One of these correspondents sent to me some time ago an able letter, undertaking to give details if I desired. I took him at his word and asked him to give me details; and the letter he has sent me in reply is abler than the first. It will compete with any well written report of an inspector. It contains a summary of reports of every organization claiming to work in the writer's province for the uplift of Harijans, and after giving me sufficient details, his one conclusion about all the organizations practically without exception is:

"They are run principally by Caste men who have their own axes to grind or who are in need of some occupation that would maintain them decently. The utmost that some of these have done is to fling a few scholarships at Harijan boys. Some others have been great at delivering lectures. All have come to us as patrons. Hardly has anyone come as a friend and equal, let alone as a servant. Your provincial organization is no exception. It is difficult for a Harijan to approach its chief man without fear and trembling. He is always in danger of being met with a frown."

My correspondent is also not without suggestions, which may be summarized thus:

"If you are to take advantage of the great awakening that has taken place, you must concentrate upon primary education in a mass scale. You will not drive out the ignorance of ages without spreading that education. We shall certainly help, but seeing that Caste Hindus want to remove untouchability and make us one with them, there is no better way of employing their money and their labour than in imparting this education."

It is necessary to know the Harijan mind in any programme of work that may be taken up. Caste Hindus, for whom removal of untouchability is a matter of penance and purification, have undoubtedly to do much more than open schools everywhere. I have discussed elsewhere where such schools may be opened. The conduct of Caste Hindus would be generally tested by its reaction upon the mass mind of the Harijans. If we have really changed towards them, they will feel the change in a thousand ways. Our activity, I mean that of Caste Hindus, will affect every department of their lives. Even in the remotest village we are inter-dependent, so much so that this interdependence cannot be dissolved all at once, even if we desired it, without resulting in the greatest harm to the nation in general; and this interdependence, which is today that of slave and master, will never be corrected unless there is absolute religious equality. It is a tremendous task, but as we progress towards the goal, the truth must dawn upon every Caste Hindu that there is no halfway house between abject slavery and perfect religious equality. Hence my humble insistence upon temple entry without losing sight of the other things we must do.

Let every organization for the service of Harijans introspect itself in the light of the criticism I have condensed and the suggestions I have made.[13] 'I have repeatedly said that this work can be done only by those who sincerely believe untouchability to be a stain on Hinduism. This is a movement requiring the change of heart of millions. It cannot be led to success by any political manoeuvres. It can be done only through self-purification. This is a great sacrificial fire in which we have to burn our load of sins and come out purified. Those who do not take to this work with faith and spirit will fail to move the hearts of millions. We shall be nowhere if we deceive ourselves or the Harijans. The success or failure of this movement depends on our getting the right type of workers. We are on our trial today. If we miss today the opportunity that God has given us, we may never hope to get the opportunity again in this generation. What we refuse to do voluntarily today we shall have to do in future perforce, and we shall repent for having lost this opportunity.[14]

Religion and God

Injustice is being done all the world over, but we have given to it the sanction of religion. These distinctions have not been created by God. The Harijans are on the lowest rung of the ladder not because of any inherent defects but only because they have been kept down by the so-called higher castes. God had bestowed on them the same talents that He had given us, but we deny them the opportunities for using them. They should surely have the same rights and privileges and the same opportunities of growth that we enjoy.

We are now awake to the wrong we have done to them, and the least we can do by way of penance now is to contribute money for their uplift and to share with them all the amenities of life that we have created for ourselves. We are all creatures of the same God and, therefore, equal in His eyes.

From the money that you give for this cause, you will reap a hundred-fold, for it is like grain sown in good, manured soil. The money spent after luxury and lust is, on the other hand, wasted like grain sown in barren soil.

I am told you have suffered heavily. But you should know that no nation has ever come to its own without having passed through the severest fire of suffering. Voluntary suffering only adds of our strength. I, therefore, congratulate you for having suffered. But I should also like to remind you that one of the causes that add to our sufferings is this curse of untouchability. We have oppressed the weak. We reap as we have sown. It is for us now to undo the wrong we have done to the Harijans and remove the yoke of serfdom from their shoulders.

Caste Hindus must first ask you to forgive the wrongs they have done to you. But I should also tell you, as a Harijan by choice, that you should give up your evil habits, especially carrion and beef-eating. The whole world looks upon carrion with abhorrence. And beef-eating should be given up because that is a *sine qua non* for a Hindu. The cow is the giver of plenty, and by killing her we kill ourselves. Then, I would urge you not to accept leavings. And above all, you should abolish the distinctions of high and low that have crept in among yourselves. And these things you should do, not in a bargaining spirit but because they are good in themselves. I would, therefore, ask you also to give up drink, irrespective of the fact that many other Hindus drink.[15]

A friend writes:

"I observe that there are some people in the Harijan service organizations not working in the spirit in which you want them to, that is, merely for the sake of serving Harijans.

They are seeking its shelter in order to satisfy other ambitions... I know that you do not desire civil resistance to be mixed up with Harijan service organizations. If you propose to make any public use of the letter you may emphasize this last point and make it clearer...."

I am thankful to the friend for giving me the benefit of his experience. It is a most difficult task to keep a big organization like the Servants of Untouchables Society with branches all over India free of all self-seekers and time-servers. I have discussed the subject fully with Seth Ghanshyamdas and Thakkar Bapa. I know that they are both anxious to keep the organization as pure as possible. Personally I can do no more. It was because of my utter helplessness that I undertook the fast of 21 days. On discovering impurities amongst Harijan servants, I saw that it was no use merely writing about impurities. I was searching for a way out of the difficulty.

Meanwhile I can only reiterate my conviction that untouchability will not be removed root and branch except through the service of men and women who take it up for its own sake and in a religious spirit. Unless we have a fair number of such servants throughout the length and breadth of India, we will never succeed in changing the hearts of millions of human beings. The *Savarna* Hindus are at one end, Harijans at the other, and the evil custom of ages, which has assumed the dignity of religious tenet, will not be uprooted without penance and purification. Whilst it gladdens my heart that thousands of people flock to the meeting that are being held in towns and villages and that they willingly give their pices as a token of their approval of the movement, I am painfully conscious of the fact that, if the thousands were suddenly called upon to enforce in their own lives what they seem to approve by their attendance at these meetings, they would fail to respond, not from want of will, but from sheer inability. I have discovered this again and again amongst my closest associates who have frankly confessed their inability to enforce immediately in their conduct what they knew was the right thing and what they knew had to be done immediately. They had to put up a brave fight against their traditional repugnance. The mere intellectual grasp that belief untouchability is an evil, corroding Hinduism, and that in it is tantamount to disbelief in God, His goodness and His Fatherhood, is not enough to destroy the monster. The vicarious penance of the comparatively pure is needed to bring about a change in the hearts of both *Savarnas* and Harijans.

So far as the connection of civil resistance with the movement is concerned, I am as emphatic as ever that Congressmen who desire to offer active civil resistance should not accept office in the various organizations, and much less can they be used for serving the purpose of civil resistance. Civil resistance is a unique weapon, it does not admit of alloy. It is a weapon of the fearless and, therefore, needs no shelter; but it has to be wielded in the open daylight. Therefore, whilst Congressmen who are also civil resisters on active service may do, as they are bound to do, such service to the cause as they can they may not belong to the Servants of Untouchables Society or any or its branches. By holding office in the organizations they will harm both civil resistance and the Harijan cause. It would be like a man going to a temple to pray and using the act of worship for advancing civil resistance. Neither God nor man will be cheated in that manner and, as I have said often enough in these columns, the great reformation of Hinduism will not be brought about, if it is to depend purely upon Congressmen. For, much as I would like to think that every Indian is a Congressman, I know that such is not the case. Nor is every Hindu a Congressman, if only because every Harijan is not a Congressmen. Therefore, a Harijan organization must in the very nature of things be strictly non-political and non-party and should contain in it both Congressman and non-Congressmen, office-holding being restricted to those who are not active civil resisters and who will not exploit the office secretly or openly to advance the cause of civil resistance.[16]

A correspondent sends me the following questions for answering:

1. In the propaganda against untouchability, should a worker make use of the Hindu Shastras and religious

texts to show that Hinduism does not sanction untouchability as we practise it today?

2. Should a Harijan sevak, even in his private capacity, take part in inter-dining functions?

3. Should a Harijan who is employed as a domestic servant sit at meals alongside all the members of the family?

These three questions, the correspondent says, have been seriously discussed in the columns of a newspaper and the readers have been advised that Harijan workers should serve with all seriousness, I, therefore, beseech you, to purify your hearts of the sin of untouchability, to treat Harijan boys and girls as if they are your own children, brothers and sisters. We have for long ages suppressed Harijans and today if we sacrifice our all for their sake we shall be only making some slight and tardy reparation for all the wrongs inflicted upon them in the name of religion. Therefore, whatever you give, whether it is a trinket or heavy piece of jewellery or silver, I want you to give as merely a token of your determination to rid yourselves of this taint of untouchability, the idea that you are high and somebody else is low. May God give you wisdom to see this very simple truth and enforce it in your life. Now you can give the things, whether jewellery, or silver or paper, whatever you want to give.[17]

In South India

In an address presented to him at a public meeting held at Calicut on 13 January, 1934, Gandhi replied:

'I am much obliged to you for these addresses that have been presented to me this evening and I thank you for the self-restraint you have imposed upon yourselves by not desiring to read those addresses to me. Only you have thereby appreciated the fact that I have been going from one place to another from day to day, now for over two months, and at the end of the day I am, therefore, fatigued. You, wise men that you are, have appreciated this fact and absolved me from the duty of having to listen to these addresses. You having exercised this self-restraint, naturally it was up to me to read those addresses and prepared. But I must say to you that I had no notion whatsoever that I was to have all these addresses nor have I been given copies of these addresses. Had I been given copies I would certainly have read them. However I have no doubt whatsoever that these addresses contain nothing more than what I have noticed in the numerous addresses that I have been receiving throughout these two months or more. Almost without exception they have expressed to me great joy, not only their sympathy with the cause that I am espousing for the time being but they have in these addresses signified their intention, nay their determination, of doing everything that these various bodies of gentlemen or ladies could possibly do in their own sphere to advance the Harijan's cause.

It has given me a great deal of satisfaction and joy to discover that there is consensus of opinion on the part of the intelligentsia. I would have been painfully surprised if it had been otherwise. Not only has it been so with reference to the intelligentsia but as far as mere assent goes, I have found to my great delight the masses also are equally with this movement. I am not easily self-deluded. I have no doubt that I have, must have, my due share of self-delusion or else life perhaps would be a positive burden to most of us if not to all of us. But due allowance having been made for self-delusion I can say that all these scenes that I witness every day cannot possibly be a matter of masses or classes coming to me to signify their praise or their satisfaction for services that I might have performed in a previous life or in days gone by. This life has rushed and with me it has rushed with such rapidity that it is impossible for me to have a photography of the events that have happened and, that being the case, I should be intensely surprised and also disappointed that these classes and masses had signified not only their satisfaction and their sympathy by their presence at these meetings but also give me donations more or less and had done certain acts also give me donations more or less and had done certain acts also as consideration for those services. I would let that pass by. I am assuming that all your addresses contain a serious and solemn pledge that you are determined to do everything that is humanly possible for you to do to render the reparation that is overdue to the Harijans. Malabar, if one were to draw the untouchability map of the whole of India, I suppose will easily wear the black crown and Malabar would be the blackest spot so far as untouchability is concerned. It is a matter of regret but it is no use ignoring the fact. I would turn this blackness to good account and I would invite you to gird up your loins and make such Herculean effort that at the end of the struggle it may be possible to say of Malabar the Malabar had been in the vanguard of progress in this battle against the monster of untouchability. Let it be said of Malabar that Malabar counted no sacrifices too great for removing this evil of untouchability. And what could be a better and more sacred reminder for this meeting than the portrait of Mr. K. Madhavan Nair?

I had the pleasure of knowing him long ago. When I first visited Calicut I had the honour of being introduced to him but I must confess that I did not know him so intimately as I came to know him when he paid me a visit at Yeravda. I came into very intimate touch with him, and when Mr. C. Rajagopalacharia was here and the Guruvayur referendum was going on, naturally I was corresponding with him as with other friends almost from day to day. Then Smt. Urmila Devi and my wife came into close contact with Mr. K. Madhavan Nair. My wife is a simple woman. She knows nothing, she does not know the English language, certainly she does not know Malayalam, but she was able to tell me in her very simple language that she was very much struck by the simplicity of his character. She merely strengthened the impression that Mr. Madhavan had left on my mind and that impression is still indelible. I have the most vivid recollection of my contact with him and what struck me most was his transparent humility. This is his faithful picture and I congratulate the artist on presenting the citizens of Calicut with this picture. I think there you can easily see humility written in his features. I don't think that the artist has enhanced the transparence of his humility. I think the artist is incapable of doing that. To look at Mr. Madhavan Nair and look at the living eye would give you a better illustration of that humility. The whole of his behaviour is on the picture. Mr. Madhavan Nair is in front of me today as I saw him in Yeravda. He stands vividly before me and this is the one peculiar impression that he left on me.

I discovered also that he was a man of very few words. You do not find many people who are economical in the use of language or their words. In his contact with me Mr. Madhavan Nair showed this quality in a supreme degree. His letters were compact, nice, neat and the briefest possible. Whatever he had to say he expressed in a few words and he had finished. That was the man. If you were to recall the men who had died in body but are even now still living, you will discover that they are living not because of their intellectual gifts but because of virtues which you and I and every one of us can cultivate if we have the will and if we will make the necessary effort in order to cultivate them. Therefore, I would say you will be doing wrong to the memory of the man whom I have described as I have known him, if you think that you have performed your duty by calling upon me to unveil his portrait and for having witnessed this ceremony and having heard a few words in praise of his memory; nay, you will be doing wrong. But you will be doing the right thing if you will treasure this as a perpetual reminder to you that you also would like to be if not wholly at least somewhat like Mr. Madhavan Nair. At the end, to put a finishing touch, Mr. Madhavan Nair died in harness so far as the Harijan cause is concerned. He was a true co-worker in the Harijan cause which is a matter of self-purification, repentance and reparation. I give you my evidence that Mr. Madhavan Nair, when he took up this cause, had the spirit in him, for every act that he did in connection with the Harijan cause was an act of sacrifice, repentance and reparation. These was no meanness about anything that he did. May his memory ever remain in my heart and in your own hearts.[18]

References

The Collected Works of Mahatma Gandhi, Senart, Emile, *Caste in India.*

Iyer, L.K.A., *Lectures on Ethnography.*

Russell, R.V., *The Tribes and Castes of the Central Provinces.*

O'Malley, L.S.S. *India's Social Heritage*, London, 1934.

Ketkar, S.V., *History of Caste in India*, New Delhi, 1995.

Talke, J., *Islam in Bengal*, 1914.

AICC Papers.

Vedic Index I.

Vedic Index II.

Census of India, Vol. XXV.

Dutt, N.K., *Origin and Growth of Caste in India.*

Memoirs of Central India, Vol. II.

Burnett and Hopkins, *Ordinances of Manu.*

Rapson, E.J., *The Cambridge History of India*, Vol. I, Ancient India.

Blunt, E. A.H., *The Caste System of Northern India.*

Indian Annual Register, relevant volumes.

1. J.B. Kripalani, *Gandhi: His Life and Thought,* Delhi, 1970, p. 383.

2. *Harijan,* 17 August 1935.

3. *Ibid.*

4.· *Harijan,* 10 October 1936.

5. *Harijan,* 10 May 1942.

6. *Harijan,* 28 July 1946.

7. *Harijan,* 9 November 1934.

8. *Harijan,* 20 April 1934.

9. *Ibid.*

10. *Harijan,* 5 January 1934.

11. *Harijan,* 15 April 1933.

12. *Ibid.*

13. *Harijan,* 4 March 1933.

14. *Harijan,* 1 December 1933.

15. *Ibid.*

16. *Harijan,* 24 November 1933.

17. *The Hindu,* 15 January 1934.

18. *Ibid.*

7

Caste System in Modern India

The leaders of independent India decided that India will be democratic, socialist and secular country. According to this policy there is a separation between religion and state. Practising untouchability or discriminating a person based on his caste is legally forbidden. Along with this law the government allows positive discrimination of the depressed classes of India.

Flexibility among Hindus

The Indians have also become more flexible in their caste system customs. In general the urban people in India are less strict about the caste system than the rural. In cities one can see different caste people mingling with each other, while in some rural areas there is still discrimination based on castes and sometimes also on untouchability. Sometimes in villages or in the cities there are violent clashes which, are connected to caste tensions. Sometimes the high castes strike the lower castes who dare to uplift their status. Sometimes the lower castes get back on the higher castes.

In modern India the term caste is used for Jat and also for *varna*. The term, caste was used by the British who ruled India until 1947. The British who wanted to rule India efficiently made lists of Indian communities. They used two terms to describe Indian communities, castes and tribes. The term caste was used for Jats and also for *Varnas*. Tribes were those communities who lived deep in jungles, forests and mountains far away from the main population and also communities who were hard to be defined as castes, for example, communities who made a living from stealing or robbery. These lists, which the British made, were used later on by the Indian governments to create lists of communities who were entitled for positive discrimination.

The castes, which were the elite of the Indian society, were classified as high castes. The other communities were classified as lower castes or lower classes. The lower classes were listed in three categories. The first category is called Scheduled Castes. This category includes in it communities who were untouchables. In modern India, untouchability exists at a very low extent. The untouchables call themselves Dalit, meaning depressed. Until the late 1980s they were called Harijans, meaning children of God. This title was given to them by Mahatma Gandhi who wanted the society to accept untouchables within their fold.

The second category is Scheduled Tribes. This category includes in it those communities who did not accept the caste system and preferred to reside deep in the jungles, forests and mountains of India, away from the main population. The Scheduled Tribes are also called Adivasi, meaning aboriginals.

The third category is called sometimes Other Backward Classes or Backward Classes. This category includes in it castes who belong to Sudra *varna* and also former untouchables who converted from Hinduism to other religions. This category also includes in it nomads and tribes who made a living from criminal acts.

Policy of Government

According to the central government policy these three categories are entitled for positive discrimination. Sometimes these three categories are defined together as Backward Classes. 15per cent of India's population are Scheduled Castes. According to central government policy 15per cent of the government jobs and 15per cent of the students admitted to universities must be from Scheduled Castes. For the Scheduled Tribes about 7.5per cent places are reserved which is their proportion in Indian population. The Other Backward Classes are about 50per cent of India's population, but only 27per cent of government jobs are reserved for them.

Along with the central government, the state governments of India also follow a positive discrimination policy. Different states have different figures of communities entitled for positive discrimination based on the population of each state. Different state governments have different lists of communities entitled for positive discrimination. Sometimes a specific community is entitled for rights in a particular state but not in another state of India.

In modern India new tensions were created because of these positive discrimination policies. The high caste communities feel discriminated by the government policy to reserve positions for the Backward Classes. In many cases a large number of high caste members compete for a few places reserved for them. While the Backward Classes members do not have to compete at all because of the large number of reserved places for them compared to the candidates. Sometimes in order to fill the quota, candidates from the lower classes are accepted even though they are not suitable for this jobs. Sometimes some reserved positions remain unmanned because there were few candidates from the lower classes causing more tension between the castes. Between the lower castes there are also tensions over reservation.

Order of Priority

In the order of priority for a reserved place of the Backward Classes, candidate from the Scheduled Castes is preferred over a candidate from the Scheduled Tribes who is preferred over a candidate from the other Backward Classes. As stated earlier Other Backward Classes are about 50per cent of India's population but only 27per cent of the Other Backward Classes are entitled for positive discrimination according to central government policy. Some Other Backward Classes communities are organizing politically to be recognized as Backward Classes entitled for positive discrimination.

The Scheduled Tribes who are seen as the aborigins of India got ownership and certain rights over Indian land. Many communities in India claim also to be aborigins of India and they are claiming the same rights as the Scheduled Tribes.

The caste identity has become a subject of political, social and legal interpretation. Communities who get listed as entitled for positive discrimination do not get out of this list even if their social and political conditions get better. In many cases, the legal system is involved to decide if a certain person is entitled for positive discrimination.

But with all this positive discrimination policy, most of the communities who were low in the caste hierarchy remain low in the social order even today. And communities who were high in the social hierarchy remain even today high in the social hierarchy. Most of the degrading jobs are even today done by the Dalits, while the Brahmans remain at the top of the hierarchy and profession by being the doctors, engineers and lawyers in Indian sub-continent.

Conversions

The conversion of untouchables to Islam or Christianity was criticized by Gandhi. He favoured religions bonds as it was a 'matter of the heart'. Others should not take advantage of the helplessness of untouchables. A remedy suggested to 'untouchables' is rejection of Hinduism and wholesale conversion of Islam or Christianity. And if a change of religion could be justified for worldly betterment. I would advise it without hesitation. But religion is a matter of the heart. No physical inconveniences can warrant abandonment of one's own religion. If the inhuman treatment of the Panchamas were a part of Hinduism, its rejection would be a paramount duty both for them and for those like me who would not make a fetish even of religion and condone every evil in its sacred name. But I believe that unsociability is no part of Hinduism. It is rather its excrescence to be removed by every effort. And there is quite an army of Hindi reformers who have set their upon heart riding Hinduism of this blot. conversion, therefore, I hold, is no remedy whatsoever.

Threat of Conversion

Those who use the threat (of conversion) do not, in my humble opinion, know the meaning of religion. Religion is a matter of life and death. A man does not change religion as he changes his garments. He takes it with him beyond the grave. Nor does a man profess his religion to oblige others. He professes a religion because he cannot do otherwise. A faithful husband loves his wife as he would love no other woman. Even her faithlessness would not wean him from his faith. The bond is more than blood- relationship. So is the religious bond if it is worth anything. It is a matter of the heart. An 'untouchable' who loves his Hinduism in the face of persecution at the hands of those Hindus who arrogate to themselves a superior status is a better Hindu than the self-hyphen styled superior Hindu, who by the very act of claiming superiority denies his Hinduism. Therefore, those who threaten to renounce Hinduism are in my opinion betraying their faith."[1]

If afflicted by the persecution and losing hope of ever receiving help from the other *Savarna* Hindus, the poor Harijans seek the shelter of Christianity, we may not be surprised. And our grief is worse than useless if we cannot turn it into powerful energy. Conversion under the stress of physical discomfort is no spiritual conversation. But we may not grumble if Harijans change their faith in order to better their socio-economic condition and to secure protection from persecution.

Men who threaten to leave their religion, because some other men, pretending to be of the same faith as they, prevent them from entering temples, have little religion about them. Such men cannot be said to be actuated by the religious spirit. Temples are houses of worship. They are for all who believe in them. Religious persecution is not a thing of today. It is as ancient as religion itself. It tries and purifies the persecuted who prove themselves staunch in their faith. If Harijans can patiently bear persecution, they are bound to come triumphant in the end.

Religion is an essentially personal matter. It is one between oneself and one's God. It should never be made a matter of bargain.[2]

Gandhi interpreted *varna* as the hereditary and traditional calling of our ancestors. He regarded this as the law of our being. Caste was a drag upon Hindu progress and he called it a weedy growth to be weeded out.

So far as I know anything at all of Hinduism, the meaning of *varna* is incredibly simple. It simply means the following on the part of us all, of the hereditary and traditional calling of our forefathers, in so far as that traditional calling is not inconsistent with fundamental ethics, and this only for the purpose of earning one's livelihood. I regard this as the law of our being, if we would accept the definition of man given in all religions. Of all the animal creation of God, man is the only animal who has been created in order that he may know his Maker. Man's aim: in life is not, therefore, to add from day to day to his material prospects and to his predominant calling is from day today to come nearer his material professions but his own Maker, and from this definition it was that the *Rishis* of old discovered this law of our being. You will realize that if all of us follow this law of *varna* we would limit our material ambition, and our energy would be set free for exploring those vast fields whereby and wherethrough we can know God. As years go by, the conviction is daily growing upon me that *varna* is the law of man's being and, therefore, as necessary for Christianity and Islam, as it has been necessary for Hinduism and has been its saving. I refuse, therefore, to believe that *Varnashrama* has been the curse of Hinduism, as it is the fashion nowadays in the South on the part of some Hindus to say. But that does not mean that you and I may tolerate for one moment or be gentle towards the hideous travesty of *varnashrama* that we see about us today. There is nothing in common between *Varnashrama* and caste. Caste, if you will, is undoubtedly a drag upon Hindu progress, and untouchability is as I have already called it or described it an excrescence upon *Varnashrama.* It is a weedy growth fit only to be weeded out, as we weed out the weeds that we see growing in wheat fields or rice fields. In this conception of *varna*, there is absolutely no idea of superiority and inferiority.[3]

Varna means pre-determination of the choice of man's profession. The law of *varna* is that a man shall follow the profession of the his ancestors for earning his livelihood. Every child naturally follows the 'colour' of his father, or chooses his father's profession. *Varna*, therefore, is in a way the law of heredity. *Varna* is not a thing that is super-imposed on Hindus but men who were trustees for their welfare disco-evered the law for them. It is not a human invention, but an immutable law of nature— the statement of a tendency that is ever present and at work like Newton's law of gravitation. Just as the law of gravitation existed even before it was discovered, so did the law of *varna*. It was given to the Hindus to discover that law. But their discovery and application of pertains laws of nature, the peoples of the West have easily increased their material possessions. Similarly, Hindus by their discovery of this irresistible social tendency have been able to achieve in the spiritual field what no other nation in the world has achieved.

An Interview

Q. If a man practises a profession which does not belong to him by birth, what *varna* does he belong to?

A. According to the Hindu belief he belongs to the *varna* in which he is born, but by not living up to it he will be doing violence to himself and becomes a degraded being, a *patita*.

Q. A Shudra does an act which belongs to a Brahmana by birth. Does he become a *patita*?

A. A Shudra has a much right to knowledge as a Brahmana but he falls from his estate if he tries to gain livelihood through teaching. In ancient times there were automatic trade guilds, and it was an unwritten law to support all the members of the profession. A hundred years ago, a carpenter's son never wanted to become a lawyer. Today he does, because he finds the profession the easiest way to steal money. The lawyer thinks that he must charge Rs. 15000 as fees for the exercise of his brain and a physician like Hakim Saheb thinks that he must charge Rs. 1,000 a day for his medical advices!

Q. But may not a man follow a profession after his heart?

A. But the only profession after his heart should be the profession of his fathers. There is nothing wrong in choosing that profession, on the contrary it is noble. What we find today are freaks, and that is why there is violence and disruption of society. Let us not confound ourselves by superficial illustrations. There are thousands of carpenters' sons following their father's callings, but not even a hundred carpenters' sons who are lawyers. In ages gone by there was not the ambition of encroaching on other's profession and amassing wealth. In Cicero's time, for instance, the lawyer's was an honorary profession. And it would be quite right for any brainy carpenter to become a lawyer for service, not for money. Later ambition for fame and wealth crept in. Physicians served the society and rested content with what it gave them, but now they have become traders and even a danger to society. The medical and the legal professions were deservedly called liberal when the motive was purely philanthropic.

Q. You have been saying that the law of *varna* curbs our worldly ambition. How?

A. When I follow my father's profession, I need not even go to a school to learn it, and my mental energy is set free for spiritual pursuits, because my money or rather liveli-hood is ensured. *Varna* is the best from of insurance for happiness and for real religious pursuit. When I concentrate my energy on other pursuits, I sell away my powers of self-realization or sell my soul for a mess of pottage.

Q. You talk of releasing the energies for spiritual pursuits. Today those who follow their father's profession have no spiritual culture at all— their very *varna* unfits them for it.

A. We are talking with crooked notions of *varna*. When *varna* was really practiced, we had enough leisure for spiritual training. Even now, you go to distant villages and see what spiritual vulture villagers have as compared to the town-dwellers. These know no self-control.

But you have spotted the mischief of the age. Let us not try to be what others cannot be. I would not even learn the Gita if every one who wished could not do it. That is why my whole soul rises against learning English for making money. We have to re-arrange our lives so that we ensure to the millions the leisure that a fraction of us have today, and we cannot do it unless we follow the law of *varna.*

Q. What is the *varna* of a man practising different professions at different times?

A. It may not make any difference in his *varna* so long as he gains his livelihood by following his father's profession.

He may do anything he likes so long as he does it for love of service. But he who changes profession from time to time for the sake of gaining wealth degrades himself and falls from *varna*.

Q. Do you not find a man exhibiting qualities opposed to his family character?

A. That is a difficult question. We do not know all our antecedents. If my father is a trader and I exhibit the qualities of soldier, I may without reward serve my country as soldier but must be content to earn my bread by trading.[4]

Time and again he asked *Savarna* Hindus to show good treatment towards Harijans and not to magnify their social disabilities. They should save them from conversions by adopting liberal views and by doing so, they would save them from social degradation. He also sought the sympathy and support of Hindu reformers in this regard.

Secession of stalwarts like Dr. Ambedkar can but weaken the defence of Harijans. We know, as a matter of fact that non-Hindu Harijans, no matter how eminent they may be, are not able to help Hindu Harijans. Indeed, they are a class apart still in their adopted faiths. Such is the hold untouchability of the Indian type has on the people in India.[5]

Ever since Dr. Ambedkar has thrown his bombshell in the midst of Hindu society in the shape of threatened conversion, frantic efforts have been made to wean him from the proposed step. Dr. Ambedkar's threat has had its repercussions on Harijans too, who are at all literate and are able to read newspapers. They have begun to approach Hindu institutions or reformers with a demand for posts, scholarship, or the like, accompanying it with the statement that the writer might, in the event of refusal, be obliged to change to another faith, aid having been offered on behalf of the representatives of that faith.

Without a doubt these threats are a portent and matter of grave concern to those who care at all for the religion of their forefathers. But it will not be served by coming to terms, with those who have lost faith in Hinduism or for that matter in any religion. Religion is not a matter of barter. It is a matter for every individual to decide for himself to which faith he will belong. It does not lend itself to purchase in any shape or from.

It is an admitted fact that the conduct of a vast number of Hindus who call themselves Sanatanists is such as to cause the greatest inconvenience and irritation to the Harijans all over India. The wonder is that many more Harijans than already have, have not left Hinduism. It speaks volumes for their loyalty or for the innate virtue of Hinduism that millions of Harijans have clang to it in spite of the inhumanities to which in the name of that very faith they have been subjected.

Loyalty of Harijans

This wonderful loyalty of Harijans and their unexampled patience render it imperative for every *Savarna* Hindu to see that Harijans receive the same treatment that every other Hindu does. The course before *Savarnas* is, therefore, on the one hand, not to interfere with Harijans wishing to leave the Hindu fold by trying to keep them within it by the offer of bribes in the shape of finding employment or scholarships; and on the other hand, to insist on full justice being done to Harijans in every walk of life. Indeed reformers should anticipate the Harijans, requirements and not wait till they begin to complain. The Harijan Sevak Sangh is the biggest institution for the removal of untouchability. It has wisely adopted a most liberal policy of giving scholarship to deserving students. It employs as many Harijans as possible. But it is in no sense a bureau for finding jobs for unemployed Harijans. Generally speaking, there is no dearth of jobs for Harijans who are fit for the jobs for which they offer themselves.

One word to the impatient and needy Harijans. They must not use treats when they approach Hindu institutions or individuals for help. They should rely upon the strength of their case demanding a hearing. The majority of Harijans do not know what change of religion can mean. They mutely suffer the continuing degradation to which *Savarnas* in their selfishness have consigned them. They must be the primary care of Hindu reformers whether they complain or do not.[6]

Dr. Ambedkar wants to scourge the *Savarna* Hindus as he has every right to do, but he may not expect the latter to be party to it. He has every right to be impatient. But prejudices and superstitions centuries old do not die in a moment. No one who has at all cared to study the reform movement will deny that every attempt humanly possible has been and is being made to bring home to the *Savarna* Hindus the message of the anti-untouchability movement. If Dr. Ambedkar's proposal were accepted, the reform movement would receive a setback which might mean death to it in the end.

If the leaders of different religions in India ceased to compete with own another for enticing Harijans, into their fold, it would be well for this unfortunate country. I have the profound convictions that those who are engaged in the competition are not serving the cause of religion. By looking at it in terms of politics or economics they reduce the religious values, whereas the proper thing would to be estimate politics and every other thing in terms of religion : Religion deals with the science of the soul. Great as the other forces of the world are, if there is such a thing as God, soul force is the greatest the force the finer it is. Hitherto electricity has held the field among the finer physical powers. And yet nobody has seen it except through its wonderful results. Scientific speculation dares to talk of a force finer even than that of electricity. But no instrument devised by man has been able to know anything positive of soul force or spritual force. It is on that force that the true religious reformer has hitherto relied and never without hope fulfilled. It is that force which will finally govern the welfare of Harijans and everyone else and confound the calculations of man, however, gifted they may be intellectually. The reformer who has entered upon the duty of riding Hinduism of the disease of untouchability has to depend in everything he does on that force and nothing else.[7]

Hinduism and Culture

Two friends write to me deploring my attitude on Dr. Ambedkar's proposal. Their argument may be summed up as follows:

Surely you are making much ado about nothing. Guru Nanak was a Hindu reformer like the others who have founded Hindu sects, Sikhs are Hindus to all intents and purposes. Their culture is the same as of the Hindus. If Harijans declare themselves as Sikhs, why do you call it change of faith?

The objectors seem to be alone in their questions. Some time after 1915 when I returned home from my self-imposed exile of fourteen years, I happened to go to the Punjab. Addressing a meeting of Sikhs, I had said they were in my opinion Hindus belonging to a sect of reformers. A well-meaning Sikh friend spoke to me aside and said I had unwillingly offended Sikhs by calling them Hindus. What they believe matters, not what I or a few individuals do. Sikhs have separate electorate. Dr. Ambedkar does not regard Sikhs as Hindus. He definitely wants a change of faith. If Sikhs were a Hindu sect, no change in the Pact would be necessary. It is open to any Hindu to change his sect and still remain a Hindu.[8]

Christians in Travancore

The Mahatma did not hesitate to narrate activities of Christians in Tranvancore and other regions of India. Christian missions were spending a lot on conversions mostly in eastern, southern and central regions of our country. Their missionaries opened educational institutions, hospitals, churches and other centres which could benefit the weaker sections of the society. The allurements given by them were the economic security for them and welfare for their children. The Mahatma stated that the Christians missions were flirting with Harijans.

Tranvancore has a large and important Christian community. Christian missions are flirting with Harijans, rightly no doubt foom their own standpoint, they are spending money on them and holding out hope of real freedom and equality of social status. It is beside the present discussion that for Harijans there is no social equality , no real freedom, anywhere except when it is first obtained in Hinduism. I am not thinking of individuals. I am thinking of the whole mass. The latter are so interwined with the other Hindus that unless they become brothers with them instead of remaining serfs which they are, no change of label can avail anything.[9]

About the 9th of October there was a meeting of Christian

denominations in London. His Grace the Archbishop of Canterbury presided. The following occurs in the report of the meeting published in the *Church Times* of the 16th October:- The next speaker was dressed as a layman, without even the smallest discernible purple patch to indicate that he was Dr. J.W. Pickett, a Bishop of the Methodist Episcopal Church. U.S.A. For some years past, Dr. Pickett has been studying the mass movements on the spot in India, and has published the results of his observations in *Christian Mass* Movements in India, described by the Archbishop of Canterbury as a remarkable and valueable book. Dr. Pickett is profoundly impressed with the spiritual significance of the movements. He said that four and a half millions of the depressed classes in India have become the disciples of our Lord, and the witness they bear to Him in their lives is making the multitudes in India marvel. Even Brahmanas have testified—albeit reluctantly— to the power of Christianity to transform the characters and lives of people whom they once thought incapable of religious feelings, and to whom they denied the right of entrance to the temples of Hinduism. It is people of this kind, said Dr. Pickett, who have now standards of church attendance and worship difficult to equal in Western Christendom. He Quoted an example in the Telugu area, where 9,00,000 people now profess the Christian Faith. Out of 1,026 villages 1,002 hold a service for the worship of God every eventing of the year, and more than two hundred also a daily morning service. It appeared to satisfy Dr. Pickett entirely as a test of the reality of the faith of the converts to hear a surprisingly high proportion of them speak of a sense of mystical union with God, and their belief that God had come into their lives. Even their Hindu neighbours admitted that the religion of Jesus Christ had lifted them to a new standard of cleanliness of person and home, and made them a trustworthy people. More impressive still is the fact that high caste people are now coming into the Church literally by dozens and hundreds in areas where this transformation of life has occurred among the untouchables. 'It is a miracle' he declared: 'One of the great miracles of Christian history'.

I have rarely seen so much exaggeration in so little space. A reader ignorant of condition in India would conclude that the figures relate to the conversions due to the movement led by Dr. Ambedkar. I am sure Dr. Pickett could not have made any such claim. He has in mind the figures to date commencing from the establishment of the first Church in India hundreds of years ago. But the figures are irrelevant to the general claim said to have been advanced by the Bishop. Where are "the multitudes in India who marvel" at the transformation in the lives of "four and a half millions of the depressed classes"? I am one of the multitude having practically travelled more than half a dozen times all over India, and have not seen any transformation on the scale described by Dr. Pickett, and certainly none of recent date. I have had the privilege of addressing meetings of Indian Christians who have appeared to me be no better than their fellows. Indeed the taint of untouchability persists in spite of the nominal change of faith so far as the social status is concerned. Needles to say I am referring to the masses, not individuals. I should like to know the Brahmanas "who have testified—albeit reluctantly—to the power of Christianity to transform the characters and lives of people whom they once thought incapable of religious feeling." But if it is of any consequence, I can show many Brahamanas who can testify to the power of the reform movement to make a radical change in the lives and outlook of Harijans who were neglected by Caste Hindus. I must pass by the other unbelievable generalizations. But I should like to know the hundreds of high Caste Hindus who "are now coming into the church in areas where this transformation of life has occurred among the untouchables". If all the astounding statements Dr. Pickett has propounded can be substantiated, truly it is "one of the great miracles of Christian history", nay, of the history of man.

But do miracles need an oratorical demonstration? Should we in India miss such a grand miracle? Should we remain untouched by it? Miracles are their own demonstration. As witness the miracle in Travancore. Nobody believed a month ago that more than 2000 temples of Travancore could be opened to Harijans and that Harijans would enter them in their hundreds without let or hindrance from the most orthodox Hindus. Yet that even has happened in Tranvancore which even he who runs may see. It is beside the point whether it can be called a miracle or not. I see in it the visible finger of the invisible God.

I believe in the Bible as I believe in the Gita. I regard all the great faiths of the world as equally true with my own. It hurt me to see any one of them caricatured as they are today by their own followers and as has been done by the learned Bishop, assuming of course that the report reproduced above is substantially correct.[10]

Dr. Mott's Questions

Dr. Mott: "Removal of untouchability is the business of your lifetime. The importantce of this movement lies beyond the frontiers of India, and yet there are few subjects on which there is more confusion of thought. Take for instance, the Missionaries and Missionary Societies. They are not of one mind. It is highly desirable that we become of one mind and find out how far we can help and not hinder. I am Chairman of the International Missionary Council which combines 300 Missionary Societies in the world. I have on my desk reports of these Societies, and I can say that their interest in the untouchables is deepening. I should be interested if you would feel free to tell me where, if anywhere, the Missionaries have gone along wrong lines. Their desire is to help and not to hinder."

Deshbandhu Andrews here asked to be permitted to put forward a concordant. He said: "There are fundamental differences between you and the Missionaries, and yet you are a friend of the Missionaries. But you feel that they are not playing the game. You want the leaders of the Church to say: 'We do not want to fish in troubled waters: we shall do nothing to imply that we are taking advantage of a peculiar situation that has arisen'."

Gandhiji: "I do not think it is a matter which admits of any compromise at all. It is a deeply religious problem and each should do what he likes. If your conscience tells you that the present effort is your mission, you need not give any quarter to Hindu reformers. I can simply state my belief that what the Missionaries are doing today does not show "spirituality".[11]

'Christian Harijans' should be a contradiction in terms. For, untouchability that is sought to be driven out of India is the special curse (according to the reformers) or the privilege (according to Sanatanists) of Hinduism. But the Hindu contact has so infected the Christian that at least in Malabar it seems to show itself among Christians almost in the same form as among Hindus. Thus writes a Malabar Christian to Shri Amritlal Thakkar:

From the days of the famous Vykom Satyagraha, the real condition of the Travancore Harijans, the worst in India, has been brought to light to a very great extent, but it is not yet suspected or detected except by a few solitary individuals like C.F. Andrews, that the Christian Harijan in Travancore is, in matter of civic or social rights and in abject poverty, absolutely the same as his Hindu Harijan brother. Pulayas or Cherumas, Pariahs or Sambhavas with Ignaoas or Ina Pulayas and some other minor communities number about 6,00,000 according to the last year's census report and are considered the lowest strata of the outcaste societies of Travancore.

Public institutions, roads, inns, rest-houses, temples, Churches, court-houses, business houses, shops, streets and even taverns that are unapproachable by the one are exactly to the same extent unapproachable by the other. To both, caste men like Nambudris are unseeable to this day.

Prosperous Christian communities like Nadars in the South and Syrians in the North, who thrived for long in the generations of the Missionaries and State endowments are to us what no change Sanatanists are to our Hindu Harijan brother. Hundreds of Churches unapproachables by us (Harijan, either Christian or Hindu) will explain why Christian Harijans of the bottom ranks have to make common cause with their fellow outcaste brothers.

We believe that the innumerable cruelties inflicted upon us by the Caste Hindus and Christians and the inhuman practice of hunting us out of human abodes, especially in Central and North Travancore, not only by touchables but also by untouchables like Ezhavas, are facts too well known to you to need our quoting in this letter specific instances to illustrate the general yet accurate observation made above.

This state of things is no doubt a disgrace to Hinduism but is no less to Christianity, if not more so.[12]

The following Press cutting has been sent to me by Thakkar Bapa:[13]

Kumbakonam—December 14. Tension prevailed yesterday during the Sunday Service in St. Mary's Cathedral, Kumbakonam, consequent upon Catholic Harijans entering in an organized body and distributing themselves admits the Caste Catholics instead of occupying the portion specifically intended for them. Commotion and uproar followed the Harijans refusing to budge an inch. The situation growing worse, the caste people withdrew from the service expressing determination not to attend until there was a final settlement of the issues involved. The Harijans held a meeting at which it was resolved to continue the fight till equality was secured. The Bishop advised the Harijans to act reasonably, assuring them that the separate accommodation implied no special distinction except for mere convenience. He wanted them not to wound other people's feelings by springing innovations without mental understanding. Not satisfied with the Bishop's assurance, the Harijan leaders are carrying out propaganda in the villages urging resistance against what they called caste arrogance and bigotry.

Whether the Harijan is nominally a Christian, Muslim or Hindu and now Sikh, he is still a Harijan. He cannot change his spots inherited from Hinduism so-called. He may change his garb and call himself Catholic Harijan, or a Muslim Harijan or neo-Muslim or neo-Sikh, his untouchability will haunt him during his lifetime. It is one and the same thing whether you call the numeral offer five half a dozen or six. Not until untouchability is removed from Hinduism will the taint be removed from Harijans, no matter what label they adopt.[14]

Temple Entry

Among the marks of untouchability to be removed was the prohibition against temple -entry by Harijans. Before, therefore, the movement of temple-entry could make headway, it had become imperative to have this anomaly removed. 'Whether, therefore, Harijans desire temple entry or not, Caste Hindus have to open their temples to Harijans, precisely on the same terms as to other Hindus...... Temple-entry is the one spiritual act that would constitute the message of freedom to the 'untouchables' and assure them that they are not out castes before God.,

Vykom Satyagraha

Vykom Satyagraha had attracted such wide public attention, and though restricted to a small area, presented so many problems for solution. Gandhi opined thus: 'There is no doubt in my mind about it that the orthodox Hindus, who still think that worship of God is inconsistent with touching a portion of their own co-religionists and that a religious life is summed up in ablutions and avoidance of physical pollutions merely, are alarmed at the development of the movement at Vykom. They believe that their religions is in danger. It behoves the organizers, therefore, to set even the most orthodox and the most bigoted at ease and to assure them that they do not seek to bring about the reform by compulsion. The Vykom Satyagrahis must stoop to conquer. They must submit to insults and worse at the hands of the bigoted and yet love them, if they will change their hearts'.

According to Gandhi, trustees were not owners of temple. Even owners ceased to have property rights over temples when they were meant for public use. True owners of the temples were the votaries who went there to worship. 'I have myself visited these temples. No one even cared to inquire as to what my sect was. It was enough that I looked like a Hindu. The same holds good of hundreds of other visitors like myself. Therefore, the Harijans must be free to visit all temples that are open to the Hindus.'

'Vykom of which till lately no one outside Travancore, at most the Madras Presidency, knew anything has suddenly leapt to fame because it has become the seat of Satyagraha. The Press contains daily bulletins of the progress of the movement. It has been undertaken on behalf of the 'untouchables' of Travancore. The movement has given us another word to describe the condition of the suppressed classes. It is unapproachability. These poor countrymen of ours may not only touch any other Caste Hindus but they may not even approach them within a stated distance. The leaders of the movement with a view to remedying the veil have taken up only a fragment of the evil, hoping no doubt that if they deal with it successfully, they will have dealt it a death-blow at least in that part of India in which direct action is now going on. In the prosecution of the campaign some of the staunchest workers of Malabar have been imprisoned. There can now be no receding. The struggle may last long if orthodox Hindu opinion is actively hostile to the movement. The Satyagrahis are certain to break down the wall of prejudice, no matter how strong and solid it may be if they continue firm, but humble, truthful and non-violent. They must have faith enough in these qualities to know that they will melt the stoniest hearts.'

'I have been asked to develop the argument against sending aid, apart from public sympathy, from outside Travancore. I have already stated the utilitarian argument in an interview. But there is a root objection too to getting, indeed even accepting, such support. Satyagraha is either offered by a few self-sacrificing persons in the name of the many weak, or by very few in the face of enormous odds. In the former case which is the case in Vykom, many are willing but weak, and a few are willing and capable of sacrificing their all for the cause of 'untouchables'. In such a case it is obvious they need no aid whatsoever. But suppose that they took outside aid, how would it serve the 'untouchable' countrymen? The weak Hindus in the absence of strong ones rising in their midst will not prevail against the strong opponents. The sacrifice of helpers from other parts of India will not convert the opponents and it is highly likely that the last stage of the 'untouchables' will be worse than the first. Let it be remembered that Satyagraha is a most powerful process of conversion. It is an appeal to the heart. Such an appeal cannot be successfully made by people from other parts of India flocking to Vykom.'[15]

'In the case too of a very few offering Satyagraha against heavy odds, outside support is not permissible. Public Satyagraha is an extension of private or domestic Satyagarha. Every instance of public Satyagraha should be tested by imagining a parallel domestic case. Thus, suppose in my family I wish to remove the course of untouchability. Suppose further that my parents oppose the view, that I have the fire of the conviction of Prahlad, that my father threatens penalties, call in even the assistance of the State to punish me. What should I do? May I invite my friends to suffer with me the penalties my father has devised for me? Or is it not up to me, meekly to bear all the penalities my father inflicts on me and absolutely rely on the law of suffering and love to melt his heart and open his eyes to the evil of untouchability? It is open to me to bring in the assistance of learned men, the friends of the family, to explain to my father what he may not understand from me, his child. But I may allow no one to share with me the privilege and duty of suffering. What is true of this supposed case of domestic Satyagraha is equally true and no less of the case we have imagined of public Satyagraha. Whether therefore the Vykom Satyagraha represent a hopeless minority or as I have been informed, a majority of the Hindus- concerned, it is clear that they should avoid aid from outside save that of public sympathy. That in every such case we may not be able to conform to the law, that in the present case too, we may not be able to do so may be true. Let us not, however, forget the law and let us conform to it as far as ever we can.[16]

Vykom Satyagraha has attracted such wide public attention, and through restricted to a small area, presents so many problems for solution that offered no apology to the reader for constantly engaging his attention for it. He received several important and well-though out letters protesting against my countenancing it in any way whatsoever. One such letter even urges me to use whatever influence I may have, for stepping it altogether. I am sorry that I am unable to publish all these letters. But I hope to cover all the points raised in these letters or otherwise brought to my notice.

The first may be cleared at once. Exception has been to Shri George Joseph – a Christian –having been allowed to replace Shri Menon as leader and organizer. In my humble opinion the exception is perfectly valid. As soon as I heard that Shri Joseph was 'invited to take the leader' and he contemplated taking it, I wrote to him as follows on 6th April:

"As to Vykom, I think that you should let the Hindus do the work. It is they who have to purify themselves. You can help by your sympathy and by your pen, but not by organising the movement and certainly not by offering Satyagraha. If you refer to the Congress resolution of Nagpur it calls upon the Hindu members to remove the curse of untouchability. I was surprised to learn from Mr. Andrews that the disease had infected even the Syrian Christians."

Unfortunately before the letter could reach him, Shri Menon was arrested and Shri George Joseph had taken his place. But he had nothing to expiate, as every Hindu has in the matter of untouchability as countenanced by the Hindus. His sacrifice cannot be appropriated by the Hindus in general as expatiation made, say by Malaviyaji would be. Untouchability is the is sin of the Hindus. They must suffer for it, they nust purify themselves, they must pay the debt they owe to their suppressed brothers and sisters. Theirs is the shame and theirs must be the glory when they have purged themselves of the black sin. The silent, loving suffering of one single pure Hindus as such will be enough to melt t he heart of millions of Hindus; but the sufferings of thousands of non-Hinuds on behalf of the 'untouchables' will leave the Hindus unmoved. Their blind eyes will not be opened by outside interference, however, well-intentioned and generous it may be; for it will not bring home to them the sense of guilt. On the contrary, they would probably hug the sin all the more for such interference. All reforms to be sincere and lasting must come from within.

The reformers, I am sure, do not seek to force their views upon the community; they strike to touch its heart. Outside pecuniary help must interfere with the love process if I may so describe the method of Satyagraha. Thus viewed, the proposed Sikh free kitchen, I can only regard, as a menace to the frightened Hindus of Vykom. There is no doubt in my mind about it that the orthodox Hindus, who still think that worship of God is inconsistent with touching a portion of their own co-religionists and that a religious life is summed up in ablutions and avoidance of physical pollutions merely, are alarmed at the development of the movement at Vykom. They believe that their religion is in danger. It behoves the organizers, therefore, to set even the most orthodox and the most bigoted at ease and to assure them that they do not seek to bring about the reform conquer. They must submit to insults and worse at the hands of the bigoted and yet love them, if they will change their hearts.

Role of Satyagrahrisa

But a telegram says   in effect, 'the authorities are barricading the roads; may we not break or scale the fences? May we not fast? For we find that fasting is effective.'

My answer is, if we are Satyagrahrisa, we dare not scale or is break fences. Breaking or scaling fences will certainly bring about imprisonment but the breaking will not be civil disobedience. It will be essentially in civil and criminal. Nor may we fast. I observe that my letter to Joseph with reference to fasting has been misunderstood. For the sake of ready refernces I reproduce below the relevant part:

"Omit fasting but stand or squat in relays with quiet submission till arrested."

"The above is the wire sent to you in reply to yours. Fasting in Satyagrahra has well-defined limits. You cannot fast against a tyrant, for it will be a species of violence done to him. You invite penalty from him for disobedience of his orders but you cannot inflict on yourselves penalties when he refused to punish, and renders it impossible for you to disobey his order so as to compel infliction of penalty. Fasting can only be resorted to against a lover, not to extort rights but to reform him, as when a son fasts for a father who drinks. My fast at Bombay and then at Bardoli was of that character. I fasted to reform those who loved me. But I will not fast to reform, say, General Dyer, who not only does not love me but who regards himself as my enemy. Am I quite clear?"

It need not be pointed out that the above remarks are of a general character. The words 'tyrant' and 'lover' have also a general application. The one who does an injustice is styled 'tyrant'. The one who is in sympathy with you is the 'lover'. In my opinion, in the Vykom movement opponents of the reform are the 'tyrant'. The State may or may not be that. In this connection I have considered the State as merely the police striving to keep the peace. In no case is the State or the opponents in the position of 'lover'. The supporters of Vykom Satyagrahis enjoy that status. There are two conditions attached to a Satyagrahi fast. It should be against the lover and for his reform, not for extorting rights from him. The only possible case in the Vykom movement when a fast will be justified, would be when the local supporters go back upon their promise to suffer. I can fast against my father to cure him of a vice, but I may not in order to get from him an inheritance. The beggars of India who sometimes fast against those who do not satisfy them are no more Satyagrahis than children who fast against a parent for a fine dress. The former are impudent, the latter are childish.

My Bardoli fast was against fellow-workers who ignited the Chauri Chaura spark and for the sake of reforming them. If the Vykom Satyagrahis fast because the authorities will not arrest them. It will be, I must say in all humility, the beggar's fast described above: If it proves effective it shows the goodness of the authorities, not that of the cause or of the actors. A Satyagrahi's first concern is not the effect of his action. It must always be its propriety. He must have faith enough in his cause and his means, and know that success will be achieved in the end.

But, say some of my correspondents, the conditions for lawful Satyagraha do not exist in Vykom. They ask:

1. Is unapproachability exclusively observed at Vykom or is it general throughout Kerala?
2. If it is general, then what is the special reason for selecting Vykom in preference to places within the British territory in Kerala?
3. Did the Satyagrahis petition the Maharaja, the local Assembly, etc.?
4. Did they consult the orthodox sections?
5. Is not the use of the road the thin end of the wedge, is it not a step towards the abolition of caste altogether?
6. Is not the road a private road?

The first two questions are irrelevant. Unapproachability and untouchability have to be tackled wherever they exist. Wherever the workers consider a place or time suitable, it is their duty to start work whether by Satyagraha or other legitimate means.

My information goes to show that the method of petition, etc., was tried not once but often.

I am assured that the use of the road is the final goal of the Satyagraha. It is, however, not to be denied that the present movement throughout India is to throw open to the suppressed classes all the public roads, public schools, public wells and public temples which are accessible to non-Brahmanas. It is in fact a movement to purify caste by ridding it of its most pernicious result.

I have letters which protest that the road in question is a public road. In fact my informants tell me it was some years ago even accessible to the unapproachable as to other non-Brahmanas.

In my opinion, therefore, there is a just cause for the Vykom Satyagraha, and so far as it is kept within proper limits and conducted with the strictest regards to non-violence and truth, it deserves full public sympathy.[17]

The representatives from Kerala asked me if they should not have a resolution of the Congress supporting the movement. I told them that I did not like the idea. What they wanted was moral support. It would have been given by the Committee for the asking, if they had sent a resolution to the President. My responsibility in dissuading them was, therefore, serious. But I am convinced that all local movements must be self-reliant and that the AICC should give its moral support only in exceptional cases.

A word now to the organizers of Vykom Satyagraha. The challenge of the *goondas* must be taken up. But the Satyagraha must not lose their heads. The Khaddar dress of the volunteers is said to have been torn from them and burnt. This is all must provoking. They must remain cool under every provocation and courageous under the hottest fire. Loss even of a few hundred lives will not be too great a price to pay for the freedom of the 'unapproachables'. Only the martyrs must die clean. Satyagraha like Caesar's wife must be above suspicion.[18]

The Vykom Satyagraha has perhaps a meaning deeper than is generally realized. The young men who have organized it are stern in discipline and gentle in their dealings with the orthodox section. But this is the least part of their trails. Some of them are suffering too the persecution of social boycott. We of the Western Presidency have no idea of what this persecution can mean. These young men who are taking part in the movement are not only being denied social amenities but are threatened even with the deprecation of their share in the family property. If they would go to law, probably they would get their due.[19]

The Vykom Satyagraha are fighting a battle of no less consequence than that of Swaraj. They are fighting against an age-long wrong and prejudice. It is supported by orthodoxy, superstition, custom and authority. There is only one among the many battles that must be fought in the holy war against irreligion masquerading as religion, ignorance appearing in the guise of learning. If their battle is to be bloodless, they must be patient under the severest trials. They must not quail before a raging fire.

The Congress Committee may give them no help. They may get no pecuniary help, they may have to starve. Their faith must shine through all these dark trials.

I make bold to state that from the very outset Satyagraha at Vykom was intended to be an educative force and never an instrument of coercion of the orthodox, it was for that reason that the fast against the orthodox was abandoned. It was to avoid coercion of the Government by embarrassment that the barricades have been scrupulously respected. It was for that reason that no attempt was made to dodge the policy. It has been recognized that what appears to the reformers as a gross and sinful superstition is to the orthodox a part of their faith. The Satyagraha's appeal has, therefore, been to the reason of the orthodox.[20] But experience has shown that mere appeal to the reason produces no effect upon those who have settled convictions. The eyes of their understanding are opened not by argument but by the suffering of the Satyagrahi. The Satyagrahi strives to reach the reason through the heart. The method of reaching the heart is to awaken public opinion. Public opinion for which one cares is a mighter force than that of gunpower. The Vykom Satyagraha has vindicated itself in that it has drawn the attention of the whole of India to the cause, and it has been instrumental in the Travancore Assembly considering in a remarkable debate a resolution favouring the reform sought for and lastly in eliciting a considered reply from the Dewan of Travancore. I am sure victory is a certainty if only the Satyagraha will retain their patience and their spirit of suffering.[21]

The conduct of Satyagraha in the Ashram must be in correspondence with their bearing at boundary line. The Ashram must be a busy hive in which every member is ever found at his own allotted task. It must be a model of simplicity and sanitation. The members are pledged to the Charkha work during all spare moments. The spinning, the carding and the weaving departments admit of considerable improvement. Every inmate should be an expert carder and spinner if everyone cannot also become an expert weaver. The members must insist on spinning and weaving at least the cloth required by them. They should also learn Hindi well. They are or should regard themselves as trustees for the prestige and dignity of Hinduism. There is a fight not to end with the opening of the roads round temples but should be considered to be the beginning of a glorious struggle for the purity of Hinduism and removal of the abuses that have crept into it. They are not reformers who would take no note of the opposite side or would violate every sentiment of the orthodox people. They would view with the tallest among the orthodox in purity of conduct and veneration for all that is good and noble in the Shastras. They would not disregards scriptural authority without the deepest thought, and to that end some of them would even study Sanskrit and explore the possibilities of reform within the four corners of the scriptures. They will not be in a hurry but having fearlessly taken all the steps that they can consistently with their creed of truth and non-violence, they will have the patience and the faith of the Rishis of old.

For the opening of the roads is not the final but the first step in the ladder of reform. Temples in general, public wells, public schools must be open to the 'untouchables' equally with the Caste Hindus. But that is not the present goal of the Satyagrahis. We may not force the pace. The schools are almost all open to the 'untouchables'. The temples and the public wells or tanks are not. Public opinion should be carefully cultivated and the majority should be converted before the reform can be successfully carried out. Meanwhile the remedy lies in founding temples and digging tanks or wells that would be open to the 'untouchables' and to the other Hindus. I have no doubt that the movement for the removal of untouchability has made tremendous headway. Let us not retard it by indiscretion or overzeal. Once the idea of pollution by the touch of a person by reason of his birth is gone the rest is easy and bound to follow.[22]

In the course of my tour, I have had the privilege of declaring open many temples amidst the acclamations of thousands of people, practically without dissentient voice. In the single instance where there was an appreciable minority against the opening. I refused to open the temple till minority was won over or it had at least ample time to act upon the majority. If I discovered that a single temple was opened without such consent or by compulsion in any form, I should move heaven and earth to have the temple enclosed to Harijans. Then take the Temple-Entry Bill. I may be allowed to say that the Temple-Entry Bill or an equivalent is absolutely necessary if the will of the majority is to prevail. Today, according to legal opinion, even one dissentient voice is enough to keep a temple closed to Harijans. But I would be no party even to such enabling legislation being passed, if there is not a clear majority of Caste Hindus in favour of it.[23]

The local Harijan Sevak Sangh should make a sustained effort to have the existing temples thrown open and even to build new ones, not for Harijans only but for all. If they are situated in healthy localities and have a school, a meeting place and a *Dharmashala* attached to them, they must prove useful and popular among all classes of Hindus. There may be public prayers held there every evening or at stated periods and religious discourses may be occasionally arranged. If these temple are properly conducted, they would go a long way towards removing the prejudice against the opening of existing temples to Harijans. Care must be taken, where temples are opened to Harijans, that no discrimination is made against them. They must be opened on precisely the same terms as they are opened to the other Hindus.

It is hardly necessary to state that in different localities different methods may be adopted for securing the desired end. Perfect non-violence must of course be maintained in all classes. An all-India simultaneous movement of the same type is not contemplated. It will vary in intensity and method according to the circumstances in each locality. Nowhere should temples be opened where there is an active nimority opposed to the opening. Practical unanimity should be scored before any temple is opened. Thus, what is required is sustained effort to convert local public opinion in favour of temple-entry.[24]

Role of Harijans

You will begin by taking the Harijans along with you to the temple if you are in the habit of going to a temple. But if you discover that you will not be allowed into the temple along with your Harijan companions, then if you have the living belief that I have that untouchableility is wrong, you will shun that temple as you shun a scorpion or fire. You will then believe with me that such a temple is not inhabited by God. I will take by way of illustration the greatest temple known all over the world, viz. Kashi Vishwanath in Banaras. The Lord who is supposed to reside there is known as the Lord of the Universe. And yet in the very name of that Vishwanath the *Savarna* Hindus have today the impudence to say to the Harijans, "You shall not come to this temple!"

I claim to be as good a Hindu as any orthodox Hindu. I have endeavoured to enforce all precepts of Harijans in my own life to the best of my ability. I admit that my ability is small. But that does not affect my attitude to and love for Hinduism. Yet, in spite of all that love for Hinduism, with a due sense of my own responsibility. I am here to tell you that so long as the doors of the Banaras Temple are closed against a single Harijan, Kashi Vishwanath does not reside in that temple, and I could not possibly approach that temple with a belief in its sanctity, or in the fact that by worshipping there, I should be purified of my sins. I can have no sense of piety in respect of such a temple. And what is true of Kashi Vishwanath is true of every other temple in India which bars its doors to Harijans.

If it was demonstrated to me to my satisfaction that the political or economic regeneration of Harijans would be enough to retains the Harijans in the Hindu fold, I should still want to open the temples and remove every trace of inequality, because for me it is, as it must be for you, a question of repentance and reparation for the wrong we have done to our fellowmen.[25]

Role of Travancore Durbar

The Travancore Durbar have earned the congratulations of the whole Hindu world and all thoughtful men, by issuing the following Proclamation:

"Profoundly convinced of the truth and validity of our

religion, believing that it is based on divine guidance and on all-comprehending toleration, knowing that in its practice it has throughout the centuries adapted itself to the need of the changing times, solicitous that none of our Hindus subjects should by reason of birth, caste or community be denied the consolation and solace of the Hindu faith, we have decided and hereby declare, ordain and command that, subject to such rules and conditions as may be laid down and imposed by us preserving their proper atmosphere and maintaining their rituals and observances, there should henceforth be no restriction placed on any Hindu by birth or religion on entering or worshipping at temples controlled by us and our Government."

If the proclamation means anything it means that in the temple conducted under the State aegis Harijans will offer worship precisely on the same terms as the highest Caste Hindu so called. In other words, in the house of God in Travancore henceforth there will be no distinction between man and man, there will be no Harijan and no high caste, all will be Harijans— children of God. If these are not the implications of the great Proclamation, it is nothing but a mere scrap of paper. But we have no reason to doubt its sincerity or suspect any mental reservations.

'I hope you will make a wise and religious use of the Proclamation', Gandhiji said at a big meeting of the Pulaya at Venganoor. It depends upon our mental condition whether we gain something or do not gain anything by going to the temples. We have to approach these temples in a humble and penitent mood. There are so many houses of God. Of course God resides in every human form, indeed in every particle of His creations, everything that is on this earth. But since we, very fallible mortals, do not appreciate the fact that God is everywhere, we impute special sanctity to temples and think that God resides there. And so when we approach these temples we must cleanse our bodies, our minds and our hearts and we should enter them in a prayerful mood and ask God to make us purer men and purer women for having entered their portals. And if you will take this advice of an old man, this physical deliverances that you have secured will be a deliverance of the soul.[26]

I should like to apply this Mantra to our condition in virtue of the Proclamation. Whilst I have unstintingly associated myself in your rejoicings over this great Proclamation and in tendering my thanks and congratulations to His Highness, Her Highness and their Diwan, in terms of this mantra I am obliged also to say that this Proclamation is a tardy carrying out of the behest contained in this verse of the Ishopanishad that I have recited. Only yesterday we were unfit to call ourselves Hindus. For if all that there is in the universe is pervaded by God, that is to say, if the Brahmana and the Bhangi, the learned man and the scavenger, the Ezhava and the Pariah, no matter what caste they belong to –if all these are pervaded by Lord God, in the light of this Mantra, there is none that is high and none that is low, all are absolutely equal, equal because all are the creatures of that Creator. And this is not a philosophical thing to be dished out to Brahmanas or Kshatriyas, but it enunciates as eternal truth which admits of no reduction, no palliation. And if that is so, how can anyone here dare to arrogate superiority to himself over any other human being? I tell you, therefore, that if this Mantra holds good, if there is any man or woman here who believes that the temples are defiled by those called *Avarna*s, that person, I declare, would be guilty of a grave sin.

I would like the Mantra I have recited to be enshrined in the hearts of all our men and women and children; and if this contains, as I hold, the essence of Hinduism, it should be inscribed on the portals of every temple. Don't you then think that we should be belying that Mantra at every   step if we excluded anyone from those temples?[27]

Great as this Proclamation is and great as is its religious merit, greater still is the responsibility that His Highness has taken upon his shoulders, and also his advisers. Whilst without the effort of every *Savarna* Hindu, the Proclamation can undoubtedly be rendered ineffective, I must also say that the Proclamation would not have its full effect unless it is backed in an ample measure by State action. So far as I can see the Proclamation demands State activities in all departments of life. Of these I propose to take the religious first; because from it must follow activities in all the other departments.

I venture to suggest that it is the duty of the State— or of the Maharaja, if there is any destination between the two, for he is the custodian of the vast majority of Hindu temples – that he should see to it that the temples are renovated spiritually, and have the authority and sanctity that they used undoubtedly to have at one time. And I believe that it can only be done if they are in charge of priests who know what they have to do, who know something of the sanctity of them, and of the duties to which they are called. In other words, they should not be ignorant people following their calling for a livelihood, but they should be men who are proud of their privilege of bringing the message of God to temple-goers, showing by their own conduct and their life that these temples are abodes of divinity.

Then there should be the correct kind of instruction given in these temples. The Harijans will be taken by the hand by someone in charge of temples and they will be told what they are expected to gain by temple-worship. This means undoubtedly, according to modern thought, a revolutions in the upkeep and conduct of these temples. But the Proclamation itself is nothing short of a revolutionary document, and if that revolution is to touch, as it ought to touch, the lives of all Hindus, naturally temples have to be abodes of the living God, and not abodes of a mass of gold or other metals worked into figures.

Trustees are not owners of the temples. Even owners cease to have property rights over temples when they are meant for public use. True owners of the temples are the votaries who go there to worship. Regarded in this light, all Jain and Swami Narayan temples are Hindu shrines. I have myself visited these temples. No one even cared to inquire as to what my sect was. It was enough that I looked like a Hindu. The same holds good of hundred of other visitors like myself. Therefore, the Harijans must be free to visit all temples that are open to the Hindus. Today awakened public opinion and the law which embodies the opinion do not regard Harijans as a separate caste, but an integral part of the four or the eighteen *varnas* comprising Hindu society. Therefore, the contrary view cannot prevail. It is the devotee's devotions that makes a temple a living shrine. The deity in the temple is only a reflection of the devotee's spirit.

Admiration and Sympathy

As you are aware, that struggle from its very inception, has commanded my deep admiration and sympathy. It is possible that the conductors of Satyagraha may have made mistakes in the campaign. Who is there in the world who is infallible? But I am satisfied that the mistakes, if any committed, were not deliberate, Satyagraha, like the name itself, is a somewhat new doctrine— rather a new presentation of an old doctrine. The question of untouchables is one of those questions which lends itself to the method of Satyagraha in a peculiar manner, for, Satyagraha is a method of suffering – not suffering imposed by those who oppose you, but suffering imposed upon oneself. No the position taken up by the Satyagraha in Vykom is that the roads that pass by the great temples should be opened to those who are considered to be untouchables and unapproachables. The claim is based upon humanity itself. Any road which is open to the public, or, so far as Hindus are concerned, any road that is open to those who are called Caste Hindus should, it is claimed be open to those who are thrown out of the caste and considered untouchables or unapproachables. In my humble opinion, it is a natural and just claim. As you know, ever since I have set my foot on the Indian soil after a long exile in South Africa, I have been speaking frankly, fearlessly, and freely on the question of untouchability. I claim to be a Sanatana Hindu. I claim to know sufficient of the Sastras for my own purpose. And I venture to suggest that untouchability and unapproachability as these are now practiced in this holy land of ours, have no place or sanction in the history of Please, Hinduism. (Hear, hear), please! neither approval nor disapproval; but simply listen to my remarks I venture to suggest to those who are Professors of Hinduism, who hold Hinduism as dear as life itself, that Hinduism like every other religion, apart from the sanctions of Sastras, has got to submit itself to the rest of universal reason.

In this age of reason, in the age of universals knowledge, in this age of education and comparative theology, any religion which entrenches itself behind Sastraic injunctions and authority merely is, in my humble opinion, bound to perish.

In my opinion, untouchability is a blot upon humanity and, therefore, upon Hinduism. It cannot stand the test of reason. It is in conflict with the fundamental precepts of Hinduism. The first among the three principles I am about to enunciate of Hinduism is *Sathyam Nasti Paramo Dharma* – there is no religion higher that truth. The second is *Ashimsa Paramo Dharma*. And, if "Ahimsa"—meaning love, non-violence —is the law of life— is the greatest religion— is the only religion, then I suggest you that untouchability is in conflict, direct conflict, with that truth. The third is that God alone is; everything else is transitory illusion. *Brahma Satyam, Jaga Anityam.* If God alone is truth, and everything else is noting, is suggest to you that it is impossible for us to reconcile untouchability and unapproachability with this doctrine. I have come, therefore, to reason with my orthodox friends: I have come to plead with them; and by their courtesy and goodwill, I was able to wait upon them this afternoon. They gave me a patient hearing and listened to me. We argued. I appealed to their reason. I appealed to their humanity. And I appealed to the Hinduism in them. I am sorry to confess to you that I was not able to produce the impression that I had expected that I would be able to. But despair is a term which does not occurs in my dictionary. I shall despair when I despair myself of God and humanity. But as I believe in God, as I believe in the fact that we are here met together, and as I believe also in humanity because I see that in spite of all our differences and quarrels, humanity lives on.

I believe also that the Truth that I claim to represent for the time being will impress itself upon my orthodox friends here. I have made three sporting offers to these friends of mine. In the name and on behalf of the Satyagrahis of Vykom, those offers are bindling on me. But I have left them free to reject or accept those offers. I have pleased with them that they should have accepted these offers even though it may be by way of trial. And I have not hesitated to enter into such a unilateral contract because I believe implicitly in the truth which I plead and stand for. For, I have come not to precipitate or enhance the quarrel, but to bring about peace and goodwill between the orthodox section and those who are today trying to act in the name of humanity and justice. Though I may seem at times to be fighting, my purpose is never to fight, or having undertaken a fight not to prolong it, but to bring about peace at the shortest possible notice. An English friend, when I embarked upon non-cooperation, told me that my non-co-operation was only skin-deep, but that I was pining for co-operation, I immediately fell in with him and told him that he had read me correctly. So it is with my orthodox friends— friend I assure them. Satyagraha is there – but to be called off as soon as they wish it. It is for them to make a sporting offer, and it will be accepted. Only let them beware of murdering truth. A Satyagrahi has always a minimum— and this is the minimum in connection with this struggle: the right of way is such a reasonable demand that it has only to be asked to be given. Let it be understood, therefore, that there is no mental reservation behind this struggle.

I have repeatedly told the Hindus of India what the removal of untouchability means to me and to those who are today engaged in that holy campaign. It does not mean that breaking up of *Varnasrama* Dharma; it does not mean inter-dining or inter-marriage. But it does mean the common relation between man and man that should exist in any civilized society. It does mean that places of worship should be open, if they are at all open, to all those who are considered to be Hindus. I grant that if there is a particular class, say Brahmins, who want to build temples and exclude non-Brahmins from them, I say it is their right to do so. But is there a temple which is open to non-Brahmins also, then I say that there is nothing like a fifth caste which may be put out of them. I see no warrant for such an exclusion in the Hindu Sastras. Similarly, I claim that public places such as schools should be opened alike to the untouchables if they are open to other classes. So would it be with watering places such as wells and lakes and rivers. That is the whole of my claim on behalf of those who are engaged in this campaign against untouchability and unapproachability. Let me clear the position a little so far as Vykom is concerned. The present Satyagraha is merely directed towards vindicating the right of the untouchables to pass through the road through which Christians and Mussalmans and the Caste Hindus are entitled to pass. Satyagrahis today are not fighting for entry into temples. They are not fighting in connection with schools— I do not know if there is any prohibition in regard to schools in Travancore. Not that such is not their claim; it is their claim. But I am presenting to you today the implications of the present struggle. But since Satyagraha is a method of conversion and conviction, it seeks never to use the lightest coercion. I, therefore, gladly endorse in its entirety the remarks made by the Dewan Bahadur in his address to the Travancore Assembly. And if I find that the Satyagraha in Vykom in denial of their own vows use violence or any coercive measure in order to put undue pressure upon the orthodox Hindus of Vykom, you will find me, on proof being given to me, entirely dissociating from these Satyagrahis – so called. But so long as the Satyagraha kept within the terms of their contract, so long shall I consider it to be my bounden duty to give all the assistance that a single individual is capable of giving.

I plead, therefore, with all the force I might command with the orthodox Brahmins and non-Brahmins of Vykom who may be opposed to this campaign, to study it in all its bearings, to apply their reason to bear upon this struggle and apply justice and humanity if they find that the struggle is just and the struggle of the Satyagrahis to vindicate the right of humanity is also fair, reasonable and non-violent. I am glad to be able to bear my testimony to the happy relations that have hitherto subsisted generally between the Police authorities and the Satyagrahis. They have shown how a decent, gentlemanly battle can be carried on without any vexation, without any heart-sore and without any violence. I know that prejudices die hard. Untouchability is an error of longstanding. I have told my Satyagraha friends that they will have to exercise tremendous patience. Time is always on the side of those who will wait upon it. Public opinion, I hope even of Vykom, is on their side. And if the Satyagrahis will only have the patience and will be able to endure silent and slow suffering, I have no doubt that victory is theirs.

The Government of Travancore so far as I can see from the Address of the Dewan Bahadur, is holding the scale evenly between the two parties. I know that my Satyagraha friends here shook their heads when I told that the presentation by the Dewan Bahadur was not open to exception. Whatever the truth may be there is no doubt about it that credit will be your own if the two sections of the community meet together and find a reasonable and honourable solution for the difficulty without the intervention of the Government. The Dewan Bahadur himself, so far as his own opinion is concerned, has told the orthodox people where his opinion lies. He invites them to march with the time—to recognize the time spirit. I hope that my orthodox friends will listen to the sound advice given to him. In any event, I can give them my best assurance that no matter what they do, no matter whether they accept my offers or reject them, I shall only do according to the behests of Hindu religion as I know it—to recognize no one as my enemy on the face of the earth. I shall, therefore, love them in spite of differences between them and myself, and I shall ever pray to God that He may guide their steps in the right direction, open the eyes of their understanding, open their eyes to the writing on the wall and render justice to the down trodden countrymen of ours. And I am humble enough also to pray to God at the same time that, if I have misread the Hindu Sastras, if I have misread humanity, and have erred in giving the advice that I have tendered to the Satyagrahis. He will open my eyes also, show me my error and give me the strength and the necessary courage to recognize my error and apologise to my orthodox friends.

One thing more and I have done. Whether there are differences between you and I on the question of untouchability. I hope there is no question of difference of opinion about another matter which also concerns the poorest of the land. I refer to the spinning wheel and khaddar. You owe it to the poorest in the land to find a sacred corner in your homes for the spinning wheel and you owe it to them that you wear the product of the spinning wheel and place a few coppers in the pockets of your country men and country women. I shall not be satisfies, as I have said repeatedly, until the prince and the peasant, the viceroy and his page are clad from top to bottom in khaddar, home-spun, hand-spun and hand-made.

The third thing—I don't need mention it to you – is Hindu-Muslim unity. You have in this connection much to teach the rest of India. All the different races and communities belonging to different religions, I am happy to be able to note and testify, are living in perfect harmony and friendship in Travancore. I hope that the rest of India will copy the admirable spirit which actuates you.

I thank you all for the very patient hearing that you have kindly given to me, and I close with the hope and the fervent prayer that the battle that is going on in Vykom may end in the only manner in which it suits.

Gospel of Spinning and Khadi

Take up the gospel of the spinning and khaddar. I have urged His Holiness to take up this in right earnest, and I ask every one of you to take to spinning, to take to weaving and wear the product of your own labour. I understand that, not very long ago, every one of you, or at least every women in your community, was a beautiful spinner. Thousand upon thousands knew how to weave. Both are noble callings. In spinning alone lies the economic salvation of India—I am convinced. Individually, spinning, I admit, is not a profitable occupation. But nationally, it is one of the most noble and the most profitable of occupations. Hence I have called spinning, the sacrifice, the *Yajna,* at this stage, for India. And I was gladdened beyond measure when His Holiness told me that he would like to spin himself. He has given me his assurance that henceforth he is going to ask everyone of his devoted disciples and to appear in his presence unless he is clad in spotless khaddar. (Applause) I expect all the educated men amongst you to feel the privilege of spinning and the privilege of wearing khaddar. It is not criminal in Travancore to wear khaddar. I expect you to go amongst your women-folk, and ask them to do likewise. You do not go in for heavy sarees that the Tamil sisters do in the Madras Presidency. You do not go in for a variety of colours. I am charmed with the spotless white dress of the women of Travancore. A few yards of cloth suffices your wants— both men and women. You must regard it as a matter of shame, humiliation and degradation that you should have to fall back upon Manchester or Ahmedabad calico. If you will attend to these things, that will be your contribution to the national cause, or to the cause of Satyagraha at Vykom. Do not be frightened that it is a long-drawn out battle. His Holiness told me yesterday that we might not see the end of this agony during our life time in this generation. He thinks: "I shall have to wait for another incarnation of mine before I have the pleasure of seeing the end of this agony." I respectfully differ from him. I hope to see the end in this very age— during my lifetime. But I do not hope to do so without your assistance. Assist me to the full measure of your ability; and I undertake to show to you that this wrong becomes a thing of the past. Do your duty manfully, and I undertake to show to you that this fifth class is entirely eradicated from Hinduism. May God grant the necessary strength and determination to His Holiness to infect him with a proper understanding. And may God grant you the wisdom and the strength to carry out the sacred task that you have undertaken.

I tender my thanks once more, publicly, to His Holiness for the extreme kindness that he has shown to me and the hospitality that he has extended to me. I thank you once more for the address that you have presented to me, and for the patience with which you have listened to me. But the best reward that I expect from you is a translation of what you have listened to from me to action."

In fact many years before Gandhi undertook Satyagraha against untouchability at Vykom, a social revolutionary trend was glaring phenomenon in this State under the leadership of Sri Narayana Guru who believed that caste was the main obstacle in the way of social, economic and political emancipation of the country. He wanted the rule of *dharma* and not the law of *varna* to guide the lives of the people. By his public speeches and personal contact with numerous people, he repudiated the relevance of *varna* by calling it mischievous in the life of an individual and proved with facts that 'it was an irrational absurdity spun into a pseudoscience by selfish philosophers'. He opined that man was not made for caste as it degenerated him. According to him, 'There is no caste: it is foolishness to think there is.' He, therefore, declared, 'One caste, one religion, one God for man'.[28]

The Satyagraha

Thus, the Satyagraha had its off-shoots from the social and economic conflicts and contradictions inherent in the caste system. These social degrading disabilities sprang from the evils of untouchability, unapproachability and unseeability of the exterior castes which were practiced with fanatical rigour unknown in many parts of India. So much so, when the high castemen went anywhere, they shouted at the low-castemen to get out of the way where they had to pass, and they did so without murmur; and if they did not do so, the Nayar might kill them without penalty. Besides, the slightest violation of the caste restrictions was viewed with grave concern by people as well as by the Government, and the heaviest punishment was awarded to the offenders.

Besides, other serious disabilities like denial of right to walk along public roads, to enter public schools, law courts, and Government offices and services, plagued the untouchables during a few decades of the twentieth century. The Government had put up sign boards on the public roads near temples, palaces and abodes of Brahmins prohibiting lower castes from entering the area, indicating the uneven justice based on injunctions of caste regulations, imparted by the rulers and their eagerness to perpetuate the caste-race superiority of the Savarnas.

The Government of Travancore strove to enforce these caste rules with extreme security. In most cases, these customary regulations and practices had no sanction in the *Dharmasastras,* but the ethics of the Brahmins gave a superior religious sanction for them, thereby making these customs stronger than law.

The officials of the State felt much disturbed when the Congress Committee announced to take out a procession of mixed castes along the prohibited roads. They also sent representations to the Travancore Durbar urging that prompt measures should be taken to protect Vykom temple from pollution. The District Magistrate issued a prohibitory order under section 127 which stated that it would be a breach of State law to encourage untouchables to walk along the roads leading to the temple.

The Maharaja of the State, though an enlightened ruler, was highly orthodox in his private life and wanted that all caste rules should be scrupulously followed by the people. Therefore, Congress interference in the social and political life of the State was deeply resented by him. He instructed the bureaucracy of the State to crush any kind of breach of peace with a severe action, and outside help, if any, should be severely dealt with.

The prominent members of the Anti-untouchability Committee, consisting of T.K. Madhavan, K.P. Kesava Menon and a few others decided to meet Government's opposition by sending three or four volunteers at a time through the prohibited road on 30 March, 1924. When the first batch of three marched on the prohibited lines, they were stopped by the police. The District Magistrate sentenced them to six month's simple imprisonment on their refusal to offer sureties. Other batches, which followed their leaders, met the same fate. Their increasing involvement in non-violent Satyagraha leading to their arrests made Gandhi to send a message of congratulations to the volunteers who courted arrests for a noble cause. Subsequently, every word uttered by Gandhi on the Vykom Satyagraha proved a source of encouragement to the numerous Satyagrahis in the State.

Meeting were held all over the State to propagate the ideal of Satyagraha in which Hindus, Muslims and Christians participated and freely discussed the spirit of inter-communal and inter-caste solidarity. Resolutions were passed entreating all people to make and wear hand-spun khadi cloth and advising them not to sell or use liquor. Thus, every village turned to be a centre for propaganda and fund collection. Leaders and volunteers from outside Kerala also joined to take active part in this campaign.

Gandhi, accompanied by his private secretary, Mahadev Desai, his son, Remadas Gandhi, C. Rajagopalachari and others reached Vykom in order to dispel the misapprehensions of the orthodox sections and to bring about a change in their attitude towards the Satyagraha. He met the Maharani Regent, Sri Narayana Guru, the Dewan and prominent orthodox leaders on 12 March, 1925 and discussed all details of the problems confronting the Satyagrahis for the cause of the untouchables at Vykom.

In a public meeting held at Vykom on March, 1925, soon after his interviews with orthodox Hindu leaders, Gandhi said, '...I am sorry to confess to you that I was not able to produce the impression that I had expected that I would be able to. But despair is a term which does not occur in my dictionary. I shall when I despair myself of God and humanity.'

Gandhi also explained thus: 'I grant that if there is a particular class, say Brahmins, who want to build temples and exclude non-Brahmins, from them, I say it is their right to do so. But if there is a temple which is open to non-Brahmins also, then I say that there is nothing like a fifth caste which may be put out of them. I see no warrant for such an exclusion in the Hindu Sastras.'

On the basis of an agreement Satyagraha was called off on 23 November, 1925. The agreement stated that all the roads round Vykom temple with the exception of two lanes were open to all castes without distinction. At a short distance, a gate was put up inside which people would be admitted only for purpose of worship in the temple. It was also declared that the enclosed portion would be open neither to Christians and Muslims, nor to Hindus who had not got the right of worship in the temple nor even to a caste-Hindu except during hours of service. A new road was to be constructed joining the eastern approach to the northern road for the convenience of the public.

K. Kelappan in a statement expressed satisfaction at this settlement and took the terms of the Government to mean that all the road lying round the temple at Vykom were now alike open to all members of the hundu ommunity, be he a Caste Hindu or a non-caste Hindu, and that no invidious distinction was made in the matter of the right of way as between the citizens of the State.

Thus, the steps for the upliftment of Harijans taken by Gandhi were unique in our history. Along with numerous other issues—political, social, economic, cultural and others—he ardently identified himself with numerous causes which had deep connection with the daily life of a down—trodden member of our society. He always wished to give the Harijan a place of honour and respect in our society which was denied to him since centuries. In this task what he preached, he professed. He spoke much in their favour by undertaking strenuous tours of all the regions of India. He castigated caste Hindus and criticized their behaviour towards the untouchables. By doing so, he demanded their financial and social co-operation for the upliftment of this neglected community. At Mahatma's persuasion, numerous affluent persons came forward and funded his schemes of reform. The money thus raised was spent on their educational, moral, social, economic and religious development. Undoubtedly much progress was visible in this regard with the passage of time. The Hindu orthodoxy in many areas had to bow down before Mahatma's humanitarian gestures.

Gandhi used to spend some time with the Harijans by living himself with them. This kind of personal identification of the Mahatma made the Harijans realize their sense of importance in our society. He taught them the sense of cleanliness and advised them to raise their economic and social standards by hard work and honest means. He raised their colonies and advised the workers to devise schemes of their upliftment.

After incessant work for more than three decades, if was realized that much headway was made in this regard. They were given numerous concessions in the educational institutions, reservations in Government departments, ministerial positions, reserved seats in the provincial Legislatures and Lok Sabha. By doing so, the social status of a sizeable population in this community has been raised.

References

1. *Young India,* 27 October 1920 and 4 June 1925.
2. *Harijan,* 23 and 29 March 1935.
3. *Young India,* 20 October 1927.
4. *Young India,* 24 November 1927.
5. *Harijan,* 26 October 1935.
6. *Harijan,* 21 March 1936.
7. *Harijan,* 22 August 1936.
8. *Harijan,* 19 September 1936.
9. *Harijan,* 21 November 1936.
10. *Harijan,* 19 December 1936.
11. *Ibid.*
12. *Harijan,* 18 March 1933.
13. *Harijan,* 26 December 1936.

14. *Ibid.*
15. *Young India,* 17 April 1924.
16. *Young India,* 24 April 1924.
17. *Young India,* 1 May 1924.
18. *Young India,* 3 July 1924.
19. *Young India,* 18 September 1924.
20. *Young India,* 19 February 1925.
21. *Young India,* 19 March 1925.
22. *Young India,* 2 April 1925.
23. *Harijan,* 4 May 1934.
24. *Harijan,* 28 March 1936.
25. *Harijan,* 20 June 1936.
26. *Harijan,* 23 January 1937.
27. *Harijan,* 30 January 1937.
28. See for details T.K. Ravindran, *Vykom Satyagraha and Gandhi,* Trichur, 1975, pp. 12-13.
29. *Ibid.,* pp.2 ff.

Ketkar, S.V., *History of Caste in India,* New Delhi 1990.

Rapson, E.J., *The Combridge History of India,* Vol. I, Ancient India.

Central Provinces Gazetteer, Calcutta, 1908.

Wilson, *Rig Veda.*

Blunt, E.A. H., *The Caste System of Northern India.*

History of the Marathas, Vol. I.

Vedic Index I.

Vedic Index II.

Talke, J., *Islam in Bengal,* 1914.

Imperial gazetteer of India, 1907.

O' Malley, LSS., *India's Social Heritage,* London, 1934.

Russell, R.V., The Tribes and Castes of the Central Provinces, Vol. I.

AICC Papers in Nehru Memorial Library, New Delhi.

Home (Political) records in the National Archives of India.

Indian Annual Register, relevant volumes.

8

Conclusion

The present volume has been designed to present the peculiar features of the centuries old caste system in India, which dominated the Hindu social order and forced millions of people to live like neomatic and vagrant tribes, slaves and, totally discarded from the main social-economic stream worst than animals. In every part of the land, they were criminally kept divided into several castes, sub-castes and groups. In fact the caste-system made the *trivarnas* or the *dwijs*, conscious of their religions pre-eminence, pride of ancestry, of family, and personal position. By birth they were all empowered with racial, professional and economic supremacy, and higher social status, while the Dalits, the Sudras, the lower castes, the mixed tribes and castes, the non-Aryans, were made untouchables, captives and braven men. They were subject to torture and harassment under the Hindu scriptures and *Manusmriti* for a long time.

A few earlier representative studies, which have been included provide enough scholarly material on the origin and growth of the caste-system and its vicious anti-social implications, to understand the psychology of the Aryan minds and later caste Hindus, towards the toiling masses and working classes. It is believed that the contact of the Aryans with the indigenous people of the natives of India is mainly responsible for the growth of caste system.

The origin of caste-system is also attributed more to Puranic stories and local traditions. Many castes take their name from their dominant occupation. For Nesfield, caste is a matter of profession. Division of labour is the soul of caste. For Risley, caste is a matter of marriage. He sees natural enemity between the conquering Aryans and the conquered indigenous people and racial distinction of colour between the conquered dark Dravidian or non-Aryan races and their conquering fair skinned Aryans. The theory of mixed castes is a proof of cross-breeding.

The *Manusmriti,* which constituted the highest authority for the laws of Hindu social order; now stands as a condemned book. However, it is not definite who actually composed it and collected the material. It is also not certain when it came into existence.

In the "Commentary on the Hindu Law", Siromani says: There is a tradition that Manu has undergone through successive reductions. The introduction, Narada states of the work of the Manu, originally consisted of 1000 chapter, and 100000 Slokas; Narada abridged it to 12000 Slokas, and Sumati again reduced it to 4000. The treatise, which we possess must be, a third abridgement, as it only extends to 2685.

Manusmriti regulates the ideals of administration, social behaviour and canons of justice according to Brahman supremacy. It can now be termed as treatise of inhuman and injustice, rather jungle law, in the modern civilised society.

In the 6th century BC Buddha revolted against the Brahmanic authority, being a Kshatriya of Koliya clan and rejected all caste barriers. He tried to unite the lower castes and initiated them into his discipline, the *Dhamma.* For him a Buddhist monk, a *Bhikhu* or *shraman* was superior to a Brahman.

After collapse of the Gupta Empire, both the Brahmanic and feudalistic forces, the upper castes strengthened their social position and supported the *Varnashram Dharma,* preserved and maintained the authority of the *Dharmashatras.* While the Kshatriya Kings were hereditary feudal rulers and warriors, the Brahmans emerged as religious leaders and lawgivers in the society. All Hindu religious thoughts discarded the cardinal virtues of

Buddhism, emphasized the superiority of Brahmans and priestly class, beside total faith in the scriptures. Thus again the Hindu revivalism opened the gates of tyranny and harassment of Dalits.

In the later period, the Brahmanism, Saivism, Vedantism, Vaishnism and Bhakti Movement extended support to feudal religious tendencies. The Buddhism and Jainism, both being liberal, humanistic, religious movements were uprooted. In the socio-economic plan the Sudras were treated as inferior class meant to serve the, Brahmans, Kshatriyas and the Vaishyas. The position and professions of all the Sudras were identified, classified and forcefully controlled under Hindu law books.

In the 12th century, the Lingayats, who were originally a religious sect revolted against the authority of the Brahmans and discarded their religion and caste distinction and became a powerful group. In the 20th Century, the leather working and cultivating Chamar community of eastern Uttar Pradesh, also popularly knows as Jatavas in western Uttar Pradesh and Delhi and Ravidasi Chamars of Punjab and Haryana revolted against Brahman supremacy and evils of caste system and untouchability. Compared to the Hindu social order they are more attracted to Buddhism. They have become a more awakened and cultural group and remodelled them into a functional progressive caste, amongst the present day Dalits.

The Mahars of Maharashtra and elsewhere have also condemned Brahmanic social order and embraced Buddhism and discarded the evils of casteism and stigma of untouchability. Now in India they are a political and social force of transformation—all due to Baba Sahib Ambedkar.

It is interesting to know that in the initial stages of the East India Company's expansion of imperialistic interests, it inducted the Mahars of Bombay Presidency in its Army. They were a martial race and helped to conquer several parts of the country. Similarly, the Pariahs of Madras and Dusadhs of Bengal and Bihar were also recruited to expand the British Empire. This contact and mobility of untouchables made them aware of their strength and martial character, besides economic stability, knowledge of their civic rights and status of their brethren in the so-called Hindu social order.

The western and cultural impact changed the mentality of Brahmans, Kayasthas and Zamindars of Bengal and local Hindu Rajas and Muslim feudal lords, and Nawabs of Bombay and Madras Presidency became envious and jealous of Dalit recruits in the army. In the beginning all these upper castes and feudal forces were very much afraid of the English men, when the untouchables, joined the regular forces of the company, but slowly changed their designs and started joining the British Army and even converted themselves to Christianity. We find a long history of such conversions from the days of Raja Rammohun Roy to Devendranath Tagore, and even afterwards. As a result the depressed classes were eased out of army and Dalit soldiers were replaced in due course; and their further entry was banned.

The educated Hindu caste openly supported the British, joined civil posts and judiciary; got higher education and many of them embraced Christianity. In the 19th Century till the first quarter of the 20th Century all the money meant for educational purposes was spent on Hindus. However, earlier generations of the caste Hindus controlled the levers of power in British India and there was a slight change after independence. This is one of the glaring examples of behaviour of Indian caste system.

For Indian and foreign students of sociology and anthropology, the study of Dalit communities and present caste system in India is still a lively and challenging subject of research. Many of the neglected, exploited and unstudied Indian societies, even today need further scientific and methodological assessment and study, which were started more than a century ago both, by the British bureaucrats, in general, and the sociologists and anthropologists attached to the Raj, in particular. The ethnological, surveys gave fruitful results in the beginning of this century. But after independence it seems no serious and genuine efforts have been made to study the complicated social structure and economic status and rank of these communities in the more changed circumstances and highly developed societies. Still there is a wide gap between higher castes and lower strata of societies. While earlier such studies have become more or less historical and of reference value. The whole problem of suppressed, exploited and underdeveloped societies has been politicalised by the vested interests, specially the social workers and the politicians. The role of the NGO's has been a saga of total failure and rather misappropriation of funds, both Indian and foreign in the direction. The study of human races and their culture alone is not so important, but their betterment and assimilation in the main social stream is more necessary and significant.

In this age of science and technology, sophisticated computers and communication skills, Jet airways and global village conceptualization, our society will not bear 100 million semi-starved Indian citizens, almost confined to the bottom of the social ladder.

The hideous urban slums, the night shelters, the pavement dwellings and all sorts of temporary JJ. sheds in the parks, near about gutters and rubbish and outskirts of human settlements and the village ghettoes can easily be seen and surveyed to know and understand the real socio-economic structure and the economics of poverty of a immensely complex and utterly neglected and underprivileged Dalit society by Nobel Laureate Amratya Sen.

All the Dalits are of the same race and culture. But very little has been done to bridge the widening gap between the haves and the have-nots, except worldly lip sympathies. Professionally, economically, socially and politically the higher castes are safe, solid and sound.

The preferential treatment, like reservation of jobs, educational concessions etc. may provide a helping hand to a few, but cannot elevate all the downtrodden, who require urgent attention of the society.

Because of the impact and repercussions of the First and Second World War, the socio-economic condition of Dalits became very grim, and problem of untouchability serious and all their handicrafts ruined. Though political weightage was given to these problems and social efforts were made by the society for eradication of untouchability the results could not be obtained to our satisfaction.

The Congress and Mahatma Gandhi as well as reformers did a lot in this direction and on the other hand Dr. Ambedkar and Babu Jagjivan Ram, the stalwarts of Dalit movement, were key figures in awakening downtrodden masses: Their ways may have been different, ideologies may have differed but aims were definitely alike.

The famous authors of the "Freedom at Midnight" Larry Collins and Dominique Lapierre interviewed Lord Mountbatten, the last Viceroy, on the partition of India and recorded last momentous days of the Raj in their book "Mountbatten and the Partition of India". They put questions on the abolition of untouchability. Lord Mountbatten had replied "... untouchability is to be abolished of course. The Hindus did not want that, you see the real caste Hindus allowed the untouchability—it made them important. And untouchability was horrible. There were 60 million, you know. If the shadow of an untouchable falls across his food, he had to throw the food away. The whole thing was absolutely, extraordinary."

One should appreciate deep knowledge and correct picture presented by Lord Mountbatten on the problem of untouchability. This country can elect a President of India, but not a Prime Minister from the Dalit. The gravity of situation demands not only effective enforcement of human rights laws, but a more radical package for those who are crying and dying for help, still neglected and oppressed by our society.

Bibliography

(A) Primary Sources
Home (Political) records, available in the National Archives of India, New Delhi.
AICC Papers in Nehru Memorial Museum and Library (NMML).
Indian Annual Register (ed.) by H.N. Mitra, relevant volumes.
The Collected Works of Mahatma Gandhi, relevant volumes.
Selected Works of Jawaharlal Nehru, (ed.) by S. Gopal.
Reading Papers
Irwin Papers in NMML
Linlithgow Papers in NMML
Speeches and Writings of Dr. B.R. Ambedkar.
Speeches and Writings by Dr. Rajendra Prasad (ed.) by Vamik Chaudhuri
Collected Works of Sardar Vallabhbhai Patel (ed.) by P.N. Chopra.

(B) Newspapers and Journals
Amrita Bazar Patrika
The Bombay Chronicle
Hindustan Times
Harijan
Hindu
Indian Review
Modern Review
Journal of Indian History
Times of India
Indian History Congress
Proceedings (relevant volumes)
The Tribune
The Pioneer
Searchlight
The Statesman
Young India

(C) **Published Works**

The Aryan Household (ed.), 1891.

Bombay Gazetteer ; *Parsis of Gujarat.*

Blunt, E.A.H., *The Caste System of Northern India.*

Banerjea, Surendranath, *A Nation in Making.*

Central Provinces Gazetteer, Calcutta, 1908.

Census of India, Vol. XXV.

Coomaraswamy, *Sati : A Defence of the Eastern Women in the British Sociological Review,* Vol. VI, 1913.

Dutt, N.K., *Origin and growth of Caste in India.*

Galenter, Mare, "Untouchability and the Law" in J. Michael Mahar (ed.) *The Untouchables in Contemporary India,* The University of Arigona Press, USA, 1972.

Hopkins's and Burnett's Code of Manu.

Imperial Gazetteer of India, Vol. I, 1907.

Iyer, L.K.A., *Lectures on Ethnography,* Ch.IV.

Khandait, *Tribes and Castes of Bengal.*

Ketkar, S.V., *History of Caste in India,* New Delhi, 1990.

Monier-Williams, *Sanskrit Dictionary.*

Marathas, History of, Vol. I.

Memoirs of Central India, Vol. II.

Mahabharata, Bhishma Parva.

Macdonell and Keith's *Vedic Index of Names and Subjects,* Vol II, London, 1912.

O'Malley, L.S.S., *India's Social Heritage,* London, 1934.

Rajputana Gazetteer, Calcutta, 1908.

Rapson, E.J., *The Cambridge History of India,* Vol. I, Ancient India.

Russell, R.V., *The Tribes and Castes of the Central Provinces.*

Richards, F.J., *Sidelights on the Dravidian Problem, Part II, The Caste System.*

Rig Veda, Muller, II.

Singh, K.S., India's Communities, relevant volumes

Senart, Emile, *Caste in India.*

Talke, J., *Islam in Bengal,* 1914.

Vedic Index I

Vedic Index II

Wilson, *Rig Veda,* Introduction.

Index